TH

Professor Tariq Ramadan received his doctorate in Arabic and ~~Islamic~~ Studies from the University of Geneva. In Cairo, Egypt, he received one-on-one intensive training in classical Islamic scholarship from scholars at the Al-Azhar University. Having taught Islamic Studies and Philosophy at Freiburg University in Switzerland for many years, he was offered the post of Professor of Islamic Studies in the Classic Department and Luce Professor of Religion, Conflict and Peacebuilding at the University of Notre Dame in the United States. He had to resign the post after the US refused to allow him entry. He is currently challenging their decision with the support of ACLU and PEN and is Senior Research Fellow at the Lokahi Foundation and Visiting Fellow at St Antony's College, Oxford.

Through his writings and lectures Tariq Ramadan has contributed substantially to the debate on the issues of Muslims in the West and Islamic revival in the Muslim world. He is active both at the academic and grass-roots levels, lecturing extensively throughout the world on ethics of citizenship, social justice and dialogue between civilizations. A member of many international organizations and steering committees, he is President of the European think-tank the European Muslim Network.

PENGUIN BOOKS

THE MESSENGER

THE MESSENGER

The Meanings of the
Life of Muhammad

Tariq Ramadan

PENGUIN BOOKS

PENGUIN BOOKS

Published by the Penguin Group
Penguin Books Ltd, 80 Strand, London WC2R ORL, England
Penguin Group (USA) Inc., 375 Hudson Street, New York, New York 10014, USA
Penguin Group (Canada), 90 Eglinton Avenue East, Suite 700, Toronto, Ontario, Canada M4P 2Y3
(a division of Pearson Penguin Canada Inc.)
Penguin Ireland, 25 St Stephen's Green, Dublin 2, Ireland (a division of Penguin Books Ltd)
Penguin Group (Australia), 250 Camberwell Road, Camberwell, Victoria 3124, Australia
(a division of Pearson Australia Group Pty Ltd)
Penguin Books India Pvt Ltd, 11 Community Centre, Panchsheel Park, New Delhi – 110 017, India
Penguin Group (NZ), 67 Apollo Drive, Rosedale, North Shore 0632, New Zealand
(a division of Pearson New Zealand Ltd)
Penguin Books (South Africa) (Pty) Ltd, 24 Sturdee Avenue, Rosebank, Johannesburg 2196, South Africa

Penguin Books Ltd, Registered Offices: 80 Strand, London WC2R ORL, England

www.penguin.com

First published in the United States of America by Oxford University Press, Inc. 2007
First published in Great Britain by Allen Lane 2007
Published in Penguin Books 2008

1

Copyright © Oxford University Press, 2007
All rights reserved

The moral right of the author has been asserted

Printed in England by Clays Ltd, St Ives plc

Except in the United States of America, this book is sold subject
to the condition that it shall not, by way of trade or otherwise, be lent,
re-sold, hired out, or otherwise circulated without the publisher's
prior consent in any form of binding or cover other than that in
which it is published and without a similar condition including this
condition being imposed on the subsequent purchaser

978-0-141-02855-2

Contents

To Najma

This book is a work of dawn
And you accompanied it, with your footsteps on the stairs,
Your mischievous, laughing, or sulky eyes.
You came to curl up in my arms.
I would then leave the screen through which I was immersed
In the infinite light of the Messenger's goodness and love,
To drown in the infinite warmth of your presence.
The Messenger taught me forgiveness, you offered me innocence.
May your path be bright, my daughter, and may He love you
Through your smiles and through your tears.
I love you.

To Muna Ali

An American encounter and a never-ending gift
Facing trials, accepting silences.
You have accompanied my thought and my questions,
And read and reread and rephrased, often better than I could have done.
Faithfulness of the heart and soul in the Light of the Most High
In the footsteps of His Messenger.
I forget nothing.

To Claude Dabbak

To tell you here of my esteem and respect
For that deep modesty and constant humility.
Behind the translator, one senses deeply rich learning
And an immense gift offered to Western Muslims.
Your name too often hides behind authors' works.
Our debt is immense, mine in particular.
In the name of us all, truly, from the bottom of my heart,
Thank you!

Acknowledgments

In the hours of dawn when this book was written, there was silence, meditative solitude, and the experience of a journey, beyond time and space, toward the heart, the essence of spiritual quest, and initiation into meaning. Moments of plenitude, and often of tears; of contemplation and vulnerability. I needed this.

As time went on, the list of the women and men who made it possible to complete this project grew longer. I am almost sure that some of these precious names are going to escape me, though this in no way lessens the importance of their presence and contribution. Others have been moved by discretion or other reasons to remain anonymous; I understand, and my heart thanks them beyond these pages with the affection and gratitude they know go out to them.

I would first of all like to thank Faris Kermani and Neil Cameron, who two years ago asked me to narrate a film, *In the Footsteps of the Prophet Muhammad*, for a British television channel. Political considerations (two Arab governments having banned me from entering their territory) unfortunately made that project impossible. I then decided to do something entirely different and write a biography of the Prophet Muhammad, endeavoring to throw light on the spiritual and contemporary teachings in the life of the last Prophet. Many people around me encouraged me to carry out this work. I am indebted to Iman, Maryam, Sami, Moussa, and Najma for their constant accompaniment and support, and to my mother for some original ideas that came up here and there in our discussions. I would like to thank Cynthia Read, of Oxford University Press (New York), very warmly for her permanent enthusiasm, faithfulness, and humanity. In her Oxford-based collaborators, I have also found thoughtful and kind women and men.

During this academic year, my work has been accompanied by the presence of Gwen Griffith-Dickson and Vicky Mohammed of the Lokahi Foundation, based in London. At Saint Antony's College, Oxford University, Walter Armbrust and Eugene Rogan (Middle East Center) as well as Timothy Garton Ash and Kalypso Nicolaidis (European Studies Center) also enabled me to complete this work in the best possible conditions through their academic support and friendship. I do not forget Polly Friedhoff (who has now gone into well-deserved retirement), Franca Potts, and Collette Caffrey, who have been constantly available. To all of them, and to all those women and men who have surrounded me with their recognition and unobtrusive support, I would here like to express my deepest gratitude.

There is of course Yasmina Dif, my assistant, who manages my European office in such a warm and efficient manner. Shelina Merani, in Canada, has also undertaken difficult work with heart and solidarity. Muna Ali, more than an assistant based in the United States, keeps reading, commenting, and sharing ideas faithfully and seriously. Claude Dabbak has translated this book and has, with great humility, never failed to put her learning at the service of the necessary corrections. This book could not have been completed without the collaboration of this team, at once fraternal, demanding, and devoted. With all my heart, I thank them for being with me on this journey and making it possible for us to advance together, in His light, against wind and tide.

My final thanks and my last prayer go to the One, the Most Near, that He may accept and receive this life of the Prophet, that He may forgive me its possible errors or failings—which are due to none but myself—and that He may allow it to be a small landmark in the human enterprise of understanding and reconciliation: with oneself, with others, with His love. I learn daily that the quest for humility cannot justify any lapse from spiritual requirements or intellectual probity.

For myself, this book has been an initiation. I pray to the Most Gracious that it may be so for others. Long is the road of exile leading to oneself. . . .

London
May 2006

Introduction

Countless biographies of the Prophet Muhammad already exist.[1] From classical sources (such as the works of Ibn Ishaq and Ibn Hisham) to more recent accounts of the life of God's Messenger, as well as other renowned works by Muslim scholars over the course of history, it seems that everything must have already been said over and over again and that the subject matter must necessarily have been exhausted. So why should we undertake yet another attempt?

The present biography does not aim to compete with classical sources (which indeed are its source material), disclose any new facts, or provide an original or revolutionary reinterpretation of the history of prophethood and its context. The aims of the present study are far more modest, though it does not make them any easier to achieve.

The Prophet Muhammad occupies a particular place in the life and conscience of Muslims today, just as he did in the past. According to them, he received and transmitted the last revealed book, the Quran, which repeatedly insists on the eminent and singular position of the Messenger of God, all at once a prophet, a bearer of news, a model, and a guide. He was but a man, yet he acted to transform the world in the light of Revelation and inspirations he received from God, his Educator (*ar-Rabb*). That this man was chosen and inspired by God but also fully accepted his own humanity is what makes Muhammad an example and a guide for the Muslim faithful.

Muslims do not consider the Messenger of Islam a mediator between God and people. Each individual is invited to address God directly, and although the Messenger did sometimes pray to God on behalf of his community, he often insisted on each believer's responsibility in his or her dialogue and relationship with the One. Muhammad simply reminds the faithful of God's presence: he initiates them into His knowledge and discloses the initiatory path of spirituality through which he teaches his Companions and community that they must transcend the respect and love they have for him in the worship and love they must offer to and ask of the One, who begets not and is not begotten.

To those who, in his lifetime, wanted miracles and concrete evidence of his prophethood, Revelation ordered him to reply: "I am but a man like yourselves; the inspiration has come to me that your God is One God."[2] This same Revelation also informs the believers, for all eternity, of the singular status of this Messenger who, while chosen by God, never lost his human qualities: "You have indeed in the Messenger of God an excellent example for he who hopes in God and the Final Day, and who remembers God much."[3] These two dimensions—the man's humanity and the Prophet's exemplarity—serve as the focus of our interest in the present biography.

This is not going to be a detailed account of historical facts, great achievements, or famous wars. Classical biographies of the Messenger give abundant information about such matters, and we see no profit in dealing with them exhaustively. Our attention is mainly focused, throughout the narration of the story of his life, on situations, attitudes, or words that could reveal Muhammad's personality and what it can teach and convey to us today. When Aishah, his wife, was once questioned about the Prophet's personality, she answered: "His character [the ethics underlying his behavior] was the Quran."[4] Since the Book addresses the believing consciousness through the ages, it seemed essential to observe how the man who best incarnated it in his behavior could "speak" to us, guide us and educate us nowadays.

The initial idea was therefore to plunge into the heart of the Prophet's life and draw out its timeless spiritual teachings. From his birth to his death, his life is strewn with events, situations, and statements that point to the deepest spiritual edification. Adherence to faith, dialogue with God, observing nature, self-doubt, inner peace, signs and trials, and so on are themes that speak to us and remind us that basically nothing has changed. The Messenger's biography points to primary and eternal existential questions, and in this sense, his life is an initiation.

A second type of lesson can nevertheless be drawn from the historical events that filled the Prophet's life. In the seventh century, at the heart of a specific social, political, and cultural environment, God's Messenger acted, reacted, and expressed himself about human beings and events in the name of his faith, in the light of his morals. Studying his actions in this particular historical and geographical setting should enable us to throw light on a number of principles about the relation of faith to human beings, brotherhood, love, adversity, community life, justice, laws, and war. We have therefore endeavored to approach Muhammad's life from the perspective of our own times, considering how it still speaks to us and what its contemporary teachings are.

The reader, whether Muslim or not, is thus invited to look into the Prophet's life and follow the steps of an account that is strictly faithful to classical biographies (as far as facts and chronology are concerned) but which nevertheless constantly introduces reflections and comments, of a spiritual, philosophical, social, judicial, political, or cultural nature, inspired by the facts narrated. The choice to focus on certain events rather than others is of course determined by the wish to draw out teachings that speak to our lives and to our times. In each section of the (deliberately short) chapters that make up this book, the reader will notice constant movements between the Prophet's life, the Quran, and the teachings relevant to spirituality and the present-day situation that can be drawn from the various historical situations.

Our aim is more to get to know the Prophet himself than to learn about his personality or the events in his life. What is sought are immersion, sympathy, and, essentially, love. Whether one believes or not, it is not impossible to try to immerse oneself in the Prophet's quest and existence and recapture the pulse—the spirit—that infused his mission with meaning. This is indeed the primary ambition of this work: making of the Messenger's life a mirror through which readers facing the challenges of our time can explore their hearts and minds and achieve an understanding of questions of being and meaning as well as broader ethical and social concerns.

This book is intended for a large audience, both Muslim and non-Muslim. The text is academically rigorous in regard to classical Islamic sources, which we hope makes it useful to scholars and the Islamic sciences. By contrast, the narrative, interwoven with reflections and meditations, is deliberately easy to follow and endeavors to convey Islam's spiritual and universal teachings. The Messenger's historical experience is clearly the privileged way to grasp the eternal principles shared by more than a billion Muslims throughout the world. This book is thus a living introduction to Islam.

The Messenger taught his Companions to love God, and the Quran taught them in return: "Say[, O Messenger]: 'If you love God, follow me: God will love you.'"[5] They strove to follow his example, driven by a love for him that itself was animated by the intensity of their love for God. This love was such that when Umar ibn al-Khattab heard of the Prophet's death, he threatened to kill whoever dared claim that the Prophet was dead: he had only been raised to heaven and would assuredly come back. Another of Muhammad's Companions, Abu Bakr, asked Umar to be quiet, and declared: "O you people, let those who worshiped Muhammad know that Muhammad is now dead! As for those who worshiped God, let them know that God is alive and does not die."[6] Then he recited the following verse: "Muhammad is no more than a messenger; many were the messengers who passed away before him. If he died or was killed, will you then turn back? If any did turn back, not the least harm will he do to God. But God will reward the thankful."[7] Those words forcefully recall the finitude of the Messenger's life but in no way reduce the infinite love and deep respect Muslims have continued to show the Last Prophet through the ages.

This love finds expression in the permanent remembrance of his life in their hearts and memories, constantly offering prayers for the Messenger, and in the human and moral requirement to follow his example in daily life. The present biography endeavors to fulfill this requirement with love and knowledge. The Prophet's life is an invitation to a spirituality that avoids no question and teaches us—in the course of events, trials, hardships, and our quest—that the true answers to existential questions are more often those given by the heart than by the intelligence. Deeply, simply: he who cannot love cannot understand.

The Messenger

CHAPTER ONE

Encounter with the Sacred

Islamic monotheism has always stood in continuity with the sacred history of prophethood. From the beginning, the One God sent humankind prophets and messengers entrusted with the message, the reminder of His presence, His commands, His love, and His hope. From Adam, the first prophet, to Muhammad, the Last Messenger, Muslim tradition recognizes and identifies with the whole cycle of prophethood, ranging from the most famous messengers (Abraham, Noah, Moses, Jesus, etc.) to the lesser known, as well as others who remain unknown to us. The One has forever been accompanying us, His creation, from our beginnings to our end. This is the very meaning of *tawhid* (the Oneness of God) and of the Quranic formula that refers to humankind's destiny as well as to that of each individual: "To God we belong and to Him we return."[1]

A Lineage, a Place

Of all messengers, the most important figure in the Last Prophet's lineage is undoubtedly Abraham. There are many reasons for this, but from the outset, the Quran points to this particular link with Abraham through the insistent and continuous expression of pure monotheism, of human consciousness's adherence to the divine project, of the heart's access to His recognition and to His peace through self-giving. This is the meaning of the word *Islam*, which is too often translated quickly by the mere idea of submission but which also contains the twofold meaning of "peace" and "wholehearted self-giving." Thus a Muslim is a human being who, throughout history—and even before the last Revelation—has wished to attain God's peace through the wholehearted gift of him- or herself to the Being. In this sense, Abraham was the deep and exemplary expression of the Muslim:

> He [God] has chosen you, and has imposed no difficulties on you in religion. It is the religion of your father Abraham. He has named you Muslims, both before and in this [Revelation]; so that the Messenger may be a witness for you [the new Muslim community], and you may be witnesses for humankind.[2]

Along with this recognition of the One, the figure of Abraham stands out most particularly among the line of prophets leading up to the Messenger of Islam for several other reasons. The book of Genesis, like the Quran, relates the story of Abraham's servant Hagar, who gave birth to his first child, Ishmael, in his old age.[3] Sarah, Abraham's first wife, who in turn gave birth to Isaac, asked her husband to send away his servant and her child.

Abraham took Hagar and Ishmael away to a valley in the Arabian Peninsula called Bacca, which Islamic tradition identifies as present-day Mecca. The Islamic account, like Genesis, relates the questionings, suffering, and prayers of Abraham and Hagar, who were compelled to experience exile and separation. In both the Muslim and Judeo-Christian traditions, this trial is recounted with the certainty and intimate comfort that the parents and child were carrying out a command from God, who will protect and bless Abraham's descendants born of Hagar. To Abraham's invocations about his son, God answers in Genesis:

> As for Ishmael, I have heard you; behold, I will bless him . . . and I will make him a great nation.[4]

Then further on, when Hagar is helpless and without food and water:

> And God heard the voice of the child, and the angel of God called to Hagar from heaven, and said to her, "What troubles you, Hagar? Fear not; for God has heard the voice of the child where he is. Arise, lift up the child, and hold him fast with your hand; for I will make him a great nation."[5]

As for the Quran, it relates Abraham's prayer:

> O my Lord! I have made some of my offspring dwell in a valley without cultivation, by Your sacred House; in order, O our Lord, that they may establish regular prayer: so fill the hearts of some among men with love toward them, and feed them with fruits, so that they may give thanks. O our Lord! Truly You know what we conceal and what we reveal: for nothing whatever is hidden from God, whether on earth or in heaven. Praise be to God, Who has granted me in old age Ishmael and Isaac: for truly my Lord is He, the Hearer of Prayer![6]

On a purely factual level, the Prophet Muhammad is a descendant of Ishmael's children and is therefore part of that "great nation" announced by the Scriptures. Abraham is hence his "father" in the primary sense, and Islamic tradition understands that the blessings of this father's prayers extend to his descendant the Last Prophet as well as to the place where he left Hagar and Ishmael, where, a few years later, he was to undergo the terrible trial of his son's sacrifice, and where he was finally to raise with him God's sacred House (the Kaba). Quranic Revelation recounts:

> And remember that Abraham was tried by his Lord with certain commands, which he fulfilled. [God] said: "I will make you a guide for the people." [Abraham] said: "And also for my offspring?" [God] said: "But My promise is not within the reach of evildoers. Remember We made the House a place of assembly for men and women and a place of safety. And take the station of Abraham as a place of prayer. And We covenanted with Abraham and Ishmael, that they should sanctify My House for those who go round it, or use it as a retreat, or bow, or prostrate themselves [there in prayer]." And remember Abraham said: "My Lord, make this a city of peace, and feed its people with fruits—such of them as believe in God and the Last Day."[7]

This is the millenary teaching of Islamic tradition: there is a God and a line of prophets whose central figure is Abraham, the archetype of the Muslim, the blood father of this lineage of Ishmael leading up to Muhammad. Abraham and Ishmael sanctified this place in Bacca (Mecca) by building God's House (*bayt Allah*) with their own hands. And this is precisely where the last of God's messengers to humankind was born: Muhammad ibn Abdullah, who bore the message reminding people of the One, of the prophets, and of the sacred House. A God, a place, a prophet.

The Trial of Faith: Doubt and Trust

These simple facts alone illustrate the remarkable bond linking Muhammad's life to Abraham's. Yet it is the spiritual lineage that even more clearly reveals the exceptional nature of this bond. The whole Abrahamic experience unveils the essential dimension of faith in the One. Abraham, who is already very old and has only recently been blessed with a child, must undergo the trial of separation and abandonment, which will take Hagar and their child, Ishmael, very close to death. His faith is trust in God: he hears God's command—as does Hagar—and he answers it despite his suffering, never ceasing to invoke God and rely on Him. Hagar questioned Abraham about the reasons for such behavior; finding it was God's command, she willingly submitted to it. She asked, then trusted, then accepted, and by doing so she traced the steps of the profound "active acceptance" of God's will: to question with one's mind, to understand with one's intelligence, and to submit with one's heart. In the course of those trials, beyond his human grief and in fact through the very nature of that grief, Abraham develops a relationship with God based on faithfulness, reconciliation, peace, and trust. God tries him but is always speaking to him, inspiring him and strewing his path with signs that calm and reassure him.

Several years after this abandonment in the desert, Abraham was to experience another trial: God asked him to sacrifice his first-born son, Ishmael.[8] This is how the Quran recounts the story:

> So We gave him [Abraham] the good news: the birth of a sweet-tempered son. Then, when [the son] was old enough to walk with him, he said: "O my son! I have seen in a dream that I offer you in sacrifice. Now see what you think!" [The son] said: "O my father! Do as you are commanded; you will find me, if God so wills, one of the steadfast." So when they had both submitted [to God], and he had laid him prostrate on his forehead, We called out to him: "O Abraham! You have already fulfilled the dream!—

thus indeed do We reward those who do right. For this was a clear trial."
And we ransomed him with a momentous sacrifice. And we left for him
among generations [to come] in later times: peace and salutation to
Abraham![9]

The trial is a terrible one: for the sake of his love and faith in God,
Abraham must sacrifice his son, despite his fatherly love. The trial of faith
is here expressed in this tension between the two loves. Abraham confides
in Ishmael, and it is his own son, the object of sacrifice, whose comfort-
ing words to his father are like a confirming sign: "O my father! Do as you
are commanded; you will find me, if God so wills, one of the steadfast."
As was the case a few years earlier with Hagar, Abraham finds in others
signs that enable him to face the trial. Such signs, expressing the presence
of the divine at the heart of the trial, have an essential role in the experience of faith and shape the mode of being with oneself and with God.
When God causes His messenger to undergo a terrible trial and at the
same time associates that trial with signs of His presence and support (the
confirming words of his wife or child, a vision, a dream, an inspiration,
etc.), He educates Abraham in faith: Abraham doubts himself and his
own strength and faith, but at the same time the signs prevent him from
doubting God. This teaches Abraham humility and recognition of the
Creator. When Abraham is tempted by deep doubt about himself, his
faith, and the truth of what he hears and understands, the inspirations and
confirmations of Hagar and Ishmael (whom he loves but sacrifices in the
name of divine love) enable him not to doubt God, His presence, and His
goodness. Doubt about self is thus allied to deep trust in God.

Indeed, trials of faith are never tragic in Islamic tradition, and in this
sense, the Quran's story of Abraham is basically different from the Bible's
when it comes to the experience of sacrifice. One can read in Genesis:

> After these things God tested Abraham, and said to him, "Abraham!" And
> he said, "Here am I." [God] said, "Take your son, your only son Isaac,
> whom you love, and go to the land of Moriah, and offer him there as a
> burnt offering upon one of the mountains of which I shall tell you." . . .
> And Abraham took the wood of the burnt offering, and laid it on Isaac his
> son; and he took in his hand the fire and the knife. So they went both of
> them together. And Isaac said to his father Abraham, "My father!" And he

said, "Here am I, my son." [Isaac] said, "Behold the fire and the wood; but where is the lamb for a burnt offering?" Abraham said, "God Himself will provide the lamb for a burnt offering, my son." So they went both of them together.[10]

Abraham must sacrifice his son, and here he experiences this trial in absolute solitude. To his son's direct question, "Where is the lamb for a burnt offering?" Abraham answers elliptically. He *alone* answers God's call. This difference between the two accounts may seem slight, yet it has essential consequences for the very perception of faith, for the trial of faith, and for human beings' relation to God.

A Tragic Experience?

This tragic solitude of the human being facing the divine underlies the history of Western thought from Greek tragedy (with the central figure of the rebel Prometheus facing the Olympian gods) to existentialist and modern Christian interpretations as exemplified in the works of Søren Kierkegaard.[11] The recurrence of the theme of the tragic trial of solitary faith in Western theology and philosophy has linked this reflection to questions of doubt, rebellion, guilt, and forgiveness and has thus naturally shaped the discourse on faith, trials, and mistakes.[12]

One should nevertheless beware of apparent analogies. Indeed, the prophets' stories, and in particular Abraham's, are recounted in an apparently similar manner in the Jewish, Christian, and Muslim traditions. Yet a closer study reveals that the accounts are different and do not always tell the same facts nor teach the same lessons. Hence, someone who enters the universe of Islam and strives to encounter and understand the Islamic sacred and its teachings should be asked to make the intellectual and pedagogical effort of casting away—for as long as this encounter lasts—the links she or he may have established between the experience of faith, trial, mistake, and the tragic dimension of existence.

Quranic Revelation tells the stories of the prophets, and in the course of this narration it fashions in the Muslim's heart a relationship to the Transcendent that continually insists on the permanence of communication through signs, inspirations, and indeed the very intimate presence of

the One, so beautifully expressed in this verse of the Quran: "If My servants ask you concerning Me: I am indeed close [to them]. I respond to
the prayer of every supplicant when he or she calls on Me."[13] All the messengers have, like Abraham and Muhammad, experienced the trial of faith
and all have been, in the same manner, protected from themselves and
their own doubts by God, His signs, and His word. Their suffering does
not mean they made mistakes, nor does it reveal any tragic dimension of
existence: it is, more simply, an initiation into humility, understood as a
necessary stage in the experience of faith.

Because Muhammad's life expressed the manifested and experienced essence of Islam's message, getting to know the Prophet is a privileged means
of acceding to the spiritual universe of Islam. From his birth to his death,
the Messenger's experience—devoid of any human tragic dimension—
allies the call of faith, trial among people, humility, and the quest for peace
with the One.

CHAPTER TWO

Birth and Education

According to Islamic tradition, the House of God (*al-Kaba*) had been built by Abraham and his son Ishmael in the name of pure monotheism, of the worship of the One God, the Creator of the heavens and the earth, the God of humankind and of all the prophets and messengers.[1] Centuries went by and Mecca became a place of pilgrimage, but also mostly a marketplace and a trading center, giving rise to extensive cultural and religious blending. After some time, worship of the One gave way to the cult of tribal or local idols, to multiform polytheism. Islamic tradition reports that when Revelation began, more than 360 idols, images, or statues were housed and worshiped in the Kaba. Only a small group of believers remained attached to the worship of the One God and refused to join in the general idol worship. They were called the *hunafa* and identified with the Abrahamic monotheistic tradition.[2] The Quran itself qualifies Abraham and/or the nature of his worship as pure (*hanif*): "Who can profess a better religion than one who submits his whole self to God, does good, and follows the way of Abraham, pure monotheism [or the pure monotheist]? For God chose Abraham as beloved friend."[3]

The most famous of the *hunafa* at the time of Muhammad was called Waraqah ibn Nawfal and had converted to Christianity. With the other believers, the Jews and Christians living in the area, Waraqah ibn Nawfal represented the expression of a now marginal monotheism, which was spurned and sometimes fought over in and around Mecca.

A Birth

In his seminal book on the life of the Prophet Muhammad, Ibn Hisham informs us that Ibn Ishaq has clearly and precisely established the Prophet's birth date: "The Messenger (God's peace and blessings be upon him) was born on a Monday, on the twelfth night of Rabi al-Awwal, in the year of the elephant."[4] Other accounts mention other months of the year, but throughout history there has been broad acceptance of that date among scholars and within Muslim communities. The Muslim calendar being a lunar one, it is difficult to determine exactly the solar month of his birth, but the "year of the elephant" to which Ibn Ishaq refers corresponds to 570 CE.

The Last Prophet was born in one of Mecca's noble families, Banu Hashim, which enjoyed great respect among all the clans in and around Mecca.[5] This noble descent combined with a particularly painful and debilitating personal history. His mother, Aminah, was only two months pregnant when his father, Abdullah, died during a trip to Yathrib, north of Mecca. Fatherless at birth, young Muhammad was to live with the tension of the dual status implied in Mecca by a respectable descent, on one hand, and the precariousness of having no father, on the other.

Ibn Ishaq reports that the name Muhammad, quite unknown at the time in the Arabian Peninsula, came to his mother in a vision while she was still pregnant.[6] This same vision is also said to have announced to her the birth of the "master of this people" (*sayyid hadhihi al-ummah*); according to the vision, when he was born she was to say the words "I place him under the protection of the One [*al-Wahid*] against the treachery of the envious."[7] Torn between her grief at her husband's death and the joy of welcoming her child, Aminah said repeatedly that strange signs had accompanied the gestation, then the extraordinarily easy birth of her child.

The Desert

Aminah soon became aware that she was the mother of an exceptional child. This feeling was shared by Muhammad's grandfather, Abd al-Muttalib, who took responsibility for him after his birth. In Mecca, it was customary to entrust infants to wet nurses belonging to the nomadic

Bedouin tribes living in the nearby desert. Because he was fatherless, one nurse after another refused to take the child into her care, fearing that his ambiguous status would bring them no profit. Halimah, who had arrived last because her mount was tired, decided with her husband that it was better for them to take the child, although he was an orphan, than to risk being mocked by their tribe when they went home. They therefore went back with the infant Muhammad, and Halimah, just like Aminah, tells of many signs that led her and her husband to think that this child seemed blessed.

For four years, the orphan was looked after by Halimah and lived with the Banu Sad Bedouins in the Arabian desert. He shared the nomads' life in the most barren and difficult natural environment, surrounded, as far as the eye could see, with horizons bringing to mind the fragility of the human being and spurring contemplation and solitude. Although he did not yet know it, Muhammad was going through the first trials ordained for him by the One, Who had chosen him as a messenger and was, for the time being, his Educator, his *Rabb*.[8]

The Quran would later recall his particular situation as an orphan as well as the spiritual teachings associated with the experience of life in the desert:

> Did He not find you an orphan and give you shelter? And He found you wandering, and He gave you guidance. And He found you in need, and made you independent. Therefore [for that reason], do not treat the orphan with harshness, nor chide him who asks. But the bounty of your Lord, proclaim![9]

Those verses of the Quran carry several teachings: being both an orphan and poor was actually an initiatory state for the future Messenger of God, for at least two reasons. The first teaching is obviously the vulnerability and humility he must naturally have felt from his earliest childhood. This state was intensified when his mother, Aminah, died when Muhammad was six. This left him utterly dependent on God, but also close to the most destitute among people. The Quran reminds him that he must never forget this throughout his life and particularly during his prophetic mission. He was orphaned and poor, and for that reason he is reminded and ordered never to forsake the underprivileged and the needy.

Considering the exemplary nature of the prophetic experience, the second spiritual teaching emanating from these verses is valid for each human being: never to forget one's past, one's trials, one's environment and origin, and to turn one's experience into a positive teaching for oneself and for others. Muhammad's past, the One reminds him, is a school from which he must draw useful, practical, and concrete knowledge to benefit those whose lives and hardships he has shared, since he knows from his own experience, better than anyone else, what they feel and endure.

An Education, and Nature

Life in the desert was to fashion the man and his outlook on creation and the elements of the universe. When Muhammad came to the desert, he was able to learn from the Bedouins' rich oral tradition and their renown as speakers to develop his own mastery of the spoken language. Later on, the Last Prophet was to stand out through the strength of his words, his eloquence, and above all his ability to convey deep and universal teachings through short, pithy phrases (*jawami al-kalim*). The desert is often the locus of prophecies because it naturally offers to the human gaze the horizons of the infinite. For nomads, forever on the move, finitude in space is allied to a sense of freedom blended, here again, with the experience of fleetingness, vulnerability, and humility. Nomads learn to move on, to become strangers, and to apprehend, at the heart of the linear infinity of space, the cyclical finitude of time. Such is the experience of the believer's life, which the Prophet was later to describe to young Abdullah ibn Umar in terms reminiscent of this dimension: "Be in this world as if you were a stranger or a wayfarer."[10]

In the first years of the Prophet's life he developed a specific relationship with nature that remained constant throughout his mission. The universe is pregnant with signs that recall the presence of the Creator, and the desert, more than anything else, opens the human mind to observation, meditation, and initiation into meaning. Thus, many verses of the Quran mention the book of creation and its teachings. The desert, apparently devoid of life, repeatedly shows and proves to the watchful consciousness the reality of the miracle of the return to life:

And among His Signs is this: you see the earth humble [because of drought]; but when We send down rain to it, it is stirred to life and yields increase. Truly, He who gives it life can surely give life to the dead, for He has power over all things.[11]

This relationship with nature was so present in the Prophet's life from his earliest childhood that one can easily come to the conclusion that living close to nature, observing, understanding, and respecting it, is an imperative of deep faith.

Many years later, when the Prophet was in Medina, facing conflicts and wars, a Revelation in the heart of night turned his gaze toward another horizon of meaning: "In the creation of the heavens and the earth, and the alternation of night and day, there are indeed signs for all those endowed with insight."[12] It has been reported that the Prophet wept all night long when this verse was revealed to him. At dawn, when Bilal, the muezzin, coming to call for prayer, asked about the cause of those tears, Muhammad explained to him the meaning of his sadness and added: "Woe to anyone who hears that verse and does not meditate upon it!"

Another verse conveys the same teaching, referring to multiple signs:

In the creation of the heavens and the earth; in the alternation of night and day; in the sailing of the ships through the ocean for the profit of humankind; in the rain that God sends down from the skies, and the life which He then gives to the earth after it had been lifeless; in the beasts of all kind that He scatters through the earth; in the change of the winds, and the clouds that run their appointed courses between the sky and the earth; [here] indeed are signs for a people who are wise.[13]

The first years of Muhammad's life undoubtedly fashioned his outlook, preparing him to understand the signs in the universe. The spiritual teaching that can be drawn from them is essential, both for the Prophet's education and for our own education throughout history: being close to nature, respecting what it is, and observing and meditating on what it shows us, offers us, or takes (back) from us requirements of a faith that, in its quest, attempts to feed, deepen, and renew itself. Nature is the primary guide and the intimate companion of faith. Thus, God decided to expose His Prophet, from his earliest childhood, to the natural lessons of creation, conceived as a school where the mind gradually apprehends signs and meaning. Far removed from the formalism of soulless religious rituals, this sort of education, in and through its closeness to nature, fosters a relationship to the divine based on contemplation and depth that will later make it possible, in a second phase of spiritual education, to understand the meaning, form, and objectives of religious ritual. Cut off from nature in our towns and cities, we nowadays seem to have forgotten the meaning of this message to such an extent that we dangerously invert the order of requirements and believe that learning about the techniques and forms of religion (prayers, pilgrimages, etc.) is sufficient to grasp and understand their meaning and objectives. This delusion has serious consequences since it leads to draining religious teaching of its spiritual substance, which actually ought to be its heart.

The Split Chest

Tradition reports that a most peculiar event took place when Muhammad was four, as he was playing with the children of the Banu Sad Bedouin tribe. Halimah says that her son came to her and her husband in fright and informed them that "two white-clad men grasped him [Muhammad] and laid him on the ground; then they opened up his chest and plunged their hands in it."[14]

Halimah and her husband ran to the spot indicated by their child and found Muhammad shaken and pale. He confirmed his foster brother's story, adding that after opening his chest, the two men "touched something there; I do not know what it is."[15]

Troubled by this story and fearing the child might have suffered some harm, the pair decided to take Muhammad back to his mother. At first, they concealed the main reason for their decision, but faced with the mother's insistent questions, they finally informed her of the event. She was not surprised, and even mentioned that she herself had witnessed signs indicating that a particular fate was being prepared for her child.

Many years later, the Prophet recalled the event and said that two men "split [his] chest, took out the heart, and opened it to take out a black clot, which they threw away. Then they washed [his] heart and chest with snow."[16] In other traditions, he explained the spiritual meaning of those events; in a discussion with some Companions, reported by Ibn Masud, he said: "'There is no one among you but is accompanied by a jinn or an angel specifically assigned to him.' They asked: 'Even you, Messenger?' 'Even me, but God has helped me and he [the jinn, here meaning the evil spirit] has submitted, so he only enjoins me to do what is good.'"[17]

Here, the Prophet guides our understanding of the event beyond the mere facts reported, to its essential spiritual dimension: from his earliest childhood, the Messenger was protected from the temptations of evil that plague everybody else's heart. The purification of his chest prepared him for his prophetic mission. About fifty years later, he was again to have a similar experience, when his heart was opened once more and purified to enable him to experience the Night Journey to Jerusalem, then the elevation to Sidrat al-Muntaha, the Lotus of the Utmost Boundary.[18] Such spiritual experiences, singular and initiatory, prepared the Chosen One (*al-Mustafa*) to receive first the message of Islam and then the command to perform ritual prayer, the pillar of religious practice.[19]

On a more general level, the Quran refers to this purification with these words: "Have We not opened your breast for you? And removed from you your burden which galled your back? And raised high the esteem in which you are held?"[20] For most commentators on the Quran, those verses primarily refer to the threefold gift granted to the Prophet: faith in the One inscribed in his heart, election as the Prophet, and, lastly, the support of God Himself throughout his mission. From his earliest childhood, as we have seen, Muhammad was to be accompanied by signs and trials that educated and prepared him for that mission.

Now back in Mecca, young Muhammad stayed with his mother for two years. When he was six, she wanted her son to get acquainted with members of her family who lived in Yathrib (which would later be known as Medina). They went there, but on the way back, Aminah fell ill and died at Abwa, where she was buried. Now both fatherless and motherless, Muhammad was surrounded by signs of his election as well as by grief, suffering, and death. Barakah, who had traveled with them as Aminah's servant, took the child back to Mecca. His grandfather, Abd al-Muttalib, immediately took him into his care. He was constantly to show deep love and particular respect for his grandson. However, he died two years later.

The Orphan and His Educator

Muhammad's story is a difficult one, as is emphasized by the repetition in these verses from the Quran: "So verily, with every difficulty there is relief. Verily, with every difficulty there is relief."[21] At the age of eight, young Muhammad had experienced fatherlessness, poverty, solitude, and the death of his mother and then of his grandfather. Yet all along his path he continually encountered signs of a destiny that, through people and circumstances, accompanied and facilitated his evolution and education. On his deathbed, Abd al-Muttalib asked his son Abu Talib, Muhammad's uncle, to look after him; Abu Talib carried out this mission as a father would have done for his own child. Later, the Prophet constantly recalled how much his uncle and his uncle's wife, Fatimah, had loved and taken care of him. "Verily, with every difficulty there is relief."

Throughout the hardships of his life, Muhammad of course remained under the protection of the One, his *Rabb*, his Educator. In Mecca, tradition reports that he was persistently protected from idol worship and the festivals, feasts, or weddings where drunkenness and lack of restraint prevailed. One evening, he heard that a wedding was to be celebrated in Mecca and he wanted to attend. On the way there, he reported, he suddenly felt tired; he lay down to rest and fell asleep. The next morning, the heat of the sun woke him from his deep slumber. This seemingly trivial story is nevertheless most revealing as to the methods used by the Prophet's Educator to prevent His future Messenger from being tempted into lack of restraint and drunkenness. The One, always present at his side, literally put him to sleep, thus protecting him from his own instincts and not allowing His protégé's heart to develop a sense of wrongdoing, guilt, or any such moral torment as a result of an attraction that was, after all, natural for a boy his age. While gentleness and diversion were used to protect him, those events—which the Prophet was later to mention— gradually built in him a moral sense shaped through the understanding of those signs and of what they protected him from. This natural initiation into morals, remote from any obsession with sin and fostering of guilt, greatly influenced the kind of education the Prophet was to impart to his Companions. With a teaching method relying on gentleness, on the common sense of individuals, and on their understanding of commands, the Prophet also strove to teach them how to put their instincts to sleep, so to speak, and how to resort to diversion to escape evil temptations. For those Companions, as for us, in all ages and societies, this teaching method is most valuable and reminds us that a moral sense should be developed not through interdiction and sanction but gradually, gently, exactingly, understandingly, and at a deep level.

In the ensuing years, young Muhammad became a shepherd to earn his living, looking after flocks on the outskirts of Mecca. He later mentioned this experience to his Companions, portraying it as a common feature characteristic of prophets: "'There was no prophet who was not a shepherd.' He was asked: 'And you too, Messenger of God?' He answered: 'And myself as well.'"[22]

As a shepherd, young Muhammad learned solitude, patience, contemplation, and watchfulness. Such qualities were necessary to all prophets to carry out their missions among their people. He also acquired a deep sense of independence in his life and work, which enabled him to be most successful in the trader's calling he was soon to take up.

CHAPTER THREE

Personality and Spiritual Quest

Abd al-Muttalib, Muhammad's grandfather, had seen his riches dwindle during the last years of his life, and Abu Talib, who was now his nephew's guardian, was also going through particularly difficult financial and commercial circumstances. Therefore, Muhammad had started to earn his own living very early, and he was always trying to help the members of his family.

The Monk Bahira

When Muhammad was twelve years old, Abu Talib decided to take him along in a merchant caravan heading for Syria. They stopped in Busra, near the dwelling of a Christian monk called Bahira. Muslim tradition reports that the hermit Bahira, just like Waraqah ibn Nawfal and most of the Christians, Jews, and *hunafa* in the peninsula, was expecting the imminent coming of a new prophet and was continually watching for signs of this.[1] When he saw the caravan approaching, it seemed to him that a cloud was accompanying the group and shielding them from the heat. Determined to learn more, he decided to invite all the travelers to partake of a meal, which was unusual among the hermits of the area. After carefully observing each member of the group, he fixed his gaze on young Muhammad; he went to him, took him aside, and asked him a number of questions about his family situation, his social position, his dreams, and so on. He finally asked if he could have a look at his back, and young Muhammad agreed. Between the boy's two shoulder blades, the monk

Bahira noticed a skin growth identified by his books as "the seal of prophethood" (*khatim an-nubuwwah*).² The monk hastened to warn Abu Talib that a particular fate awaited this boy and that he must protect him from adversity and from the attacks that would undoubtedly befall him, like all previous messengers of God.

We have seen that the first years of Muhammad's life were strewn with many signs. Everyone around him felt and thought that this child was different and that a particular fate lay in store for him. The monk Bahira confirmed this impression and integrated it into the sacred history of prophethood. At the age of twelve, the boy beloved of everybody was told that the human beings around him would later oppose him; while he could already feel that his uniqueness caused people to love him, now he knew that in the future it would give rise to hatred.

For several years, Muhammad continued to look after sheep in the hills around Mecca. Although he was young and somewhat removed from the active life of the settled inhabitants of Mecca, he would sometimes hear of or witness the ceaseless quarrels and conflicts among the various tribes, which resulted in constantly shifting alliances. In Mecca, interclan war was the rule rather than the exception, and some exploited this by dealing unfairly with traders or visitors whom they knew to be unprotected by any treaty or agreement and unable to rely on any alliance. This was what happened to a visiting merchant from Yemen; he had been wronged, but he decided not to let it pass, and so he publicly explained his situation and appealed to the nobleness and dignity of the Quraysh tribe to give him justice.³

The Pact of the Virtuous

Abdullah ibn Judan, the chief of the Taym tribe and a member of one of the two great alliances of Meccan tribes (known as the People of the Perfume), decided to invite to his home all those who wanted to put an end to the conflicts and establish a pact of honor and justice that would bind the tribes beyond alliances based merely on tribal, political, or commercial interests.

Chiefs and members of numerous tribes thus pledged that it was their collective duty to intervene in conflicts and side with the oppressed against the oppressors, whoever they might be and whatever alliances might link them to other tribes. This alliance, known as *hilf al-fudul* (the Pact of the Virtuous), was special in that it placed respect for the principles of justice and support of the oppressed above all other considerations of kinship or power. Young Muhammad, like Abu Bakr, who was to become his lifelong friend, took part in that historic meeting.

Long after Revelation had begun, Muhammad was to remember the terms of that pact and say: "I was present in Abdullah ibn Judan's house when a pact was concluded, so excellent that I would not exchange my part in it even for a herd of red camels; and if now, in Islam, I was asked to take part in it, I would be glad to accept."[4] Not only did the Prophet stress the excellence of the terms of the pact as opposed to the perverted tribal alliances prevailing at the time, but he added that even as the bearer of the message of Islam—even as a Muslim—he still accepted its substance and would not hesitate to participate again. That statement is of particular significance for Muslims, and at least three major teachings can be derived from it. We have seen that the Prophet had been advised to make good use of his past, but here the reflection goes even further: Muhammad acknowledges a pact that was established before the beginning of Revelation and which pledges to defend justice imperatively and to oppose the oppression of those who were destitute and powerless. This implies acknowledging that the act of laying out those principles is prior to and transcends belonging to Islam, because in fact Islam and its message came to confirm the substance of a treaty that human conscience had already independently formulated. Here, the Prophet clearly acknowledges the validity of a principle of justice and defense of the oppressed stipulated in a pact of the pre-Islamic era.

The second teaching is no less essential: at a time when the message was still being elaborated in the course of Revelation and of the Prophet's experiences, he acknowledged the validity of a pact established by non-Muslims seeking justice and the common good of their society. The Prophet's statement is in itself a blatant denial of the trend of thought expressed here and there throughout the history of Islamic thought—and to this day—according to which a pledge can be ethically valid for Muslims only if it is of strictly Islamic nature or/and if it is established between Muslims. Again, the key point is that the Prophet clearly acknowledges the validity of adhering to principles of justice and defending the oppressed, regardless of whether those principles come from inside Islam or outside it.

The third teaching is a direct consequence of this reflection: the message of Islam is by no means a closed value system at variance or conflicting with other value systems. From the very start, the Prophet did not conceive the content of his message as the expression of pure otherness versus what the Arabs or the other societies of his time were producing. Islam does not establish a closed universe of reference but rather relies on a set of universal principles that can coincide with the fundamentals and values of other beliefs and religious traditions (even those produced by a polytheistic society such as that of Mecca at the time). Islam is a message of justice that entails resisting oppression and protecting the dignity of the oppressed and the poor, and Muslims must recognize the moral value of a law or contract stipulating this requirement, whoever its authors and whatever the society, Muslim or not. Far from building an allegiance to Islam in which recognition and loyalty are exclusive to the community of faith, the Prophet strove to develop the believer's conscience through adherence to principles transcending closed allegiances in the name of a primary loyalty to universal principles themselves. The last message brings nothing new to the affirmation of the principles of human dignity, justice, and equality: it merely recalls and confirms them. As regards moral values, the same intuition is present when the Prophet speaks of the qualities of individuals before and in Islam: "The best among you [as to their human and moral qualities] during the era before Islam [*al-jahiliyyah*] are the best in Islam, provided they understand it [Islam]."[5] The moral value of a human being reaches far beyond belonging to a particular universe of reference; within Islam, it requires added knowledge and understanding in order to grasp properly what Islam confirms (the principle of justice) and what it demands should be reformed (all forms of idol worship).

The "Truthful" and Marriage

The Prophet's life itself, before and after the beginning of Revelation, illustrates the relevance of the above analysis: the recognition of his moral qualities preceded his prophetic mission, which confirmed a posteriori the need for such qualities. After being a shepherd, young Muhammad became a trader and built a reputation for honesty and efficiency acknowledged all over the area. People started to call him as-Sadiq al-Amin, "the truthful, the trustworthy," when he was only about twenty. One of the wealthiest traders in Mecca was a woman called Khadijah bint Khuwaylid. Twice married, then finally a widow, she was a cousin of the Christian Waraqah ibn Nawfal. For some years already she had been hearing of a young man who was "honest, fair, and efficient," and she eventually decided to test him, asking him to take some goods of hers to Syria and sell them there; she would let him take along a young servant of hers called Maysarah, and promised to double his commission if he was successful. He accepted and set out with Maysarah. In Syria, Muhammad managed a commercial operation that more than doubled Khadijah's expectations.

They came back to report to Khadijah, who silently listened to Muhammad's explanations, carefully observing the appearance and behavior of the young man, who was now about twenty-five. A light seemed to emanate from his face. Later Maysarah told her that all along the journey he had noticed a series of signs—in Muhammad's attitude and behavior—attesting that he was like no other man.[6] Khadijah then asked one of her friends, Nufaysah, to approach Muhammad and ask whether he would be interested in marriage. Muhammad told Nufaysah that he could not afford marriage, and when she mentioned the name of Khadijah, with whom he would find "beauty, lineage, nobility, and wealth," he responded that he was interested but that because of his status, he could not contemplate such a union. Nufaysah did not say that she was already acting at Khadijah's request and suggested he leave things to her, that she could arrange the match. She informed her friend Khadijah of Muhammad's favorable frame of mind. Khadijah invited him to her home and made him a proposal of marriage, which he accepted. There remained the task of speaking to relatives in both clans in order to finalize the arrangements, but no obstacle—whether their respective statuses or the interests of the tribes—was able to prevent their marriage.

Tradition reports that Khadijah was forty years old when they married, but other opinions have it that she was younger: for instance, Abdullah ibn Masud mentions the age of twenty-eight, which does seem more likely considering that Khadijah gave birth to six children in the following years.[7] The firstborn, a boy named Qasim, lived only two years; then came Zaynab, Ruqayyah, Um Kulthum, Fatimah, and at last Abdullah, who also died before he reached the age of two.[8] During those years, the Prophet decided to free and adopt as his son his slave Zayd ibn Harithah, gifted to him by his wife a few years earlier. Later, when his own son Abdullah died, he sought to help his uncle Abu Talib—in great financial difficulty and burdened with a very large family—by taking his young cousin Ali ibn Abi Talib into his home. Ali was later to marry Muhammad's youngest daughter, Fatimah.

Zayd

The story of Zayd, the adopted son, is interesting for many reasons. Captured during a battle, he had been sold several times before becoming Khadijah's slave, then Muhammad's. He remained in the Prophet's service for several years, during which time he learned that his parents were still alive, as news circulated from tribe to tribe through verse spread by merchants and travelers as they went from village to village. Zayd then composed some verse and arranged for several members of his tribe visiting Mecca to hear it and report it to his family. On hearing he was there, his father and uncle decided to leave for Mecca immediately to find Zayd and bring him back to his tribe. They heard he was at Muhammad's and came to him proposing to buy Zayd back. Muhammad in turn suggested they should let Zayd choose for himself: if he decided to go back with his father and uncle, Muhammad would let him go without asking for any compensation, but if on the contrary Zayd wanted to stay with his master, his relatives would have to accept his choice. They agreed, and they went together to ask Zayd what he wanted. He decided to stay with his master, and explained to his relatives that he preferred slavery with Muhammad to freedom away from him, so far did the qualities he had found in him exceed what he could expect of other men. He therefore remained with his master, who immediately freed him and announced publicly that Zayd was now to be considered as his son, that he would be called Zayd ibn Muhammad (Zayd, son of Muhammad), and that he would inherit from him.[9]

This story—Zayd's choice, while still a slave, of his master over his father—adds another dimension to the portrait of Muhammad that is gradually emerging, and it tells a lot about Muhammad's personality before Revelation. Simple, meditative, and courteous, but also honest and efficient in business, he expressed constant respect toward all women, men, and children, who in turn showed him gratefulness and deep love. He was as-Sadiq, a man of truth and of his word; he was al-Amin, a trustworthy and dignified person; he had been surrounded with signs announcing his fate; he was rich with extraordinary human qualities that already pointed to his singularity.

Rebuilding the Kaba

Another event shows that to his qualities of heart and his moral distinction must be added a sharp intelligence, which he used in the service of respect and peace between people and between clans. After protracted hesitation due to the interdiction against touching the sacred House, the Quraysh had finally decided to rebuild the Kaba. They destroyed the upper part of the walls, down to the foundations (which were those of the initial construction, built by Abraham and Ishmael, and which they left untouched). They rebuilt until they reached the place where the Black Stone was to be enshrined, in one corner of the Kaba. At that point bitter quarrels broke out among members of the different clans over who would have the honor of putting the Black Stone back in its place. Some were nearly ready to take up arms in order to determine to which clan the privilege would fall. An old man among them suggested that the first man who entered the sacred space be asked to judge the issue, and a consensus formed on that idea. Muhammad was the first to enter the sacred space, and clan elders were happy that chance had chosen him to arbitrate the dispute. He listened to them, then asked for a cloak; he placed the Black Stone on it and asked the chiefs of each clan to hold the cloak's edges and lift the stone together. Once they had lifted it to the desired height, he himself placed the Black Stone in the required space—to the satisfaction of all, since nobody had been wronged. This intuitive intelligence had immediately managed to reconcile the pride of each clan with their need for union. Later, during his mission, this characteristic feature of his mind was to be often illustrated by his ability to maintain the first Muslim community's unity despite the presence of very strong personalities with widely differing temperaments. In the quest for peace, he constantly strove to achieve again what he had done in this difficult situation between the Quraysh clans: teach the heart not to give way to proud emotions and arrogant thinking; bring the mind to heart-soothing solutions that make it possible to control oneself gently and wisely. In the years before Revelation, the Messenger's Educator had granted him this particular quality, an alliance between a deep heart and a penetrating spirit, of knowing how to be reasonable in all circumstances, with oneself and among other people.

By the time Muhammad was thirty-five, he had built such a reputation for himself that many among the Banu Hashim thought that he would soon take up the mantle of his forefathers and restore the greatness of his clan by becoming its leader. With his marriage, his own activities, and his personal qualities, he became politically and financially prominent, and he was already starting to receive marriage proposals for his daughters, as for instance from his uncle Abu Lahab, who wished to marry his two sons, Utbah and Utaybah, to Ruqayyah and Um Kulthum. Clan ties were woven in the expectation of the benefits that would accrue should Muhammad become clan chief.

The Quest for Truth

Muhammad himself, however, was not concerned with such matters and showed little interest in public affairs. During this time he started to spend periods of retreat in one of the caves near Mecca, as Mecca's *hunafa* and Christians already did. When the month of Ramadan came, he would go to the cave of Hira with some supplies and remain in seclusion, returning periodically for additional food, for a period of about a month. To reach that cave, he had to climb up a small mountain and go to the other side of a second small peak, following a narrow path. The cave itself was totally secluded and so small that it would have been difficult for even two people to be there together. From the mouth of the cave, one could see the Kaba far below and, a greater distance away, the barren plain stretching out as far as the eye could see.

Away from other people, facing nature, Muhammad was searching for peace and meaning. He had never taken part in idol worship, had not shared the beliefs and rites of the region's tribes, and had remained aloof from superstition and prejudice. He had been protected from false gods, whether the veneration of statues or the worship of power and riches. For some time already he had been telling his wife, Khadijah, about some dreams that turned out to be true and which troubled him because of the strong impressions they left when he woke up. It was indeed a quest for truth: dissatisfied with the answers offered by those around him, driven by the intimate conviction that he must search further, he decided to isolate himself in contemplation. He was nearing forty and had reached a point in his spiritual development that made deep introspection the necessary next step. Alone with himself, in the cave of Hira, he meditated on the meaning of his life, his presence on earth, and the signs that had accompanied him throughout his life. The spaces stretching out all around him must have reminded him of the horizons of his childhood in the desert, with the difference now that maturity had filled them with myriad fundamental existential questions.

He was searching, and this spiritual quest was naturally leading him toward the calling that signs had tacitly and inevitably pointed to throughout this life. The signs that had protected and calmed him, the visions that first appeared in dreams and then came to pass in waking life, and the questions asked by the mind and heart allied to the horizons offered by nature were insensibly leading Muhammad to the supreme initiation into meaning, to the encounter with his Educator, the One God. At the age of forty, the first cycle of his life had just come to an end.

It was when he was approaching the cave of Hira during the month of Ramadan in the year 610 that he first heard a voice calling and greeting him: "*As-salamu alayka, ya rasul Allah!* Peace be upon you, Messenger of God!"[10]

CHAPTER FOUR

Revelation, Knowledge

Alone in the cave of Hira, Muhammad continued to search for truth and meaning. Then the Angel Gabriel suddenly appeared to him and ordered: "Read!" Muhammad answered: "I am not of those who read." The angel held him so tightly that he could hardly bear it and again ordered: "Read!" Muhammad repeated: "I am not of those who read!" The angel held him tightly again, almost choking him, and repeated the order for the third time: "Read!" The same answer was repeated: "I am not of those who read!" The angel, maintaining his hold, recited: "Read in the name of your Lord [*Rabb*, "Educator"], Who created humankind out of a clinging clot. Read, and your Lord is most bountiful, He who taught by means of the pen, taught humankind that which they did not know."[1]

Those words were the first verses of the Quran revealed to the Prophet through the Angel Gabriel. Muhammad himself, then much later his wife Aishah, some Companions, and traditionists down to Ibn Ishaq and Ibn Hisham, reported this event and those that followed in generally similar terms, though with a few differences as to some (mostly minor) facts and their chronology.

After speaking these words, the Angel Gabriel went away, leaving the Prophet in a deeply troubled state. He was afraid and did not know whether he had had a devilish vision or whether he was simply possessed.

He decided to go back to his wife. He eventually arrived in great distress and said: "Cover me! Cover me!" Khadijah wrapped him in a cloak and asked what was the matter. Muhammad explained what had happened and expressed his fear: "What is happening to me? I fear for myself."[2] Khadijah comforted him and whispered: "You have nothing to fear. Have

29

a rest and calm down. God will not let you suffer any humiliation, because you are kind to your kinsfolk, you speak the truth, you help those in need, you are generous to your guests, and you support every just cause."[3]

Waraqah ibn Nawfal

Khadijah thought of seeking the opinion of her cousin, the Christian Waraqah ibn Nawfal. She went to him (whether alone or with the Prophet is not clear) and told him of Muhammad's experience.[4] Waraqah recognized the signs he had been waiting for and answered without hesitation: "Holy! Holy! By He who holds Waraqah's soul, it is the sublime Namus [the friend of the secrets of Supreme Royalty, the angel bringing the sacred Revelation] who has come to Muhammad; the same who had come to Moses. Indeed, Muhammad is the prophet of this people."[5]

Later, during an encounter with Muhammad near the Kaba, Waraqah was to add: "You will certainly be called a liar, ill-treated, banished, and attacked. If I am still alive then, God knows I will support you to bring His cause to victory!"[6] Aishah reports that Waraqah also said: "Your people will turn you away!" This startled the Prophet, and he asked, "Will they turn me away?" Waraqah warned him: "Indeed they will! No man has ever brought what you have brought and not been treated as an enemy!"[7]

The Prophet's mission had only just begun, and already he was allowed to grasp some of the fundamentals of the final Revelation as well as some of the truths that had been present throughout the history of prophecies among peoples.

Faith, Knowledge, and Humility

The first verses revealed to the Prophet, who could neither read nor write, directly turn his attention toward knowledge. Though he is unable to read when relying on his own faculties, God calls on him to read "in the name of your Lord" (*Rabb*, "Educator"), immediately drawing a link between faith in God and knowledge. The following verses confirm this relationship: "He who taught by means of the pen, taught humankind that which they did not know." Between the Creator and humankind, there is faith that relies and feeds on the knowledge granted to people by the Most Bountiful (*al-Akram*) to allow them to answer His call and turn to Him. The first verses establish an immediate correspondence with what Revelation was later to recount about the creation of humankind: "He [God] taught Adam the names of all things."[8] Reason, intelligence, language, and writing will grant people the qualities required to enable them to be God's khalifahs (vicegerents) on earth, and from the very beginning, Quranic Revelation allies recognition of the Creator to knowledge and science, thus echoing the origin of creation itself.[9]

Numerous traditions report that the second Revelation corresponded to the beginning of the surah "Al-Qalam" (The Pen): those verses confirmed the divine source of this inspiration as well as the necessity of knowledge. They also mentioned the Messenger's moral singularity, as witnessed by the first forty years of his life:

Nûn. By the pen and by that which they write. You [Muhammad] are not, by the grace of your Lord [*Rabb*, "Educator"], possessed. Verily, yours is an unfailing reward. And surely you have sublime morals. You will soon see, and they will see, which of you is afflicted with madness.[10]

Nûn is one of the letters of the Arabic alphabet; in the same way, various other letters introduce some surahs (chapters) of the Quran, while no commentator—nor even the Prophet himself—is able to say exactly what they mean or what their presence at the beginning of a chapter symbolizes. Thus, at the very moment when the Creator swears "by the pen" and confirms the necessity of the knowledge conveyed to human beings, He opens the verses with a mysterious letter, *nûn*, expressing the limits of human knowledge. The dignity of humankind, conferred by knowledge, cannot be devoid of the humility of reason aware of its own limits and thereby recognizing the necessity of faith. Accepting, and accepting not to understand, the mysterious presence of the letter *nûn* requires faith; understanding and accepting the unmysterious statements of the verses that follow require the use of a reason that is active but necessarily—and indeed naturally—humbled.

Faith, Morality, and Persecution

To the essential teaching of Islam that knowledge exists only with human awareness of its limits, the surah quoted above, "Al-Qalam," adds another dimension when it speaks of the Prophet's "sublime morals." This verse, recalling what we already knew of the Prophet's exceptionally noble behavior since his birth, draws a specific link between knowledge, faith, and action. In the light of faith, knowledge must be based in and rely on the individual's moral dignity; indeed, it is the nobleness of the Prophet's behavior that confirms to him, a posteriori, that he is not possessed, that he is in the right, and that his reward will be endless. Faith in God and knowledge, in the light of the divine, must have as their immediate consequence a behavior, a way of acting, that respects an ethic and promotes good.

Those verses convey another teaching, predicted by Waraqah ibn Nawfal as by the monk Bahira before him: there were to be insults, adversity, hatred, and even banishment by his own people. The Prophet was warned that he would certainly be rejected, but for the moment, after the first Revelations, he had to face his own doubts: he had been comforted by his wife, then by Waraqah ibn Nawfal's confirmation, but he had received nothing from the Angel Gabriel himself to reassure him thoroughly. Sometimes, when the Prophet was walking, he would see the image of Gabriel filling the horizon, and if he turned away he would still see Gabriel facing him.

There are no precise data as to the number of Revelations the Prophet received during this first phase, but Aishah reports that the Prophet said that one day he heard a noise and suddenly "the angel who had come to me in the cave of Hira appeared to me, sitting between the sky and the earth; I was frightened, and [as had happened on the occasion of the first Revelation] I rushed home and said: 'Cover me! Cover me!' which was done."[11] This was when the following verses were revealed: "O you wrapped up in a mantle! Arise and deliver your warning! And your Lord [*Rabb*] glorify! And your garments purify! And all abomination shun!"[12]

In each of these initial Revelations, God presents Himself to His Messenger as "your *Rabb*" (*Rabbuk*), or Educator, who has chosen him, raised him, then called him to bear the final Revelation of the One God. It was not without purpose that Muhammad had been orphaned and poor and that he had gone through a period of contemplation, even though at that particular moment worry and distress prevailed over the awareness of his election and mission.

Silence, Doubt

The situation was to get even worse, for during the following months Revelation stopped. This period of silence (*al-fatra*), which lasted between six months and two and a half years, depending on the tradition cited, caused the Prophet great doubt and suffering. He thought that he was no longer worthy of receiving Revelation, that he had been forsaken, or that he had merely been bewitched. Aishah reports how intensely he suffered:

> Revelation stopped for some time, so the Prophet was hurt; his sorrow was such that on several occasions, he left home to go and throw himself from a steep mountain. But each time he reached the top of the mountain to throw himself into the chasm, the Angel Gabriel would appear to him and say: "O Muhammad, you are truly God's Messenger." Those words would calm his heart and bring peace to his soul.[13]

Those apparitions and signs around him helped the Prophet resist the feelings of doubt and solitude. He was actually undergoing the same experience as Abraham: in the ordeal of this silence, he doubted himself, his capacities, and his power, but God was constantly strewing his path with signs and visions that prevented him from doubting God. This trial of silence was an initiation shaping the Messenger's spiritual quest. Revelation had verbally told him about the necessity of humility, but God's silence was now teaching it to him practically. God had revealed His presence to him, and in the course of those long weeks empty of His word, He was fostering the need for Him in His Messenger's heart. God at last spoke to him again, invoking the rising day and the spreading night as much for their physical reality, which is a sign of the Creator's power, as for their symbolism, which expresses the fragility of being and the heart between the rising light of Revelation and the obscure emptiness of silence:

> By the morning light! By the night when it is still! Your Lord [*Rabb*, "Educator"] has not forsaken you, nor is He displeased. And verily the

Hereafter will be better for you than the present. And soon will your Lord give you that with which you will be well pleased.[14]

This was good news, and Revelation was not to stop again for over twenty years.

The verses were to be revealed in an irregular way (sometimes only a few verses, sometimes a whole chapter) and the Prophet was told where exactly to insert the new revelation he received in order to constitute the final Book. Even though the Arabs were used to the oral traditional, the Prophet commanded the new converts around him who knew reading and writing (among them was the well-known Zayd ibn Thâbit) to transcribe the verses on planks or even camel's shoulder blades (and to keep them according to the order he was mentioning to them). At the same time, numerous Companions were memorising the verses as they were revealed.

Khadijah

It is important to stress here the role played by Khadijah throughout those years ridden with events, some extraordinary and others deeply painful. She was the one who had first noticed and then chosen Muhammad for his honesty, his fairness, and the nobleness of his character. Widely courted in Mecca because of her wealth, she had been able to measure the disinterested and reserved attitude of that young man, who was nonetheless so enterprising and efficient. And against usual practice, she had the courage to propose marriage to him through her friend Nufaysah. Their union was to bring them their lot of happiness, sorrow, and grief: they lost their two sons, Qasim and Abdullah, in infancy and only their four daughters survived.[15] This family destiny was difficult enough, but among the Arabs, the birth of a daughter was considered shameful; tradition reports how much, on the contrary, Muhammad and his wife surrounded their daughters with deep love and constant care, which they never hesitated to express in public.

When at the age of forty Muhammad received the first Revelation, it was to his wife he immediately turned, and she was the first to stand by him and comfort him. During all the previous years, she observed a man whose nobleness of character was a distinctive feature. When he came back to her from the cave of Hira, troubled and assailed with deep doubt as to what he was and what was happening to him, she wrapped him in her love, reminded him of his qualities, and restored his self-confidence. The first Revelations were both an extraordinary gift and a terrible trial for a man who no longer knew whether he was possessed or the prey of devilish delirium. He was alone and confused; he turned to his wife, who immediately lent him comfort and support. From that moment on, there were two of them facing the trial, trying to understand its meaning and then, after the silence of Revelation had ended, answering God's call and following the path of spiritual initiation. In this respect, Khadijah is a sign of God's presence at the heart of Muhammad's trial; she is to the Prophet Muhammad's spiritual experience what Ishmael and Hagar were to Abraham's trial. Both women and the son were the signs sent by the One to manifest His presence and His support in their trial, so that they should never doubt Him. Khadijah was to be the first to accept Islam, and throughout the first ten years of Muhammad's mission, she was to remain at his side, an unfailingly faithful companion. This woman's role in the Prophet's life was tremendous. She was, for twenty-five years, his only wife, whose presence alone protected the Prophet but who also underwent with him rejection by his kin, persecution, and isolation.[16] He loved her so much. This was so obvious that, many years after Khadijah's death, Aishah—who later married the Prophet—was to say that Khadijah was the only woman of whom she had ever been jealous. Khadijah received the good news of his election by God; she was a woman, independent, dignified, and respected, then a wife, strong, attentive, faithful, and confident; she was a pious Muslim, sincere, determined, and enduring. Muhammad, the Last Prophet of the One, was not alone, and one of the clearest signs of God's bounty and love for him was a woman in his life, his wife.

A Revelation, Truths, a Book

God had manifested Himself. The first Revelations oriented the Prophet's consciousness toward His supreme, educating presence, since He constantly spoke to him as *Rabbuk*, Muhammad's Educator, his Lord. The

Angel Gabriel had transmitted the first fundamentals of the message and of the recognition of God—the essence of faith—while expressing the centrality of knowledge (reading and writing) allied to good behavior. The announcement of good tidings was also accompanied by a warning about others' future opposition to Muhammad, for never did a person of truth appear on earth without giving rise to a fury of hatred, lies, and calumny. Even some of his own kin, who had loved him, came to hate him so much as to want to kill him.

The Angel Gabriel appeared to him several times. The Prophet was later to report that the angel sometimes appeared to him in his angelic persona and sometimes as a human being. At other times, Muhammad would hear a bell-like sound and Revelation would come suddenly, requiring of him such extreme concentration that he came close to asphyxiation. This last mode was particularly painful, even though at the end of the process he was able to repeat word for word the contents of Revelation he had received.[17] For twenty years, the Angel Gabriel was to accompany him and reveal, irregularly and as the situation warranted, the verses and surahs that would ultimately constitute the Quran. Revelations were not placed chronologically in the book that was taking shape; they followed an order that the Angel Gabriel indicated to the Prophet each time and which the latter scrupulously respected. Every year, during the month of Ramadan, the Prophet would recite to the Angel Gabriel all that he had received of the Quran so far in the order the angel had indicated. Thus was effected a regular verification of the contents and form of the Book that was slowly being constituted over a period of twenty-three years.

CHAPTER FIVE

The Message and Adversity

After recovering from the distress caused by the initial experience of Revelation, and as he began to receive the subsequent Revelations, the Prophet began to share the message with those closest to him. He had not yet received instructions on how to present the message to his people, but he anticipated fierce opposition, as had been foretold by Waraqah ibn Nawfal.

The First Conversions

After Khadijah, his wife and the first convert to Islam, the circle of those who accepted the message was to widen to include members of his close family, then his friends. Ali ibn Abi Talib, who was the young cousin in his charge; Zayd, his adopted son; Um Ayman, the nursemaid who had cared for him after he returned to Mecca at age four; and his lifelong friend Abu Bakr were thus among the first to recognize the truth of the message and to pronounce the profession of faith (*ash-shahadah*) expressing their adherence to Islam: "I bear witness that there is no god but God and that Muhammad is His Messenger." The number of converts slowly grew as a result of the Prophet's own discreet preaching and the very determined involvement of Abu Bakr, who was always ready to speak about the new faith and take action for its sake: he would buy slaves from their masters and set them free in the name of Islam's principles stressing the equality of all human beings. During those years, Muhammad's presence in Mecca, his action, and his example were to attract a large number of women and men who were gradually to embrace the new faith.

The number of conversions nevertheless remained small during the first few months. Tradition reports that during the first three years, only thirty to forty Quraysh became Muslims. They would meet with the Prophet at the home of one of the converts, al-Arqam ibn Abi al-Arqam, and learn the basics of their religion while new Revelations kept arriving. The surrounding atmosphere was becoming more and more hostile as the inhabitants of Mecca learned about the essentials of this new message and took stock of its impact on the poor and the young. The Prophet, aware of those upheavals and of the dangers ahead, decided to concentrate on discreetly giving a solid education to a small group, who he knew would face criticism, rejection, and most probably exclusion. It was this very group who were later, thanks to the quality of their spiritual education and the sincerity of their involvement, to remain steadfast in the face of difficulties and persecution. From the beginning, the Prophet had given priority to quality over quantity, and preferred to concern himself with the nature of the hearts and minds he addressed rather than their number. For three years, he quietly built up the first community of believers, whose particular feature was that it gathered, without distinction, women and men of all clans and all social categories (although the bulk were young or poor).

The Public Call

After those years, Muhammad received a Revelation enjoining him to make his call public: "And admonish your nearest kinsmen."[1] The Prophet understood that he now had to convey his message to the members of the clans to which he was linked by kinship ties. He began to call them to Islam. One day, he climbed up Mount as-Safa and called the tribal chiefs one by one. Thinking he had an urgent or important announcement to make, they gathered at the foot of the hill to listen to him. From where they stood, they could not look into the valley, whereas Muhammad was facing it. He called out to them: "If I warned you that down in this valley, armed horsemen are closing in to attack you, would you believe me?" They answered, almost with one voice: "Certainly—you are trustworthy and we have never heard you tell lies!" The Prophet then went on: "Well, I am here to forewarn you of violent torments! God has ordered me to admonish my nearest kinsmen. I have no power to protect you from anything in this life, nor to grant you blessings in the life to come, unless you believe in the Oneness of God." He added: "My position is like that of he who sees the enemy and runs to his people to warn them before they are taken by surprise, shouting as he runs: 'Beware! Beware!'"[2]

His uncle Abu Lahab's response was immediate and scathing: "Woe to you [*taban laka*]! Is this why you have gathered us?" He turned away instantly, taking the assembled chiefs with him: he was thus to come to epitomize those who rejected Muhammad's message and opposed him most fiercely.[3] Later on, when the Prophet organized two meals to present the same message, the first was a failure because Abu Lahab again intervened to prevent his nephew from speaking. During the second meal, Muhammad was able to convey the substance of his message, which was heard and secretly accepted by some members of the clans he had invited.

His kinsmen and the tribe's elders had reacted in a rather cold and distant manner because they understood that the nature of Muhammad's message threatened the age-old balance in their society. Both their gods and their power could be challenged, and the danger was serious. Muhammad continued to speak to his kinsfolk until he received another Revelation ordering a forthright, determined attitude: "Therefore expound openly what you are commanded, and turn away from those who join false gods with God."[4]

The prophetic mission was entering a new phase. Now the message was addressed to all and required a clear-cut distinction between *tawhid*, faith in one God, and the polytheism of the Quraysh. The Prophet had gathered around him a solid core of trustworthy women and men; some were his relatives, but many came from different social categories and tribes, and he had been providing them spiritual and religious education for the previous three years. With steadfastness and forbearance, they were to face rejection, persecution, and exclusion in a Meccan society that was beginning to split apart.

The Message

During the first years of Revelation, the Quranic message had gradually taken shape around four main axes: the oneness of God, the status of the

Quran, prayer, and life after death. The first Muslims were called to a profound and radical spiritual conversion, and this had been well understood by opponents within their own clans, who feared the considerable upheavals the new religion was bound to bring about in the beliefs and organization of their society.

The Oneness of God

The Quranic message primarily focused on asserting the oneness of God (*at-tawhid*). Together with the notion of God as *Rabb*, or Educator, which we saw emerge in the first Revelations, the divine name Allah was of course to appear, as well as phrases associating His being with peace and mercy. Thus, the Angel Gabriel addressed the Prophet with the phrases "Peace be upon you, Messenger of God" (*as-salam alaykum, ya rasul Allah*) and "God's peace and mercy be upon you" (*salam Allah wa rahmatuhu alayk*). Those phrases have been used by Muslims since the beginning to greet one another and invoke God through His two names: Peace (*as-Salam*) and the Most Merciful (*ar-Rahman*, also translated as the Most Gracious or the Most Kind). Furthermore, each chapter of the Quran begins with a phrase of sanctification with which the speaker recalls the presence of the One and His supreme qualities: "In the name of God [I begin with the name of God], the Most Gracious, the Most Merciful." Very early on, the Quran made the name *ar-Rahman* equivalent to the name *Allah*: "Call upon God [Allah] or call upon the Most Kind, the Most Merciful, the Most Gracious [*ar-Rahman*]: by whatever name you call upon Him, to Him belong the most beautiful names."[5]

This omnipresence of the reference to the One and His different names is essential. Indeed, it was to shape the type of relationship the first believers established with God: the recognition of His Presence and the assurance that His benevolence is a gift as well as a promise of peace. This is most aptly illustrated by the surah "Ar-Rahman," which addresses both human beings and jinns and enjoins them to observe nature and recognize His Being and His beneficence:[6]

The Most Gracious! It is He Who has taught the Quran. He has created humans. He has taught them intelligent speech. The sun and the moon follow courses exactly computed. And the stars and the trees bow in adoration. And the firmament has He raised high, and He has set up the balance [of justice] in order that you may not transgress [due] balance. So establish weight with justice and do not fall short in the balance. It is He Who has spread out the earth for [His] creatures: in it are fruit and date palms, producing spathes; also corn, with its leaves and stalk for fodder, and sweet-smelling plants. Then which of the favors of your Lord will you [humans and jinns] deny?[7]

The Status of the Quran

From nature to the requirement of ethics and equity in human behavior, everything points to remembrance of the Creator, whose primary manifestation is goodness and mercy. Indeed, He has revealed the text itself in the name of His benevolence toward people. Revelation is both a gift and a burden, and this, from the very beginning, introduces the second axis of early Islamic teachings. The status of the Quran—which in the verses quoted above establishes the link between God and humankind—is one of the essentials of the Muslim creed (*al-aqidah*).[8] The Quran is the divine word revealed as such to humankind—in "Arabic pure and clear"—and it is all at once a reminder, a light, and a miracle.[9] It is a reminder of the monotheistic messages of the past, the light of divine guidance for the future, and the miracle of the eternal and inimitable word conveyed to human beings at the heart of their history.

From the outset, the Quran presents itself as the mirror of the universe. The term that the first Western translators rendered as "verse"—referring to biblical vocabulary—literally means, in Arabic, "sign" (*ayah*). Thus, the revealed Book, the written text, is made up of signs (*ayat*), just as the universe, like a text spread out before our eyes, is teeming with signs. When the heart's intelligence, and not only analytical intelligence, reads the Quran and the world, then the two texts address and echo each other, and each of them speaks of the other and of the One. The signs remind us of what it means to be born, to live, to think, to feel, and to die.

By its highly evocative form and contents, as well as by its spiritual power, the Quran is Islam's miracle. It also represents a huge, twofold responsibility for Muslims: both on the level of the ethical demands that Quranic teachings impress upon them and in their capacity as witnesses of those same teachings before humankind. This dimension is present from the earliest Revelations: thus, the surah "Al-Muzzammil" (The

Enshrouded One), one of the first revealed, contains the warning "Soon We shall send down to you a weighty Word."[10] Another verse uses a powerful image to express the spiritual status of the Quran: "Had We sent down this Quran on a mountain, verily, you would have seen it humble itself and cleave asunder in awe of God."[11] The revealed text, God's Word (*kalam Allah*), presents itself both as a benevolent reminder and as a particularly demanding moral injunction that spreads spiritual inspiration as much as it structures the definite form of religious ritual.

Prayer

While he was walking in the surroundings of Mecca, the Prophet received a visit from the Angel Gabriel, who taught him how to perform ablutions and practice ritual prayer.[12] This teaching came very early on, immediately associating the act of purification through water with the injunction to perform prayer based on reciting the Quran and on a precise, cyclical series of gestures (*raka*). The Prophet followed the Angel Gabriel's instructions one by one, then went home and taught his wife, Khadijah, how to pray. During those early years, ritual prayer was performed only twice a day, in the morning and in the evening.

The surah "Al-Muzzammil," quoted above, also refers to the night prayer, which became an obligation for all Muslims at the beginning of the Meccan period and remained so until the duty to perform five daily prayers was finally established. The spiritual training and the ritual were particularly demanding:

> O you enshrouded one! Stand [to prayer] by night, but not all night—half of it, or a little less, or a little more; and recite the Quran in slow, measured rhythmic tones. We shall soon send down to you a weighty Word. Truly the rising by night is a time when impression is more keen and speech more certain. True, there is for you by day prolonged occupation with ordinary duties. But keep in remembrance the name of your Educator [*Rabb*] and devote yourself to Him [commune with Him] wholeheartedly.[13]

At the heart of Mecca, in an increasingly hostile environment, the women and men who had accepted Islam were training unsparingly, quietly: they rose at night to pray to God lengthily, reciting by heart the signs (*ayat*) of the Quran, which the One has established as the privileged link between His infinite Kindness and the heart of each being. This deep and intense spiritual training determined the most significant characteristic of the first believers: pious, discreet, and determined, they prayed to the God of mercy and peace; kept reciting His Revelation, which is a reminder (*dhikr*) and a light (*nur*) and followed the example and teachings of the Last Prophet. The essence of the Islamic message is wholly expressed in this intimate relationship of trust and love with the Most High, establishing a direct link between the individual and his or her Creator, Who has chosen to demonstrate exemplary behavior through a Messenger, a human being, whom He has set as a model. Three verses were later to synthesize the exact substance of this teaching:

> When My servants ask you concerning Me, I am indeed close [to them]: I respond to the prayer of every supplicant when he or she calls on Me.[14]

The Prophet, at the heart of this intimate relationship, opens the way:

> Say: If you love God, follow me: God will love you and forgive you your sins.[15]

He is the epitome of the human being aspiring to the divine beyond the finitude of life:

> You have indeed in the Messenger of God an excellent example for the person who hopes in [aspires to get close to] God and the Final Day and who remembers God intensely.[16]

The initial group of believers lived on this teaching: in their prayers, they faced Jerusalem, thus expressing the clear linkage of this message to the Jewish and Christian monotheisms, which share the same aspiration to the eternal and life in the hereafter.

The Hereafter and the Last Judgment

The verses repeatedly express the theme of life after death. In the face of people's incredulity, the Quran relies, as we have seen in preceding chapters, on examples drawn from nature, specifically the desert, a seemingly dead land that comes back to life after a rain. Very early on, the Prophet's attention was turned toward the priority of this other life: "And verily the Hereafter will be better for you than the present."[17]

In reality, the message is meant very clearly not to appease doubts and fears about inescapable death but to impress on the believers' minds and hearts the firm belief that this life has a meaning and that to God we shall return. This constant presence of the reminder of the hereafter does indeed convey the idea of the Last Judgment, for which God will establish the balance of good and evil that each being has been responsible for during his or her earthly life. Thus, consciousness of the Last Judgment points to the relationship between faith and morals, between contemplation and action: the "straight path" that pleases the Most High is the way of those who "believe and do righteous deeds" (*al-ladhina amanu wa amilu as-salihat*).[18]

Being with God, being for God, giving oneself, thus involves "enjoining what is right" (*al-maruf*) and "forbidding what is wrong" (*al-munkar*); it is opting to meet the ethical demand.[19] Being with God necessitates changing one's behavior and deciding to be part of "a community inviting to all that is good."[20] Islam, like other monotheistic traditions, insists on the return to God, on His judgment, on heaven and hell, and numerous verses associate the meaning of life with the hereafter. In the spiritual experience that determines the meaning of life and links it to the requirement to behave ethically, this initiatory phase is essential, even though it is not the ultimate teaching of the relationship with God. Beyond the hope for His paradise and the fear of hell, the pinnacle of the relationship with the Most Near is primarily to love Him and to aspire to contemplating His face (*wajh*) for eternity, as the Prophet was later to teach his Companions with this invocation: "O God, offer us the grace and pleasure of looking upon Your infinitely bounteous face [*wajhika*]." The moral demand constitutes the necessary path toward the intimate and loving presence of God.

Adversity

The call was now public, and even though the training new converts received at al-Arqam's home was discreet, they did not hesitate to speak to their relatives and to the people around them. Day after day, clan chiefs became increasingly aware of the danger the new religion posed: this was a straightforward rebellion against their gods and their customs, and it was eventually bound to endanger the chiefs' power. They first decided to send a delegation to the Prophet's uncle, Abu Talib, who had so far been protecting his nephew. They asked him to speak to Muhammad and make him stop spreading his message, which they considered dangerous and unacceptable because it directly attacked their gods and their ancestors' heritage. Abu Talib took no action after their first visit, so they came back and insisted that the matter was urgent. Abu Talib then sent for his nephew and tried to convince him to terminate his activities in order not to embarrass him. Muhammad's answer was firm: "O my uncle, I swear to God that, should they place the sun in my right hand and the moon in my left hand in order for me to abandon this cause, I would not abandon it before He [God] had made it triumph or I had perished for its sake!"[21] In the face of such determination, Abu Talib did not insist; in fact, he assured his nephew of his permanent support.

A new delegation came to the Prophet and offered him goods, money, and power. He refused their offers one by one and confirmed that he was interested only in his mission: calling people to recognize and believe in God, the One, whatever the price might be.

> I am not possessed, nor do I seek among you honors or power. God has sent me to you as a messenger, He has revealed me a Book and has ordered me to bring you good news and warn you. I have conveyed to you my Lord's message and I have given you good advice. If you accept from me what I have brought, this will cause you to succeed in this world and in the hereafter; but if you reject what I have brought, then I shall wait patiently until God judges between us.[22]

With those words, Muhammad was setting the limits of possible compromise: he would not stop conveying his message, and he would trust in God and be patient as to the consequences of this decision in this world. In practice, hostilities had now begun: clan chiefs kept insulting the Prophet and saying that he was insane, possessed, or a sorcerer. Abu Lahab, his uncle, pressured his two sons to divorce the Prophet's daughters, whom they had married, while his wife relished tossing the household garbage out into the street as Muhammad passed by.

Rumors spread that Muhammad was actually a sorcerer, that he broke up families, separated parents from their children and husbands from their wives, and was a troublemaker. When the time for the annual market period grew near, the clan chiefs, fearing that Muhammad might spread his message among visitors, had men posted at the various entrances of Mecca: they were to warn arriving visitors of the mischief caused by Muhammad and his Companions. The isolation strategy worked fairly well, although some people did not allow themselves to be influenced, such as the highway robber Abu Dharr, from Banu Ghifar. Having heard of this new message calling for faith in one God, he came to the Prophet in spite of the Quraysh people's warnings. He found Muhammad lying in the shade near the Kaba. He called the Prophet's name and asked about his message: he listened, then immediately pronounced the profession of faith, surprising the Prophet, who said, looking at him: "God guides whom He will!" Abu Dharr al-Ghifari was to become one of the Prophet's most famous Companions; he was known for his devotion, his rigor, and his criticism of luxury and laziness.

The Prophet was facing humiliation and mockery. People asked him for miracles and proofs, and he tirelessly answered by quoting the Quran and saying, "I am but a messenger!" The pressure grew, and increasingly violent manifestations of opposition started to appear. Clan chiefs particularly attacked poor Muslims and those who were not protected by any clan. Thus the slave Bilal had been tied up by his master in the desert, in the sun. His master placed a boulder on his stomach to force him to abjure his faith, but Bilal kept repeating: "He is One, He is One." Abu Bakr later bought Bilal (as he did for many other slaves) and set him free. Bilal was later to become the muezzin of Medina, unanimously respected for the sincerity of his faith, his devotion, and the beauty of his voice.[23]

A man from the Makhzum tribe, named Amr, was to express his opposition to Islam in the most cruel manner. His kin called him Abu al-Hakam (father of wise judgment), but the Muslims, confronted with his refusal to see and his coarseness, called him Abu Jahl (father of ignorance). He once went to meet the Prophet and insulted him with such hatred that those who heard him, even though they were not Muslims, considered he had transgressed the honor code by humiliating Muhammad in this way. Hearing this, Hamzah, the Prophet's uncle, intervened. He went up to Abu Jahl and threatened him with reprisals if he behaved in that way again; at the same time, he announced that he himself had become a Muslim and that he would now personally take on his nephew's protection.[24] As a result, Abu Jahl stopped abusing Muhammad: instead, he started to mistreat the Prophet's poorest and most vulnerable Companions. Ammar, a young man of Yemeni origin, had adhered to Islam's message very early and received training from the Prophet in al-Arqam's home. His father, Yassir, and then his mother, Sumayyah, became Muslims shortly after he did, and assiduously learned the new religion. Abu Jahl chose them as the object of his vengeful hatred: he took to beating them, tying them up in the sun, and torturing them. The Prophet could not do anything because of the still complex nature of clan alliances; he witnessed this debasing treatment without being able to intervene. One day, as he passed by Yassir and his wife, who were being ill-treated, the Prophet called out to them: "Be strong, Yassir's family, our meeting point is in paradise." Despite those tortures, which went on for weeks, Sumayyah and Yassir refused to abjure their faith. Sumayyah even shouted at Abu Jahl what she thought of him and his cowardly behavior. Infuriated, he stabbed her to death, then, in the same raging anger, he turned to her husband and beat him to death as well. Sumayyah and Yassir were the first martyrs (*shuhada*) of Islam: persecuted, tortured, then killed for refusing to deny God, His Oneness, and the truth of the last Revelation.[25]

The situation was getting increasingly difficult for Muslims, particularly for the most vulnerable among them as far as social status and clan affiliation were concerned. The Prophet's protection was ensured by his uncles Abu Talib and Hamzah, but this protection by no means extended to the first spiritual community of Muslims. Insults, rejection, and ill-treatment became the rule, and Muhammad began looking for a solution to alleviate the trials and suffering endured by the first Muslims. He thought of approaching Walid, the chief of the Makhzum clan, to which Abu Jahl belonged; Walid wielded considerable power over the whole of Meccan society. If the Prophet could convince him of the truth of his message, or at least bring him to intercede and stop the persecutions, this would be an important achievement for himself and his Companions. But while he was setting forth his arguments and trying to win Walid's support, the Prophet was interrupted by a blind man, poor and old, who had already converted to Islam and was asking him to recite some surahs from the Quran for him. Muhammad first turned aside calmly, but he soon became irritated by the insistence of this old man, who was preventing him from presenting his case to Walid. The chief, full of contempt, eventually refused even to hear the matter. A surah was to be revealed as a result of this incident, requiring Muslims to draw a lesson from it for eternity:

> In the name of God, Most Gracious, Most Merciful. He [the Prophet] frowned and turned away, because the blind man came to him. But what could you tell but that perhaps he might grow in purity? Or that he might receive admonition, and the reminder might profit him? As to one who regards himself as self-sufficient, you attend to him, though it is no blame to you if he does not grow in purity. But as to he who came to you striving earnestly, and with fear [in his heart], of him you were unmindful. By no means [should it be so]! For it is indeed a message of remembrance. Therefore let who will, keep it in remembrance![26]

The Prophet, moved by his desire to protect his community, is here reproached by his Educator, who teaches him never to turn away from a human being, regardless of whatever difficult circumstances the Prophet might be facing, even though the person might be poor, old, and blind. Seeking the protection of a person of distinction, socially and politically useful, Muhammad had neglected a poor man, apparently of no significance to his cause, who was asking for spiritual solace; this mistake, this moral slip, is recorded in the Quran, which through this story teaches Muslims never to neglect a human being, never to turn away from the poor and needy, but rather to serve and love them. The Prophet was never to forget this teaching, and he repeatedly invoked God, saying: "O God, we implore You to grant us piety, dignity, [spiritual] wealth, and love of the poor."[27]

Thus the Prophet is a model for Muslims not only through the excellence of his behavior but also through the weaknesses of his humanity, revealed and mentioned by the Quran so that Muslim consciences may never forget this message through the ages. No one must ever let power or social, economic, or political interests turn him or her away from other human beings, from the attention they deserve and the respect they are entitled to. Nothing must ever lead a person to compromise this principle of faith in favor of a political strategy aimed at saving or protecting a community from some peril. The freely offered, sincere heart of a poor,

powerless individual is worth a thousand times more in the sight of God
than the assiduously courted, self-interested heart of a rich one.

The Prophet constantly strove to be the example of and witness to this
message, but in the course of their history, Muslims have often forgotten
and neglected this injunction to treat the needy with respect and dignity.
Even while the Prophet was still alive, his Companion Abu Dharr al-
Ghifari, mentioned above, spoke out in a forceful and determined manner against the failings of some Muslims increasingly attracted by power,
comfort, and riches. He saw in this the beginning of an inversion of the
spiritual order, evidence of deep alienation, and the first signs of foretold
disasters. History, with its many examples of how the thirst for power and
wealth has led individuals to compromise their principles, has since taught
us how true this intuition was. In this respect, another of the Prophet's
warnings echoes in our minds, addressing his spiritual community for the
centuries to come: "For every [spiritual] community there is an object of
discord, tension, and disorder [*fitnah*], and for my community, this object
is money."[28]

CHAPTER SIX

Resistance, Humility, and Exile

The clan chiefs kept mocking Muhammad and encouraging others to criticize and humiliate him. The man who claimed to be a prophet was asked for miracles and tangible evidence. People questioned God's choice in electing a man who held no particular power, who went about in marketplaces without any sign setting him apart from other men. They mocked the man and his claims as much as the message.

Nevertheless, as we have seen, the Prophet stood his ground. When one of the Quraysh leaders, Utbah ibn Rabiah, came to see him to offer him money and power, the Prophet's response was first of all to quote the Quran at length:

In the name of God, Most Gracious, Most Merciful. *Hâ, mîm*. A Revelation from the Most Gracious, Most Merciful. A Book, of which the messages are clearly explained; a Quran in Arabic, for people with inner knowledge, giving good news and admonition: yet most of them turn away, and so they do not hear. They say: "Our hearts are under veils, [concealed] from that to which you invite us, and in our ears is a deafness, and between us and you is a screen: so do [what you will]; as for us, we shall do [what we will]." Say [O Prophet]: "I am but a man like you: it is revealed to me by inspiration, that your God is One God. So take the straight path unto Him and ask for His forgiveness. And woe to those who associate other gods with Him, those who do not pay the purifying social tax [*zakat*] and who even deny the hereafter! For those who believe and work deeds of righteousness is a reward that will never fail." Say: "Do you deny He Who created the earth in two days [*cycles*], and do you join equals with Him?[1] He is the Lord of [all] the worlds. He set on the earth mountains standing firm, high above it, and bestowed blessings on the earth, and measured therein its sustenance in four days [cycles] alike for those who seek."[2]

The Prophet went on reciting up to verse 38, which mentions those who prostrate themselves; when he reached it, he prostrated himself in reverence to the One God. Utbah had come to him to offer him the riches and power of this world, and he was now faced with a man prostrated in the name of his faith in the Eternal and thereby expressing his clear rejection of the proposal that had just been made to him. Utbah was very strongly impressed by the form and content of the Quranic message, and he went back to his kin and suggested that they should not oppose this message. But they, persuaded that he had been bewitched by the magic of those words, paid no heed to this advice and carried on with their persecutions.

Jihad

As for the Prophet, he also persevered: whenever his opponents attacked him, he used the Quran to answer, protect himself, and resist. This is what Revelation clearly taught him with this verse, which marks the first occurrence of the word *jihad* in the Quran:

> Therefore do not obey the negators, but strive against them [*jahidhum*] with the Quran with the utmost resistance [*jihadan kabira*].[3]

Confronted with pressures of all sorts, from the mildest to the most violent, Muhammad received a verse that pointed to the way and means of the resistance—of the *jihad*—he was to undertake. What we find here is the initial and essential meaning of the concept of *jihad*, the root of which, *ja-ha-da*, means "making an effort" but also, in this instance, "resisting" (that is, resisting oppression and persecution). God orders His Messenger to resist the Quraysh's ill-treatment of him by relying on the Quran. The text is actually his spiritual and intellectual weapon against their aggression. To those who sneer, insult, and humiliate, to those who attack, torture, and kill, to those who want miracles and proofs, the Prophet invariably answers with the weapon and shield of the Quran, which in itself constitutes, as we have seen, the miracle and the proof. The text liberates the real strength in people, that which has the power to resist and overcome all the persecutions in this world, because it calls for the Life beyond the illusions of this life: "The life of this world is but amusement and play. But verily, the home of the hereafter—that is Life indeed, if they but knew."[4]

The essence of the notion of *jihad fi sabiliLLah* (resistance in the way of God) is wholly circumscribed in this first occurrence of the word at the heart of the surah "The Criterion." It is a matter of distinguishing, through the miracle of the two Revelations (the universe and the text), the presence of the One, and of resisting the lies and terror of those who are moved only by the desire to protect their own interests, powers, or pleasures. The first attitude this requires is to stay aloof:

Therefore shun those who turn away from Our message and desire nothing but the life of this world. That is their attainment of knowledge. Verily, your Lord knows best those who stray from His path, and He knows best those who receive guidance. To God belongs all that is in the heavens and on earth: so that He rewards those who do evil, according to their deeds, and He rewards those who do good with what is best.[5]

The criterion also has an ethical dimension, as we can see in the above verses, since what distinguishes the believer in this life is not only faith but also a way of being and behaving. Armed with this knowledge, the Prophet and his Companions first of all tried to convey their message freely while avoiding confrontation. The Quraysh leaders did not want it to be so, and they intensified their persecutions as Revelations followed upon each other in rapid succession. The first Muslims, like the Prophet, engaged in resistance—in *jihad*—reminding people of the existence of the One God, of Life after life, of the Last Judgment, and of the necessity for good, and the Quran was always the weapon of their spiritual discernment and their shield in the face of physical brutality.

However, the persecution was so violent and continuous that this *jihad* was sometimes difficult to bear. One day, a group of Muslims came to the Prophet while he was lying in the shade near the Kaba. They asked him:

"Won't you invoke God for us, that He may help us?" The Prophet firmly answered: "Among the believers who came before you, many were thrown into ditches dug for them and were sawed in two from head to foot, and this did not turn them away from their religion; their flesh was torn apart from their bones and sinews with iron combs, and this did not turn them away from their religion. By God, this cause will certainly prevail, so it will be possible for a lone traveler to go from Sanaa to Hadramout [regions in Yemen] without fearing anything but God, or the wolf for his sheep. But you are too impatient!"[6]

They therefore had to be patient, endure, persevere, and never despair of God and of His will. The Prophet was teaching his Companions the difficult association of trust in God with pain. The experience of physical and moral suffering made it possible to reach the state of faith where one accepts adversity, where one can doubt oneself without doubting God. In this respect, young Ammar's story is edifying: he had seen his mother, then his father, being executed because they refused to deny God. Then Ammar himself was tortured in the cruelest manner. One day while he was being tortured, unable to bear any more, he denied God and praised the gods of the Quraysh. His tormentors let him go, satisfied that they had achieved what they wanted. Ammar was alive, but he was besieged and undermined by a feeling of guilt he could not get rid of, as he was convinced that his denial could not be atoned for. He went to the Prophet in tears and confessed to him the cause of his misery and his doubts as to his own value and fate. The Prophet asked him about his innermost beliefs, and Ammar confirmed to him that they were unchanged, firm, and solid, and that he harbored no doubt as to his faith in God and his love. Muhammad calmed and reassured the young man, for he had done what he could and need not be angry with himself. Revelation even mentioned "one who, after accepting faith in God, utters unbelief . . . under compulsion, his heart remaining firm in faith."[7] He advised Ammar that if he ever again underwent the same unbearable torture, in order to save his life he should say with his lips what his torturers wanted to hear, keeping his faith and his prayers to God firmly in his heart.

Thus the Prophet recognized and accepted both attitudes: that of those who never denied their faith and who went so far as to die for it, and that of those who, under unbearable torture, escaped death by verbally denying their belief while it remained unshakeable in their mind and heart. Later on, Muslim scholars were to rely on this example, among others, in asserting that Muslims could, in an extreme situation where their lives were at risk at the hands of an unjust power, say with their lips what their torturers wanted to hear. This refers to the notion of *taqiyyah* (implying the act of dissimulating) and has been legitimated, as here in Ammar's case, only when an individual has to save his or her life in an extreme situation involving unbearable torture. In any other situation, as we shall see, Muslims were to say the truth, whatever the price might be.

Stakes

The Quraysh's opposition was not merely to a man and a message. Indeed, if all of God's messengers have met with the same reception—the same opposition and hatred from a considerable part of their own community—it is because the contents of what they brought meant a radical revolution in the order of things in society.

The Quran reports the words that greeted the messengers, in different ages, when they came to convey the message to their respective peoples. The first response was most often a rejection of change mingled with the fear of losing power, as in the answer given to Moses and Aaron by Pharaoh's people: "Have you come to us to turn us away from the ways we found our fathers following, in order that you and your brother may have greatness in the land? But we shall not believe in you!"[8] Understanding this relationship to memory, ancestors, and habits is essential to understanding how different peoples reacted when confronted with the transformations that were bound to come in the wake of a new belief and, consequently, of a new presence in the social body. The reaction is always reflexive and passionate, because what is at stake has to do with the identity and stability on which the society involved relies. The Prophet Muhammad, with his message and the increasingly visible development of his community, elicited the same reactions most intensely, and the Quraysh, carried away by the fear of what seemed to threaten their landmarks, opposed him fiercely and relentlessly.

The issue of power is obviously a crucial one: all the peoples who received prophets initially believed that they sought nothing but power and status, and Muhammad's case was no exception. People obviously use their own standpoint to try to interpret and understand the messengers' intentions and objectives: in the human order, one does not upset traditions, and consequently a social and political order, unless one seeks power. The logic of human relationships imposes this interpretation, and this explains the doubts and deafness of leaders faced with a message that, although its content is in itself far removed from such considerations, has explicit consequences for their power.

By calling for recognition of the One God, for the rejection of former idols, for Life after life, for ethics and justice, Muhammad initiated an outright revolution in mentalities as much as in society. It mattered little, all things considered, whether he sought power for himself or for anyone else; what remained self-evident was the fact that the inversion of perspectives contained in his message, which was oriented toward the hereafter, shook the underpinnings of worldly power.

Recognition of the One God and consciousness of Eternity allied to the ethical teaching appeared to the new believers as elements of their spiritual, intellectual, and social liberation. The Quraysh leaders' insight was, after all, lucid and to the point: the stakes underlying their radical opposition to a message of radical liberation were far-reaching and had essential implications for their fate. They sensed, without always being able to hear or understand it, the significance of the essential affirmation of faith in the One, which all at once expresses an intimate conversion and a general transmutation of order:

> Say: "He is God, the One; God, the Absolute; he does not beget, nor is he begotten; and there is none like Him."[9]

This statement points to the existence of a frontier:

> Say: "O you who reject faith [whose hearts are veiled]! I do not worship what you worship, nor do you worship what I worship! I am not a worshiper of that which you worship, nor are you worshipers of what I worship. To you be your religion, and to me mine."[10]

Questions

The Quraysh were at a loss about how to prevent Muhammad's message from spreading further. They decided to send a delegation to Yathrib to ask

Jewish dignitaries about the nature and truthfulness of this new Revelation. The Yathrib Jews were known to profess this same idea of the One God, and Muhammad often referred to Moses, their prophet; they were therefore best suited to express an opinion or even to suggest a strategy.

Consulted about the new prophet, the rabbis suggested the people of Mecca should ask him three key questions in order to find out whether what he said was actually revealed or whether he was a fraud. The first question involved the knowledge of a story about a group of young men's exile from their people; the second was about a great traveler who had reached the confines of the universe; the third was a direct request to define *ar-ruh* (the soul). The Quraysh delegation left, convinced that they now had the means to entrap Muhammad. Back in Mecca, they went to him and asked him the three questions. He replied almost instantly: "I shall answer your questions tomorrow!"[11]

But the next day, the Angel Gabriel did not appear. There was no Revelation. Nor did the angel come the day after, or during the next fourteen days. The Quraysh gloated, certain they had at last managed to prove the duplicity of the so-called prophet, who could not answer the rabbis' questions. As for Muhammad, he was sad, and as the days went by, he was increasingly afraid of having been forsaken: without doubting God, he again underwent the experience of self-doubt amplified by his opponents' sneers. Two weeks later, he received a Revelation and an explanation:

> Never say of anything, "I shall do that tomorrow," except: "If God so wills," and remember your Lord [*Rabb*, "Educator"] when you forget, and say: "I hope that my Lord will guide me ever closer than this to the right course."[12]

This Revelation once again involved a reproach and a teaching: it reminded the Prophet that his status, his knowledge, and his fate depended on his *Rabb*, on the One and Sovereign God, and that he must never forget it. This is how one should understand the meaning of the phrase *in sha Allah*, "if God so wills": it expresses the awareness of limits, the feeling of humility of one who acts while knowing that beyond what he or she can do or say, God alone has the power to make things happen. This is by no means a fatalistic message: it implies not that one should not act but, on the contrary, that one should never stop acting while always being aware in one's mind and heart of the real limits of human power. For the second time, the Prophet was called to account by the Transcendent. Whatever adversity one faces, one's strength and freedom on earth consist in remaining constantly aware of one's dependence on the Creator.

Only later was the Prophet to receive the answers to the three questions he had been asked. The delay was paradoxically to strengthen the believers' conviction and to baffle the Prophet's interlocutors: his initial inability to answer and then the belated communication of Revelation proved that Muhammad was not the author of the Book that was being constituted and that he did actually depend on his *Rabb*'s will.

The answer to the question about *ar-ruh* (the soul) directly referred—in the same way as the requirement of humility he had previously been reminded of—to the One's superior knowledge:

> They ask you concerning the soul [*ar-ruh*]. Say: the soul is of the command [the exclusive knowledge] of my Lord [*Rabb*, "Educator"]; of knowledge, it is only a little that is communicated to you.[13]

As for the two stories (that of the Seven Sleepers of Ephesus and that of the traveler Dhu al-Qarnayn), they are also told in surah 18, "The Cave." The stories are teeming with information and details the Quraysh and the Yathrib rabbis could not have expected and of which the Prophet knew nothing before Revelation. The same surah also tells the story of Moses, who in a moment of forgetfulness and oversight had lapsed into saying that because of his status as a prophet, "he knew." God then tried him by confronting him with one who knew more than he did, the character of al-Khidr in the Quran, who initiated him to understanding God's superior knowledge, to patience, and to the wisdom of remaining humble and refraining from asking too many questions.[14]

From the experience of Moses (who was so impatient) to that of Muhammad (who forgot his dependence) as well as the teaching addressed to all human beings (who, of knowledge, have received "only a little"), everything reminds Muslims of their own fragility and of their need for God, whatever their status, and this teaching is present throughout the surah "The Cave." Later, the Prophet was to recommend that every Muslim should read this surah in its entirety every Friday so as to remember, week after week, that they must not forget—forget themselves, forget Him.

Abyssinia

The humiliations and persecutions increased as Revelation of Quranic verses went on. Now they were no longer aimed only at the most vulnerable among Muslims but also at men and women whose status normally would have protected them, such as Abu Bakr. Muhammad, protected by his uncle Abu Talib, was the butt of jeers and ridicule, but he was not physically harmed. Seeing that the situation in Mecca was getting worse, the Prophet suggested: "If you went to the land of the Abyssinians, you would find there a king under whose command nobody suffers injustice. It is a land of sincerity in religion. You would remain there until God delivered you from what you suffer at present."[15]

The Prophet was referring to the king of Abyssinia, the Negus, who was a Christian and who was reputed to be respectful and fair with his people.[16] Part of the community therefore started to prepare for departure, and eventually a number of individuals and families discreetly left Mecca to undertake the first emigration (*al-hijrah al-ula*): there were in all about a hundred people, eighty-two or eighty-three men and close to twenty women.

This took place in the year 615, five years after the beginning of Revelation and two years after the beginning of the public call. The situation had become particularly difficult, so much so as to prompt those Muslims to take the risk of going into exile very far from Mecca. Uthman ibn Affan and his wife, Ruqayyah, the Prophet's daughter, were part of the group; so was Abu Bakr, but he came back when, on the way, he met a Meccan dignitary who granted him his protection. It also included Um Salamah, who was later to become the Prophet's wife, and through whom accounts of the various episodes of the emigration to Abyssinia have come down to us.

The Quraysh leaders soon found out that some Muslims—paradoxically, not the most vulnerable—had left Mecca. It was not long either before they knew where the Muslims had gone. They had some reason to worry: if this small group of Muslims managed to settle elsewhere, they were bound to tarnish the Meccans' reputation and perhaps arouse animosity toward them or even try to constitute an alliance against them with a king who they knew shared that faith in one God. After the Muslims had been gone some time, the Quraysh leaders decided to send the Negus two emissaries, Amr ibn al-As and Abdullah ibn Rabiah, in order to dissuade him from granting those immigrants his protection and to convince him to send them back to Mecca. The two emissaries went to the Negus's court, carrying many presents that they knew to be particularly valued by Abyssinian dignitaries. They met the dignitaries one by one, gave them the gifts, and received assurances of their support when the Meccans submitted their request to the king.

Facing the Negus

Amr ibn al-As and Abdullah ibn Rabiah would have liked the king to agree to send the Muslims back without even hearing the migrants' case. The Negus refused, arguing that those who had chosen him to protect them had the right to present their case. He called for an audience that would include the emissaries from Mecca and a delegation of Muslim immigrants. The latter group chose Jafar ibn Abi Talib, who was wise and a good speaker, to represent them and answer the king's questions. The king asked them about the cause of their exile and particularly about the contents of the new message brought by the Prophet. Jafar explained to the king the basic principles contained in Revelation and embodied in Muhammad's teaching: faith in one God, the rejection of idol worship, the injunction to respect kinship ties, to say the truth, to oppose injustice, and so on. Jafar added that it was because of this message that the Quraysh people persecuted the Muslims, and this was why they had decided to seek refuge in Abyssinia near the Negus, who was reputed to be a just and tolerant ruler.

The king asked Jafar whether he had a copy of or could recite a passage from the text of Revelation brought by the Prophet. Jafar answered in the affirmative and started to recite some verses from the surah "Maryam" (Mary):

Relate in the Book [the story of] Mary, when she withdrew from her family to a place in the East. She placed a screen [to screen herself] from them: then We sent to her our angel, and he appeared to her as a man in all respects. She said: "I seek refuge from you in the shelter of the Most Gracious, if you fear Him." He said: "I am only a messenger from your Lord [to announce] to you the gift of a pure son." She said: "How shall I have a son, seeing that no man has touched me, and that I am not unchaste?" He said: "So [it will be]; your Lord says: 'That is easy for Me and [We wish] to appoint him as a sign to men and a mercy from Us': it is a matter decreed."[17]

The king and his dignitaries were moved by the beauty of the text recited in Arabic, and they were even more so when the text was translated for them and they understood that it announced the miraculous birth of Jesus. The Negus exclaimed: "Indeed, this comes from the same source as what Jesus brought."[18] And he turned to the two Meccan emissaries to reject their request and inform them that he would not hand over the Muslim immigrants, to whom he would continue to grant refuge.

Amr and Abdullah went out, most annoyed, but Amr rapidly decided that he would go to the Negus again to inform him about what this new message actually said of Jesus, and which by no means coincides with Christian beliefs. He did so the next day, and after listening to him, the king again sent for Jafar and his delegation and demanded to know more about what the Prophet said about Jesus. The Muslims were aware of the dangers this encounter involved: an explanation of the differences between the two religions might lead the Negus to send them back. They nevertheless decided to keep to the contents of the message and explain what it said truthfully. To the Negus's direct question, "What do you profess about Jesus, son of Mary?" Jafar answered no less directly: "We say what our Prophet has taught us: he is God's servant, His messenger, His Spirit, His Word that He has breathed into Mary, the Holy Virgin." There was no reference to his status as "son of God," yet the Negus responded by taking hold of a stick and exclaiming: "Jesus, son of Mary, does not exceed what you have just said by the length of this stick."[19] The religious dignitaries were surprised at this answer and expressed it by coughing discreetly, but the Negus ignored them and required that the two emissaries from Mecca be sent back and that they take all their presents with them. To the Muslims he renewed his welcome, assuring them that they would find protection and security in his land.

This was a major setback for the Meccans, whose revenge was soon to come with the stepping up of reprisals against Muslims after the two emissaries' return. As for Jafar and his community, they had found a predominantly Christian country where, although they were exiles and did not share the population's faith, they were received, protected, and tolerated. They had decided to say the truth: at the most hazardous moment of the encounter with the Negus, they had neither tried to evade the question nor lied about what the Prophet Muhammad said of Jesus, son of Mary. They indeed risked being sent back and extradited, but they were not in the same situation as Ammar, who under torture had verbally denied his faith to save his life. In this case, then, in spite of the dangers involved, there was no way out: the Muslims kept to their beliefs, which they expressed with sincerity and honesty. They had no other choice but to say the truth, and so they did.

Besides, it should be noted that Jafar had at first set forth the similarities between the two Revelations. The first verses he had recited clearly showed that the source of the message was the same and that Muslims, when accepting the new Revelation, worshiped the same God as Christians and recognized their prophet. It was the Meccan emissaries who had tried to point out the differences in order to make trouble, but Jafar was just as quick to staunchly explain the message of his faith with its distinctions and differences. The mere presence of the Muslims in Abyssinia basically sent the Christians another message: that the Muslims had recognized in the Negus a man of principle and justice, and this was why they had decided to seek refuge in his land. The Negus was not a Muslim, but he had perfectly heard the twofold meaning, explicit and implicit, of the message brought by the Muslims: their God is the same, whatever the differences between their texts and our beliefs; their values, of respect and justice, are the same whatever the discrepancies between the religions' texts. The king heard and welcomed those believers of another faith.

Subsequently, the Negus converted to Islam and remained in continuous contact with the Prophet Muhammad. He represented the latter at a wedding ceremony, and the Prophet performed the prayer for the absent deceased (*salat al-ghaib*) when he learned of the Negus's death. The majority of the Muslims exiled in Abyssinia stayed there for about fifteen years, until the Khaybar expedition (in 630), at which time they joined the Prophet in Yathrib, which had by then become Medina. Others had gone back to Mecca earlier upon receiving positive news from there (though some of these returned yet again to Abyssinia), but none ever met with any trouble in the Negus's kingdom.

CHAPTER SEVEN

Trials, Elevation, and Hopes

In Mecca, the situation was getting worse. Islam's fiercest opponents, along with Abu Lahab and the so-called Abu Jahl, included Umar ibn al-Khattab. The last of these had already stood out by violently beating a newly converted woman.

Umar ibn al-Khattab

Umar was exasperated by the turn of events. He decided the only thing that could be done was to kill the Prophet. This was the surest means of putting an end to the disorder and sedition that were welling up and endangering Meccan society as a whole.

He went out of his house, his sword in his hand, to look for Muhammad. On the way, he met Nuaym ibn Abdullah, who had secretly converted to Islam. Nuaym asked him why he looked so angry, and Umar told him about his intention to kill the Prophet. Nuaym quickly thought of a means to divert him from his plan: he advised Umar to restore order in his own family before setting upon Muhammad. He informed him that his sister Fatimah and his brother-in-law Said had already converted to Islam. Astonished and infuriated, Umar changed his plans and made straight for his sister's home.

She and her husband were reading and studying the Quran with a young companion, Khabbab, when they heard someone approaching their house. Khabbab stopped reading and hid. Umar had heard the sound of the recitation inside, and he accosted them coldly, bluntly asking what they had been reciting. They both denied the fact, but Umar insisted that he definitely had heard them reciting a text. They refused to discuss the matter, which caused Umar's anger to flare. He sprang to his brother-in-law to strike him, and when his sister tried to intervene, he struck her, causing blood to gush out. The sight of blood on his sister's face produced an immediate effect and Umar stopped short. At that very moment, his sister exclaimed with spirit: "Yes, indeed, we are Muslims and we believe in God and His Messenger. As for you, you can now do as you please!"[1] Umar was taken aback; he was torn between remorse at having hurt his sister and bewilderment at the news he had just received. He asked his sister to give him the text they had been reading when he arrived. His sister demanded that he should first perform ablutions to purify himself. Sobered but still upset, Umar accepted, performed ablutions, then started reading:

> *Tâ, hâ.* We have not sent down the Quran to you to [cause] your distress, but only as an admonition for those who fear [God]. A Revelation from Him who created the earth and the heavens on high. The Most Gracious is firmly established on the throne. To Him belongs what is in the heavens and on earth, and all between them, and all beneath the soil. Whether [or not] you speak aloud, verily He knows what is secret and what is yet more hidden. He is God! There is no God but Him! To Him belong the most beautiful names.[2]

Those were the first verses, and Umar went on reading the rest of the text, which was an account of God's call to Moses on Mount Sinai, until he reached this verse:

> Verily, I am God: there is no God but I: so serve Me, and establish regular prayer for My remembrance.[3]

Umar then stopped reading and expressed his enthusiasm about the beauty and nobleness of those words. Khabbab, encouraged by Umar's apparent good disposition, then came out of his hiding place and informed him that he had heard the Prophet praying to God to grant his community support through the conversion of Abu al-Hakam or of Umar ibn al-Khattab.[4] Umar asked him where Muhammad was, and when told he was at al-Arqam's dwelling place, Umar went there. When he reached the door, the occupants were afraid because Umar was still carrying his sword in his belt. But the Prophet told them to let him in, and Umar immediately announced his intention of becoming a Muslim. The Prophet exclaimed, *"Allahu akbar!"* (God is the Most Great) and received this conversion as an answer to his prayer.

The Prophet knew he had no power over hearts. In the face of persecution, in great difficulty, he had turned to God, hoping that He would guide one or the other of those two men who he knew possessed the human qualities as well as the power necessary to reverse the order of things. The Prophet of course knew that God alone has the power to guide hearts. For some individuals, conversion was a long process that required years of questioning, doubt, and steps forward and backward, while for others conversion was instantaneous, immediately following the reading of a text or responding to a particular gesture or behavior. This cannot be explained. The conversions that took longest were not necessarily the most solid, and the reverse was not true either: when it comes to conversion, the heart's dispositions, faith, and love, there is no logic, and all that remains is the extraordinary power of the divine. Umar had gone out of his home determined to kill the Prophet, blinded by his absolute negation of the One God; there he was, a few hours later, changed, transformed, as the result of a conversion induced by a text and the meaning of God. He was to become one of the most faithful Companions of the man he had wished dead. Nobody among the Muslims could have imagined that Umar would recognize the message of Islam, so forcefully had he expressed his hatred for it. This heart's revolution was a sign, and it carried a twofold teaching: that nothing is impossible for God, and that one should not pronounce final judgments on anything or anybody. This was a new reminder of the need for humility in all circumstances: for a human being, remembering God's infinite power should mean healthy self-doubt as to oneself and suspending one's judgment as to others. Thus, the more he moved forward with God, every day becoming more of a model for his Companions and for eternity, the more the Prophet was attaining humility and modesty as expressed in being, knowledge, and judgment.

Umar, with his spirit and courage, had decided to make his conversion public. He immediately went to Abu Jahl to tell him the news, and he suggested to the Prophet that they should pray publicly at the Kaba.[5] This certainly involved risks, but it was also a matter of showing the Quraysh clan chiefs that Muslims were present among them and were determined. Umar and Hamzah, both known for their strong personalities, entered the Kaba enclosure ahead of the group, and the Muslims prayed in a group without anyone daring to interfere.

Banishment

Nevertheless, things had gone too far. The tension was rising daily, and the Quraysh leaders, meeting to try to put an end to this slow expansion, felt it necessary to take more radical measures. The first converts came from all tribes, and this situation made it impossible to resort to a strategy based on the usual alliances. After protracted discussions and heated arguments, which themselves divided clans from within, they decided to banish all the Banu Hashim, which was Muhammad's clan, and set up a total boycott directed at the clan and its members.

A covenant was signed by about forty Quraysh leaders and hung up inside the Kaba to signal the solemnity and finality of the decision. Abu Lahab, who himself belonged to the Hashim clan, decided to disavow his clan and support the banishment, a move that violated the traditional honor code. Abu Talib adopted the opposite attitude and continued to support his nephew, thus obliging the Quraysh to de facto include the Muttalib clan in the boycott. The decision was a radical one, for it meant avoiding any contact with members of the clan—they would no longer marry their daughters and sons, trade with them, establish any other type of contract, and so forth. The boycott was to be comprehensive and last as long as the two clans allowed Muhammad to go on preaching his message; they wanted him to put an end to his mission and never again refer to the One God.

Fearing for their security, the Banu Hashim and Muttalib clans decided to move together to the same area in the Mecca valley. Even though the boycott was not total—relatives covertly had food and goods brought to the Banu Hashim—the situation became serious, and more and more of them suffered from sickness and hunger. The banishment lasted for more than three years, and it economically weakened the two clans. Abu Bakr had lost most of his fortune as a result of the boycott, and the social and psychological pressures were unbearable.

Among the Quraysh, many thought that this boycott was unnecessary, if not useless. Some of course were linked to the clan by kinship ties, which were impossible to forget or disown. There were numerous attempts to put an end to the banishment in the course of those three years, but they never succeeded because a number of key figures, such as Abu Lahab and Abu Jahl, refused to discuss the matter. Finally, change came through the initiative of a few individuals seeking allies in each of the clans. While the people were gathered near the Kaba, one of them addressed the others, objecting to the boycott on the Banu Hashim; another man in the crowd joined him, then another, then a fourth. Abu Jahl attempted to intervene, but the assembly, many of whom were of the same opinion but dared not speak out, was overwhelmingly opposed to the boycott. One of the members of the group who had initiated this little uprising went into the Kaba, took hold of the text stipulating the boycott decision, and tore it up. The hard-liners felt there was no point in resisting, and the ban was lifted. The relief was palpable in the two clans excluded, so intolerable had the situation become.

The Year of Sorrow

For several months after the boycott ended, the situation improved for the small Muslim community. They again were able to develop ties of friendship and working relationships with the Quraysh people. The Prophet continued to convey his message, and the visibility sought by Umar ibn al-Khattab had become an everyday reality in Mecca, although the insults and persecutions had not stopped.

Things were soon to change dramatically, however. Khadijah, the Prophet's wife, died shortly after the boycott was lifted. She had been Muhammad's wife, companion in faith, and most reliable support for over twenty-five years, and God called her back to Him nine years after the beginning of the mission, in 619 CE. The Prophet's grief was very deep: he had, at a very early stage, received from the Angel Gabriel the news of his wife's election, and he knew that Khadijah's presence by his side had been one of the signs of God's protection and love. In the light of her presence and of the role she played in his life, one can grasp the multiple possible meanings in a verse that was to be revealed much later, which describes the relationship between husband and wife: "They are your garments as you are their garments."[6] She had been the garment that protects (emotionally as much as physically), conceals (weaknesses and doubts as well as riches), and brings warmth, strength, status, dignity, and modesty.

It was not long before the Prophet's uncle, Abu Talib, thanks to whom he had so far enjoyed immunity among the Quraysh, fell seriously ill as well. Muhammad visited him just as he was about to breathe his last. Abu Talib confirmed that he had been happy to protect his nephew, who had always been moderate and just. Muhammad invited him to pronounce the profession of faith before departing, so that he could intercede for his uncle with God. Abu Talib, prompted by his clan's honor code, said that he feared the Quraysh would think he had uttered the profession of faith out of fear of death. They did not have the time to discuss the matter any further: Abu Talib died with the Prophet by his side. This man who, with dignity and courage, had granted the younger man his protection, as well as his love and respect, had not embraced Islam. Muhammad loved and respected him, and his sorrow was all the more intense. From this sorrow and powerlessness, a verse, revealed in relation to this event, draws an eternal teaching as to the disposition and the secrets of hearts: "You will not be able to guide [toward faith] everyone whom you love; but God guides those whom He will, and He knows best those who receive guidance."[7]

In the space of a few months, the Prophet seemed to have become doubly vulnerable: he had lost the person who had offered him love and the person who had granted him protection. In spite of his grief, he needed to react quickly and find the means to protect the community of Muslims who had remained in Mecca. Muhammad decided to seek support outside the city.

At Taif, a Slave

The Prophet went to the town of Taif and spoke to the leaders of the Thaqif tribe, hoping that they would hear the message of Islam and agree to protect the Muslims from their enemies. He met with a very cold reception, however, and the chiefs mocked his claim to be a prophet. If he was, they asked, how could God allow His Messenger to beg for the support of strange tribes? Not only did they refuse to discuss the matter, but they mobilized the population against him: as he was leaving, insults followed him and children threw stones at him. More and more people gathered and jeered at him as he passed; he finally had to seek refuge in an orchard in order to escape his pursuers. Alone, having found no protection among his fellow human beings, he turned toward the One and prayed:

> O God, to You alone I complain of my weakness, the meagerness of my resources and my insignificance before men. O Most Merciful of the Merciful, You are the Lord of the weak and You are my Lord [*Rabb*, "Educator"]. Into whose hands do You entrust me? To some remote stranger who will ill-treat me? Or to an enemy to whom You have granted authority over my affairs? I harbor no fear so long as You are not angry with me. Yet Your gracious support would open a broader way and a wider horizon for me! I seek refuge in the light of Your face, by which all darkness is illuminated and the things of this world and the next are set aright, so that I do not incur Your anger and am not touched by Your wrath. Nevertheless, it is Your prerogative to admonish as long as You are not satisfied. There is no power nor strength but in You.[8]

It was toward the One, his Protector and Confidant, that he turned when there appeared to be no way out. His questions did not express doubt about his mission, but it clearly voiced his helplessness as a human being as well as his ignorance of God's purposes. At that particular moment, away from other people, in the solitude of his faith and of his confidence in the Most Gracious, he literally and wholly put himself in God's hands; in this sense, this prayer reveals all the confidence and serenity Muhammad drew from his relationship to the Most Near. This prayer, which has become famous, tells of humanity's helplessness and of the Messenger's extraordinary spiritual strength. Seemingly lonely and without support, he knew that he was not alone.

The two owners of the orchard had seen Muhammad from a distance as he entered, and they had observed him as he raised his hands and prayed to God. They sent their slave Addas, a young man who was a Christian, to take him a bunch of grapes. When Addas gave him the grapes, he heard the Prophet say the formula: *"BismiLLah!"* ("In the name of God," "I begin with God"). Addas was most surprised and inquired about the identity of this man, who said words that he, a Christian, had never heard polytheists say. Muhammad asked him where he was from, and Addas answered that he came from Nineveh. The Prophet added: "The land of Jonah the Just, son of Matta!" The young man was puzzled and wondered how this man could know of that. After informing him that he was a Christian, Addas in turn asked Muhammad who he was and how he had received his knowledge. The Prophet told him: "Jonah is my brother. He was a prophet and I am a prophet."[9]

Addas gazed at him for a while, then kissed his head, hands, and feet; his masters were shocked at this, and when he went back to them he told them that only a prophet could know what that man knew. Addas accepted Islam immediately, after a few minutes' discussion. The Christian king of Abyssinia had immediately recognized the linkage between the two messages, and now it was a young slave, also a Christian, who shared the same intuition. Twice already, in sorrow and isolation, Muhammad had encountered on his path Christians who offered him trust, respect, and shelter: a king welcomed Muslims and granted them security, a slave served their Prophet when everybody else had rejected him and his message.

The Prophet then set off back toward Mecca. On his way, he met a horseman and requested that he ask a Meccan dignitary who was a relative of the horseman whether he would agree to grant Muhammad his protection. The horseman complied, but the dignitary refused, as did another leader whose support Muhammad sought. The Prophet did not wish to enter Mecca in such circumstances and sought refuge in the cave of Hira, where he had received the first Revelation. It was finally the third person he approached, Mutim, the leader of the Nawfal clans, who agreed to grant Muhammad his protection, greeting the Prophet in the Kaba enclosure to publicize the fact.

The Night Journey

The Prophet liked to go to the Kaba enclosure at night. He would stand there in prayer for long hours. One evening, he suddenly felt deeply tired and in great need of sleep.[10] He therefore lay down near the Kaba and fell asleep.

Muhammad has related that the Angel Gabriel then came to him. Gabriel shook him twice to awaken him, but Muhammad slept on; the third time the angel shook him, Muhammad awoke, and Gabriel took him to the doors of the mosque, where a white animal (looking something like a cross between a mule and a donkey, but with wings) was waiting for them. He mounted the animal, which was called al-Buraq, and started with Gabriel toward Jerusalem. There Muhammad met a group of prophets who had preceded him (Abraham, Moses, and others), and he led a group prayer with them on the Temple site. When the prayer was over, the Prophet was raised with the Angel Gabriel beyond space and time. On his way, rising through the seven heavens, he again met the various prophets, and his vision of the heavens and of the beauty of those horizons permeated his being. He at last reached the Lotus of the Utmost Boundary (*Sidrat al-Muntaha*). This was where the Prophet received the injunction of the five daily prayers and Revelation of the verse that established the elements of the Muslim creed (*al-aqidah*):[11]

> The Messenger believes in what has been revealed to him from his Lord, as do the believers. Each one believes in God, His angels, His books, and His Messengers. We make no distinction between one and another of His Messengers. And they say: "We hear, and we obey: [we seek] Your forgiveness, our Lord, and to You is the end of all journeys."[12]

Muhammad was taken back to Jerusalem by the Angel Gabriel and al-Buraq, and from there to Mecca. On the way back, he came upon some caravans that were also traveling to Mecca. It was still night when they reached the Kaba enclosure. The angel and al-Buraq left, and Muhammad proceeded to the home of Um Hani, one of his most trusted Companions. He gave her an account of what had happened to him, and she advised him not to tell anybody about it, which Muhammad refused to do. Later on, the Quran was to report this experience in two different passages. One is in the surah whose title, "Al-Isra" (The Nocturnal Voyage), directly refers to the event:

> Glory to He Who took His servant for a journey by night from the most sacred mosque to the farthest mosque, whose precincts We blessed, in order that We might show him some of Our signs: for He is the One Who hears and sees [all things].[13]

It is also in the surah "An-Najm" (The Star):

It is no less than inspiration sent down to him: he was taught by one mighty in power, endowed with wisdom. For he appeared in angelic form while he was in the highest part of the horizon. Then he approached and came closer, and was at a distance of but two bow lengths or nearer. So did God convey by inspiration to His Servant what He meant to convey. The heart in no way belied that which he saw. Will you then dispute with him concerning what he saw? For indeed he saw him at another descent, near the Lotus of the utmost boundary—near it is the Garden of Abode—when that which covered the Lotus covered it. His sight never swerved, nor did it go wrong. For truly did he see, of the signs of his Lord, the Greatest![14]

The Night Journey and ascension were to give rise to many comments, both when the Prophet recounted the facts and later among Muslim scholars. When Muhammad went to the Kaba and reported his experience, jeers, sniggers and criticisms quickly followed. The Quraysh believed that at last they had proof that this so-called prophet was indeed mad, since he dared claim that in one night he had made a journey to Jerusalem (which in itself required several weeks) and that he had, furthermore, been raised to the presence of his One God. His madness was obvious.

The Night Journey experience, presented in classical accounts of the Prophet's life as a gift from God and a consecration for the Messenger, the Elect (*al-Mustafa*) was a real trial for Muhammad and those around him. It marked the boundary between those believers whose faith radiated in their trust in this Prophet and his message and the others, who were taken aback by the improbability of such a story. A Quraysh delegation hastened to go and question Abu Bakr about his mad and senseless friend, but his immediate, forthright answer surprised them: "If he says such a thing, it cannot but be true!" Abu Bakr's faith and trust were such that he was not in the least disturbed, even for a second. After that, he personally went to question the Prophet, who confirmed the facts; as a result, Abu Bakr repeated forcefully: "I believe you, you have always spoken the truth."[15] From that day on, the Prophet called Abu Bakr by the epithet As-Siddiq (he who is truthful, who confirms the truth).

The trial that Muhammad's Night Journey presented for his fellow Muslims occurred at a moment when they were struggling with a most difficult situation. Tradition reports that a few Muslims left Islam, but most trusted Muhammad. A few weeks later, facts confirmed some elements of his account, for instance the arrival of caravans whose coming he had announced (having seen them on his way back) and of which he had given a precise description. Thanks to the strength of this faith, the community of Muslims would be able to face future adversity. From then on, Umar ibn al-Khattab and Abu Bakr were always to stand in the front line of this spiritual force.

Muslim scholars have, from the outset, pondered the question of whether the Night Journey was of a purely spiritual nature or whether it was also physical. The majority of scholars consider that the journey was both physical and spiritual. All things considered, however, this question is not essential in the light of the teachings that can be drawn from this extraordinary experience undergone by the Messenger. There is first of all, of course, the centrality of the city of Jerusalem: at the time, the Prophet prayed facing the holy city (the first *qibla*, or direction of prayer), and during the Night Journey it was on the site of the Temple that he led the prayer together with all the prophets. Jerusalem thus appears at the heart of the Prophet's experience and teaching as a dual symbol, of both centrality (with the direction of prayer) and universality (with the prayer of all the prophets). Later, in Medina, the *qibla* (direction of prayer) was to change—from Jerusalem to the Kaba—to distinguish Islam from Judaism, but this by no means entailed a diminution of Jerusalem's status, and in the abovementioned verse the references to the "most sacred mosque" (the Kaba, in Mecca) and the "farthest mosque" (al-Aqsa, in Jerusalem) establish a spiritual and sacred link between the two cities.

The other teaching is of a purely spiritual essence: all Revelation reached the Prophet in the course of his earthly experience, with the exception, as we have seen, of the verses that establish the fundamental pillars of faith (*al-iman*) and the duty of prayer (*as-salat*). The Prophet was raised to heaven to receive the teachings that were to become the foundation of Islamic worship and ritual, *al-aqidah* and *al-ibadat*, which require that believers should accept their form as well as their substance.[16] Unlike the field of social affairs (*al-muamalat*), which calls for the creative mediation of people's intellect and intelligence, human rationality here submits, in the name of faith and as an act of humility, to the order imposed by Revelation: God has prescribed requirements and norms that the mind must hear and implement and the heart must love. Raised to receive the injunction of ritual prayer, the Prophet and his experience reveal what prayer must in essence be: a reminder of and an elevation toward the Most High, five times a day, in order to detach from oneself, from the world, and from illusions. The *miraj* (the elevation during the Night Journey) is thus more than simply an archetype of the spiritual experience; it is pregnant with the deep significance of prayer, which, through the Eternal Word, enables us to liberate our consciousness from the contingencies of space and time, and fully comprehend the meaning of life and of Life.

Toward Exile

It was 620, a year after the deaths of Muhammad's wife, Khadijah, and his uncle Abu Talib, and the time of the yearly pilgrimage to the Kaba and Mecca's annual market period was drawing near. Muhammad was still dispensing his teachings in a climate of rejection, exclusion, and persecution. About a hundred Muslims now lived under protection in Abyssinia, but no solution seemed to present itself for the faithful who lived in Mecca. The pilgrims, coming from all areas of the peninsula, started to settle in the Mina area, to remain there throughout the festival period. Muhammad often went there and conveyed his message to women and men who, in their distant dwelling places, had heard about it but did not know its actual contents. He was far from always receiving a favorable response.

At al-Aqabah, not far from Mina, the Prophet met a group of people from Yathrib. They were from the Khazraj tribe, one of the two great rival tribes in Yathrib (the other being the Aws), and he began to deliver his message to them. They had already heard of the message from the Jewish tribes who lived in their city, and they wished to know more about it. They listened to the Prophet and eventually accepted the message of Islam: they promised to inform the members of their tribe of the substance of the message and to keep in permanent contact with the Prophet.[17] They went back home and started preaching in Yathrib.

In Mecca, conversions kept increasing, and Muhammad carried on with his public call. As far as his private life was concerned, many advised him to think of remarrying. Proposals had been made, but the Prophet had never pursued the matter. He had, however, had two dreams in which the very young Aishah, Abu Bakr's daughter, who was then six years old, was offered to him in marriage. When Khawlah, who had taken care of the Prophet's needs since Khadijah's death, advised him to remarry and suggested two names—Sawdah, a widow in her thirties who had very recently come back from Abyssinia, and Aishah, Abu Bakr's daughter— Muhammad saw in this strange coincidence a sign of the truthfulness of his dreams, and he asked Khawlah to do what was necessary to find out whether the two unions were possible. Polygamy was the norm in Arabia then, and the Prophet's situation was the exception, since he had remained monogamous for twenty-five years. The union with Sawdah was particularly easy to concretize: Sawdah immediately, and most favorably, answered the proposal made to her, and they married a few months later. Aishah had already, in keeping with Arabian customs, been promised by Abu Bakr to Mutim's son, and her father had to negotiate with Mutim in order to break the engagement. Aishah then officially became Muhammad's second wife, though the union would not be consummated for several years.

A year later, pilgrims and traders were again flocking to Mecca for the celebrations of 621. A second meeting was organized at al-Aqabah between the Prophet and the Yathrib delegation that had come to report on the evolution of the situation in their city. Twelve people from Yathrib, two of whom belonged to the Aws clan, took part in the meeting: they pledged allegiance to the Prophet, stipulating that they would worship only the One God, no others, and that they would honor the duties and interdictions of Islam. They were therefore to constitute the first Muslim community in Yathrib. Muhammad sent back with them a Companion, Musab ibn Umayr, who had just returned from Abyssinia and who was known for his calm, his wisdom, and the beauty of his recitation of the Quran.

Back in Yathrib, the delegation kept spreading the message and Musab taught Islam, recited the Quran, and answered questions. In spite of age-old and still very sharp divisions between the Aws and Khazraj, members of both tribes converted to the new religion and realized that their former rivalries had become pointless: Islam's message of brotherhood united them. Clan chiefs nevertheless remained very reluctant to embrace Islam. Musab never reacted to their attacks nor to their aggressive attitude; rather, he invariably answered: "Sit down and listen to the message: if you like it, accept it, if you do not, leave it."[18] As a result, the number of conversions was high, even among leaders.

During the following year's pilgrimage, the Prophet met an important delegation of Yathrib Muslims, composed of seventy-three people, two of them women. They belonged to both the Aws and the Khazraj, and they had come to bring the Prophet the good news of their commitment to Islam. After a few discussions about the nature of their future relationship, they concluded a second covenant stipulating that the Yathrib Muslims pledged to protect the Prophet, as well as Mecca's Muslim women and children, against any aggression. This second covenant, granting refuge and protection and a commitment of Yathrib Muslims to support their Meccan brothers, opened before the Prophet the prospect of a promising future. From then on, Muhammad encouraged Muslims to emigrate to Yathrib discreetly, while his closest Companions still remained by his side.

With Non-Muslims

Muhammad had always retained very strong ties with the members of different clans and with his kin who had not accepted Islam. His uncle Abu Talib, whom he loved so much and whom he accompanied until he breathed his last, was one such example. Another uncle, Abbas, remained by the Prophet's side even though he had not yet converted. Muhammad's trust in him was tremendous, and he did not hesitate to confide in him or have him take part in private meetings involving the future of the community (later, Abbas would be present when the second covenant of al-Aqabah was concluded; the Prophet would also keep him informed of the highly confidential preparations for his emigration to Yathrib). His remaining a polytheist never prevented the Prophet from showing him the greatest respect and deepest confidence in situations where his very life was at risk.

It was a similar attitude of trust that had made it possible for Muslims to emigrate to Abyssinia, under protection of a king whom the Prophet trusted even though he was not a Muslim. This attitude is to be found throughout the Prophet's life: he established his relationships in the name of trust and the respect of principles, and not exclusively on the basis of similar religious affiliation. His Companions had understood this as well, and they did not hesitate to develop solid ties with non-Muslims in the name of kinship or friendship, on the basis of mutual respect and trust, even in perilous situations. Thus, Um Salamah, who had been separated from her husband, found herself alone with her son on her way to Medina. Uthman ibn Talhah, who was not a Muslim, offered to escort and protect her until she reached the place where her husband was. She did not hesitate to trust him: he accompanied her and her son to their destination, then took leave of them in the most respectful manner. Um Salamah was often to tell this story, always praising Uthman ibn Talhah's noble character.

Examples of this nature abound, and neither the Prophet nor the other Muslims ever restricted their social and human relations to their coreligionists. Later, the Quran was to establish the rightfulness and the principle of such relationships formed on the basis of mutual respect:

> God does not forbid you, with regard to those who do not fight you for [your] faith, nor drive you out of your homes, from dealing kindly [showing affection] and justly with them: for God loves those who are just. God only forbids you, with regard to those who fight you for [your] faith, and drive you out of your homes, and support others in driving you out, from turning to them [for friendship and protection]. It is those who turn to them [in these circumstances] who do wrong.[19]

The Prophet himself was a model of equity toward those who did not share his faith. Through all the years of his mission, he had continued to receive important deposits from non-Muslim traders who went on dealing with him and wholly trusted him. On the eve of his departure for Medina, Muhammad asked Ali to give back one by one to their respective owners the deposits he still held; he scrupulously applied the principles of honesty and justice that Islam had taught him, whomever he dealt with, be they Muslims or non-Muslims.

During the same period, the Prophet also showed a most understanding attitude toward those who, under persecution or pressure from their families, had left Islam. This was the case with two young Muslims, Hisham and Ayyash, who abjured Islam after prolonged resistance. No particular decision or sanction was taken against them. Later on, Ayyash again came back to Islam, full of remorse and sadness. Revelation was subsequently to ease his exceedingly harsh vision and judgment about himself:

Say: "O those who have transgressed against themselves! Do not despair of God's mercy: for God forgives all sins; for He is the All-Forgiving, the Most Merciful. Turn to your Lord and submit to Him, before the chastisement comes on you: after that you shall not be helped."[20]

On hearing those verses, Hisham also came back to Islam. Yet one who did not return was Ubaydallah ibn Jahsh, who had gone to Abyssinia with the first group of emigrants and who had then converted to Christianity and abandoned his wife, Um Habibah bint Abi Sufyan.[21] Neither the Prophet, from Mecca, nor any of the Muslims who lived in Abyssinia took any measure against him: he remained a Christian until he died without ever being harassed or ill-treated. This attitude of respect for everyone's freedom remained constant throughout the Prophet's life, and the authoritative accounts of his life contain no mention whatsoever of a different attitude. Later on, in Medina, he was to speak out harshly and take firm measures against those who falsely converted to Islam for the sole purpose of gathering information about the Muslims, then denied Islam and went back to their tribes to bring them the information they had managed to obtain. These were in fact war traitors, who incurred the penalty of death because their actions were liable to bring about the destruction of the Muslim community.

Permission to Emigrate

The Prophet's most recent protector, Mutim, had just died. The situation was becoming particularly difficult, and the Quraysh, who had noticed that the Muslims were beginning to leave Mecca, were in their turn becoming more and more violent in their opposition. The clan chiefs decided to unite, and at Abu Lahab and Abu Jahl's instigation, they resolved that the Prophet must be done away with. Their plan was to mandate an executioner from each clan in order to prevent the Banu Hashim from taking revenge and asking for blood money. They agreed that no time must be lost and that they must get rid of the Prophet as soon as possible.

The Angel Gabriel had come to confirm to the Prophet the meaning of a dream he had had a few days before, when in a vision he had seen a flourishing city appear and welcome him. The angel announced to him that he must prepare to emigrate to Yathrib and that his companion was to be Abu Bakr. Muhammad went to impart the news to Abu Bakr, who wept with joy; however, they still had to organize the final details of their departure. They had heard that the Quraysh had devised a plan to get rid of the Prophet. Muhammad asked Ali to take his place in his bed the following night, and not to leave Mecca until he ordered him to.

The Prophet's would-be murderers hid in front of his home and waited for him to go out, as he usually did, to attend prayer before sunrise. When they heard some noise inside the house, which they took to be Muhammad arising and preparing to leave, they were almost ready to launch their attack when they realized that they had been deceived and that the man inside the house was his cousin Ali. Their plan had failed. In the meantime, the Prophet had gone to Abu Bakr's and had already finalized the last details of his departure for Yathrib.

CHAPTER EIGHT

Hijrah

The Prophet Muhammad was neither fatalistic nor reckless. His trust in God was absolute, but that had never caused him to drift with the tide of events. Revelation had reminded him that he must never forget to say "*in sha Allah*" (if God so wills) when he planned to act, and that the memory of God must be associated with humility (especially in regard to his own powers as a human being). Still, this by no means implied that he should forget to show responsibility and foresight in his choices in the world of human beings. Thus, Muhammad had been planning an emigration to Medina (*hijrah*) for almost two years, and nothing had been left to chance. Only after making intelligent and thorough use of his human powers had he trusted himself to the divine will, thereby clarifying for us the meaning of *at-tawakkul ala Allah* (reliance on God, trusting oneself to God): responsibly exercising all the qualities (intellectual, spiritual, psychological, sentimental, etc.) each one of us has been granted and humbly remembering that beyond what is humanly possible, God alone makes things happen. Indeed, this teaching is the exact opposite of the temptation of fatalism: God will act only after humans have, at their own level, sought out and exhausted all the potentialities of action. That is the profound meaning of this Quranic verse: "Verily never will God change the condition of a people until they change what is in themselves."[1]

With Abu Bakr

Muhammad and Abu Bakr decided to leave Mecca during the night and head toward Yemen to avoid attracting attention. Abu Bakr provided

Muhammad with a camel named Qaswa; the Prophet insisted on paying for it, since he wished this emigration to belong to him alone, and he wanted to be debtless when he departed for Yathrib. Similarly, he would refuse the gift of a patch of land that two orphans wanted to make him when he arrived in the city that was henceforth to be known variously as al-Madinah (Medina, meaning "the city"), Madinah ar-Rasul (the city of the Messenger), or al-Madinah al-Munawwarah (the enlightened city).

Having headed south, they went into hiding for a few days in the Thawr cave (*ghar Thawr*). Abu Bakr's son, Abdullah, was to gather intelligence about the Quraysh's intentions and bring it to his father and Muhammad. As for Abu Bakr's daughters, Asma and Aishah, they would prepare food and secretly carry it to the cave at night. Thus Abu Bakr mobilized all his children, the girls as well as the boy, to protect his and the Prophet's escape, despite the serious danger the situation posed for his daughters in particular. He constantly showed such an equitable attitude in his dealings with his sons and daughters, in the light of the Prophet's teachings.

Notwithstanding all those arrangements, a group of Quraysh men, suspecting a trick, went south to look for the Prophet. They arrived in front of the cave and prepared to enter. From where he stood, Abu Bakr could see them, and in alarm he told the Prophet that should the men happen to look down they could not fail to see the two of them. Muhammad reassured him and whispered, "Have no fear, for God is with us."[2] Then he added, "What do you think of two [people] whose third is God?"[3] Those words soothed Abu Bakr. In the front of the cave, the group noticed that a spiderweb covered the entrance and also that a dove had nested there: it seemed obvious that the fugitives could not be hiding in the cave, and they decided to look for them somewhere else.

Once again, in spite of their carefully planned strategy, the Prophet and his Companion were going through the trial of vulnerability. Their lives had been preserved by nothing but that fragile spiderweb; trust in God (*at-tawakkul ala Allah*), of which the Prophet reminded Abu Bakr at that particular moment, thus took on its full meaning and strength. God alone had the power to save His Messenger. When Muhammad emigrated, he took care to owe nothing to anyone (he refused gifts, settled his debts, and gave back the deposits he held), but he also knew that he owed everything to the One, that his indebtedness and obligation to Him were infinite.

Hijrah is primarily this essential teaching at the heart of the Prophet's experience: a trust in God that entails, without arrogance, absolute independence from people, as well as the humble recognition of absolute dependence upon God.

Abu Bakr had enlisted the services of a non-Muslim Bedouin, Abdullah ibn Urayqat, to guide them to Yathrib by an inconspicuous, unfamiliar route. At the time appointed for departure, ibn Urayqat came to meet them at the cave with the camels, and they headed west, then south, before eventually going north toward Yathrib. It was a very perilous journey, and were the Quraysh to catch up with the three travelers, they were sure to kill them so as to put an end to Muhammad's subversive activities. The Prophet and his Companion had entrusted themselves to God, yet they had not hesitated to enlist the help of a Bedouin who, although he shared their enemies' polytheistic beliefs, was well known to them for his trustworthiness (he was proudly true to his word) and his abilities as a guide (he knew better than anyone else the steep, out-of-the-way paths they took). Again, such an attitude is present throughout the Prophet's life: the women and men he surrounded himself with might not share his faith, but they were known to him for their moral qualities and/or their human abilities. Muhammad, like those who came after him, would not hesitate to rely on them.

Mosques

The journey to Quba lasted twenty days. The Messenger and Abu Bakr eventually reached the little village of Quba, which lay outside Yathrib. The people were waiting for them and gave them a warm welcome. They spent three days in the village and began construction of a mosque there, the first of the emigration period.[4] The Prophet was to proceed in this way at each of the three stages of the journey to Yathrib. When he left Quba, the Prophet headed toward Yathrib and halted at noon, prayer time, in the Ranuna valley, where he performed the first Friday prayer with his Companions: there again, construction of a mosque was begun. He then headed for the center of the city. Many people stopped him, inviting him to reside with them. He asked them to let Qaswa, his camel, go unhampered, for she would indicate the exact spot where he would settle.

She moved back and forth through the crowd, then at last stopped near some land belonging to two orphans. As mentioned previously, the Prophet paid the price due to them. On this spot, building of his dwelling place and a mosque immediately began.

In building these three mosques, the Prophet was pointing to the importance and centrality of the mosque in the relation to God, to space, and to human communities. The building of a *masjid* (the place where one prostrates oneself) institutes a specific sacralized space within the primary and essential sacrality of the universe as a whole; as the Prophet said, "The whole earth is a *masjid*, a mosque."[5] Once built, the mosque becomes the axial space of the Muslim spiritual community in which it is situated, but it also expresses the reality of settlement, of acceptance of the hosting space, which is then turned into a space for oneself, a home. Indeed, the presence of the mosque reveals that a place has been adopted as home, and that the believing conscience is "at home" because the place of worship, a reminder of meaning, has been set up. The Prophet's repeated act is in itself a teaching: whatever the exile or journey, whatever the movement or departure, one must never lose sight of meaning and direction. Mosques tell of meaning, direction, and settlement. Yathrib had become Medina.

Exile: Meaning and Teachings

The Prophet and all his Companions had had to leave Mecca because of persecutions and adversity from their own brothers and sisters within their respective clans. The situation had become unbearable: women and men had died, others had been tortured, and the Quraysh had finally decided to set upon Muhammad himself and get rid of him. The emigration is first of all the objective reality of believing women and men who were not free to practice their faith and who decided to make a clean break for the sake of their beliefs. Because "God's earth is spacious," as the Quran puts it, they decided to leave their homeland, to break with their universe and habits, and to experience exile, all for the sake of their faith.[6] Revelation was to praise the courage and determination of those believers who, by taking such a difficult and humanly costly step, expressed their trust in God:

To those who leave their homes in the cause of God, after suffering oppression, we will assuredly give a goodly home in this world; but truly the reward of the Hereafter will be greater, if they only realized [this]! Those who persevere in patience, and put their trust in their Lord.[7]

Exile is, then, another trial of trust. All prophets have intensively experienced this trial of the heart, as all believers have after them. How far are they prepared to go, how much are they prepared to give of themselves and of their lives, for the One, His truth and His love? Those are the eternal questions of faith, which accompany every temporal and historical experience of the believing conscience. *Hijrah* was one of the Muslim community's answers at the dawn of its existence.

In effect, exile was also to require that the first Muslims learn to remain faithful to the meaning of Islam's teachings in spite of the change of place, culture, and memory. Medina meant new customs, new types of social relationships, a wholly different role for women (who were socially far more present than in Mecca), and more complex intertribal relations, as well as the influential presence of the Jewish and Christian communities, which was something new to Muslims. Very early on, the community of faith, following the Prophet's example, had to distinguish between what belonged to Islamic principles and what was more particularly related to Meccan culture. They were to remain faithful to the first while learning to adopt a flexible and critical approach to their original culture. They even had to try to reform some of their attitudes, which were more cultural than Islamic. Umar ibn al-Khattab was to learn this to his cost when, after he had reacted most sharply to his wife answering him back (which was unthinkable in Mecca), she retorted that he must bear with it and accept it just as the Prophet did. This was a difficult experience for him, as it was for others, who might have been tempted to think that their habits and customs were in themselves Islamic: *hijrah*, exile, was to reveal that this was not the case and that one must question every single cultural practice, both to be faithful to Islamic principles and to open up to other cultures and gain from their wealth. For instance, having learned that a wedding was to take place among the Medina Muslims (the Ansar), the Prophet had two singing maids sent to them, for, he said, the Ansar enjoyed singing.[8] Not only did he thereby recognize a cultural feature or taste that was not in itself opposed to Islamic principles, but he integrated it as an enrichment of his own human experience. *Hijrah* was also, then, a trial of intelligence, spurring the need to distinguish between principles and their cultural manifestations; moreover, it implied opening up and confidently welcoming new customs, new ways of being and thinking, new tastes. Thus, the universality of principles merged with the necessity of recognizing the diversity of ways of life and cultures. Exile was the most immediate and profound experience of this, since it implied uprooting oneself while remaining faithful to the same God, to the same meaning, in different environments.

Hijrah is also the experience of liberation, both historical and spiritual. Moses had liberated his people from Pharaoh's oppression and led them toward faith and freedom. The essence of *hijrah* is of exactly the same nature: persecuted because of their beliefs, the faithful decided to break away from their tormentors and march to freedom. In so doing, they stressed that they could not accept oppression, that they could not accept the status of victim, and that basically the matter was simple: publicly speaking the name of God implied either being free or breaking free. This same message had already been conveyed by the Prophet, then by Abu Bakr, to all the slaves in Mecca: their arrival in Islam meant their liberation, and all the teachings of Islam pointed to the ending of slavery. Henceforth, a broader call was addressed to the Muslim spiritual community as a whole: faith requires freedom and justice and one must be prepared, as was the case with *hijrah*, to pay the personal and collective price for it.

The spiritual dimension of those teachings is near at hand; indeed, it underlies them and endows them with meaning. From the very first Revelations, Muhammad had been invited to exile himself from his persecutors and from evil: "And have patience with what they say, and keep your distance from them in a good exile."[9] Then: "And all abomination [sin, evil] shun."[10]

Abraham, whose nephew Lot was one of the few people to believe and recognize him, adopted the same attitude when he addressed his people in the following terms:

And [Abraham] said: "For you, you have taken [for worship] idols besides God, out of mutual love and regard between yourselves in this life; but on the Day of Judgment you shall disown each other and curse each other. And your abode will be the Fire, and you shall have none to help." But Lot believed him. [Abraham] said: "I will leave home for the sake of my Lord [*inni muhajirun ila Rabbi*], for He is almighty and wise."[11]

Hijrah is the exile of the conscience and of the heart from false gods, from alienation of all sorts, from evil and sins. Turning away from the idols of one's time (power, money, the cult of appearances, etc.); emigrating from lies and unethical ways of life; liberating oneself, through the experience of breaking away, from all the appearances of freedom paradoxically reinforced by our habits—such is the spiritual requirement of *hijrah*. Later on, questioned by a Companion about the best possible *hijrah*, the Prophet was to answer: "It is to exile yourself [to move away] from evil [abominations, lies, sins]."[12] This requirement of spiritual exile was to be repeated in different forms.

Thus, the Muslims who performed *hijrah*, emigrating from Mecca to Medina, in effect experienced the cyclical dimension of Islam's teachings, since they had to achieve a new return to themselves, an emigration of the heart. Their physical journey to Medina was a spiritual exile toward their inner selves; in leaving their city and their roots, they came back to themselves, to their intimacy with God, to the meaning of their lives beyond historical contingencies.

Physical *hijrah*, the founding act of the first Muslim community's and the axis of its experience, is now over and will not happen again, as Aishah forcefully explained to those in Medina who wanted to relive the experience. Umar ibn al-Khattab was later to decide that this unique event would mark the beginning of the Islamic era, which begins in 622. What remains, and is open to everyone through the ages and for eternity, is the experience of spiritual exile, which brings the individual back to him- or herself and frees him or her from the illusions of self and of the world. Exile for the sake of God is in essence a series of questions that God asks each individual being: *Who are you? What is the meaning of your life? Where are you going?* Accepting the risk of such an exile, trusting the One, is to answer: *Through You, I return to myself and I am free.*

Settlement and Covenants

The Prophet's first words on arriving at Quba informed the Muslims of their basic responsibilities: "Spread peace [*salam*], feed the hungry, honor kinship ties, pray while people sleep, you shall enter paradise in peace [*bisalam*]."[13] The two references to peace, at the beginning and at the end of his address, point to how the Prophet wished his Companions to understand their settlement in their new city. Caring for the poor and honoring kinship ties appear as reminders of the ethical basis of the Muslim presence, which each believer must pledge to permanently respect. Night prayer—"while people sleep"—makes for the spiritual exile mentioned above, and thereby provides the heart with the strength and serenity in faith that make it possible to fulfill the requirements of respecting ethics and of spreading peace. This quest for inner peace (alone, but in the warm light of one's family's love) is the path the believer must follow to be able to spread peace in the world and serve the poorest people.

Those teachings were present throughout the Prophet's life, including at each stage of his settlement in Medina. On arriving in Medina, he already possessed a symbolic and political power that none of the city's dignitaries could ignore. Many of Yathrib's inhabitants had converted to Islam and recognized him as God's Messenger; those converts came from both the Aws and Khazraj clans, which had been at war for ages. The message of Islam had been powerful enough, as had been the case in Mecca, to transcend former divisions and unite women and men from different clans, different social classes, and different origins. This new presence could not but be seen as a threat by all those who had enjoyed some power before the Prophet arrived. Similarly, the Jewish and Christian tribes, long settled in the area, could only take a wait-and-see attitude, as they were divided between recognizing the similarity of Islam's monotheistic message and wondering about the intentions of the new Prophet, whom they naturally did not recognize as such (Jewish leaders had spoken out on this even before he arrived). Muhammad was of course aware of the complexity of the situation and of the religious, social, and political stakes his settlement in Medina involved.

He immediately drew up a mutual assistance agreement between the Muslims and the Jews who lived in the oasis.[14] The terms of the covenant were primarily based on the recognition of diverse affiliations and did not demand any conversion. The principles of justice, equality, and equal dignity for all the signatories (whether Jewish or Muslim, Medina natives or immigrants from Mecca, Aws, or Khazraj) were mentioned in it. Referring to the Jews, the text stipulates: "They have the same rights and the same duties" (*lahum ma lana wa alayhim ma alayna*), which in effect implied that they fully and equally belonged to the local community (*ummah*).[15] It stated that the rights of each person would be defended by all, and should a conflict with the polytheists break out, they were all to stand together and not enter into separate alliances or peace agreements.[16] The text stipulated that in case of dispute, the Prophet would be answerable for the strict and equitable implementation of this agreement. The Prophet's recognition of the value of such contract-based relationships, which he came to in the light of Revelation, was a constant throughout his life and teachings. A contract determines a framework; it asserts the autonomy and recognition of the parties involved (provided its essence is respected) and makes it possible, a posteriori, to set up means of regulation and evaluation. The contract (*al-ahd*) was to become central in Islam, from marriage contracts to social or commercial contracts and those drawn up to settle conflict or war situations.[17] Revelation clarified the importance of contracts and the need to stand by their conditions: "For every engagement will be inquired into."[18] The Prophet said in this respect: "Muslims must stand by the terms of their contracts."[19]

With the Jews

Revelation, the terms of the covenant, and the Prophet's attitude toward the Jews from the moment he arrived in Medina were the factors that determined the general framework of the relationship between the faithful of the two religions. There was first of all the acknowledgment of a link: the same God had sent both Moses and Muhammad. The Jews are, with the Christians, "the people of the Book" (*ahl al-kitab*), those who received a revealed message from God. The Quran clearly states this recognition: "God! There is no god but Him, the Living, the Supporter of all. It is He who sent down to you step by step, in truth, the Book, confirming what went before it; and He sent down the Torah and the Gospel before this, as a guide to humankind."[20]

When he settled in Medina, the Prophet did not require anybody to convert, and he made it clear that he wanted relations within the new society to be egalitarian. Later, when conflicts arose and alliances were betrayed, the situation decayed and relations with one or another of the

Jewish tribes deteriorated greatly. Nevertheless, those developments by no means affected the principles underlying the relationship between Muslims and Jews: mutual recognition and respect, as well as justice before the law or in the settlement of disputes between individuals and/or groups.

For instance, a few years later, at a time when the Muslims were in latent conflict with a Jewish tribe whom they suspected of double dealing and treason, a Muslim thought he might escape responsibility for a theft he had perpetrated by laying the blame on a Jew. An eight-verse Revelation denounced the serious treachery committed by the Muslim culprit and revealed the Jew's innocence.[21] The Muslim's culpability is explicit: "But if anyone earns a fault or a sin and throws it onto one who is innocent, he burdens himself with a false charge and a flagrant sin."[22]

Whatever conflict may occur with other groups, the inalienable principles of respect and justice remained and transcended historical realities, requiring that the Muslim conscience not yield to blinding passions and hatred. The Quran states that any hatred that may incidentally arise from a war cannot obviate the principles to which believers must remain faithful:

> O you who believe! Stand out firmly for God, as witnesses to fair dealing, and let not the hatred of others to you make you depart from justice. Be just: that is next to piety; and fear God [be intimately conscious of God]. For God is well acquainted with all that you do.[23]

Muhammad kept distinguishing between situations and the people involved in them, and he showed the utmost respect toward individuals and their beliefs. For many years, a young Jew was his companion and followed him everywhere, for he loved the Prophet's company. The Prophet never asked him to abandon his faith. Eventually the boy fell seriously ill, and on his deathbed he asked his father to allow him to embrace Islam, but during all his time by the Prophet's side he had remained what he was and enjoyed the Prophet's love and regard.

Later on, as the Prophet was with a group of Muslims, a funeral procession passed by, and the Prophet stood up to show his respect for the deceased. Surprised, the Muslims informed him that this was a Jew's funeral. The Prophet answered with clarity and dignity: "Was this not a human soul?" The teaching was to remain the same in spite of difficulties, treason, and wars: no one was compelled to convert, differences were respected, and all were to be treated equally. This is Revelation's key message and the heart of its Prophet's action; all the later verses of the Quran that refer to conflicts, killing, and fighting must be read in the context of their Revelation (Muslims being in a situation of war and needing to defend themselves) and by no means alter the essential contents of the message as a whole.

Hypocrites

In spite of this covenant, in spite of Muhammad's efforts to reassure the different tribes and the different religious leaders, the situation was far from simple. It involved dealing with some people's jealousy, greed, and struggle for power, and with others' frustration. The Prophet was confronted with attitudes he had had little opportunity to know in Mecca, where conversion required such sacrifices in human terms that it could spring only from sincere and deeply believing hearts. Henceforth, things were to be different. The social configuration in Medina, the different power centers there, and the very nature of the Prophet's role—exerting such obvious influence over hearts and social affairs alike—entirely transformed the situation: some individuals saw an opportunity to gain power (a quasi-political interest) in publicizing their conversion to Islam. The Quran refers, in the first surah revealed in Medina, to this troubling apparition of the *munafiqun*, the "hypocrites," who are a major danger since they attack the Muslim community from within.[24] As Ibn Kathir points out in his commentary on the Quran, four verses at the beginning of the surah "Al-Baqarah" (The Cow) speak of sincere believers, and only two mention unbelievers, but thirteen long verses describe the hypocrites' attitudes and speech, laden with duplicity and treachery:[25]

> Of the people, there are some who say: "We believe in God and the Last Day": but they do not believe. They attempt to deceive God and those who believe, but they only deceive themselves, and realize it not![26]

Then further on:

> When they meet those who believe, they say: "We believe," but when they are alone with their evil ones, they say: "We are really with you, we were only jesting [when pretending to believe]."[27]

The danger was real, and it was to become permanent. Some of those people stirred up ancient quarrels between the Aws and the Khazraj, and one of those attempts would almost have succeeded if one member had not, just in time, reminded them of the superior nature of their brotherhood in Islam. One member of the Khazraj clan, Abdullah ibn Ubayy, had converted to Islam but appeared to many believers as a troublemaker, the typical figure of the hypocrite as described in Revelation. Abu Amir, of the Aws clan, was perceived in the same way, so much did he spread the venom of strife. No particular measure had been taken against them, but people were wary of them and took care not to fall into the snares that could cause division in Muslim ranks.

The Pact of Brotherhood

In order to tighten the bonds between Muslims, and in particular between those Muslims who were from Medina (the Ansar) and those who had emigrated from Mecca (the Muhajirun), the Prophet decided to set up a formal pact of brotherhood (*al-muakhah*) between the Muslims. This meant that each Muhajir was bound by a pact to an Ansar, who was to help him settle down, share his belongings with him, and enable him to live in Medina in the best possible circumstances. On a broader level, their relationships were based on brotherhood, sharing, and mutual spiritual assistance (the Muslim exiles from Mecca would teach their sisters and brothers in Medina what they knew). This pact was to provide the new Muslim community settled in Medina with particular strength and unity. Extremely deep relationships were created between believers who were later to attest to the intensity of their mutual love in God. In a *hadith qudsi*, the Prophet had presented this love as the pinnacle of brotherhood in faith, and his Companions strove to achieve it in their daily actions and commitments: "On the Day of Resurrection, God will say: 'Where are those who loved one another for the sake of My grace [My glory]? Today, I shall shade them with My shade, on a day when there is no shade but Mine.'"[28]

The way the Muslims dealt with the many painful, difficult, and dangerous situations they encountered show that they had achieved a degree of brotherhood and trust that no adversity could ever manage to destroy.

Those bonds constituted the Muslim community's spiritual and social strength, and in this lay the secret of their success before God and among men: faith in God, love for parents, fraternity among people, and ethics at the service of the universe and of all beings.

The Call to Prayer

As months went by, ritual practices had been gradually instituted: fasting in the month of Ramadan and a more precise imposition of *zakat* (the purifying social tax), were added to the profession of faith and to prayer. The Muslims met in the mosque at precise times and prayed together.

The Prophet was looking for a means to call the faithful to prayer. He had been considering the possibilities of imitating Jewish or Christian practices, with bells or with a horn. One day, however, Abdullah ibn Zayd, an Ansar who had taken part in the second covenant of al-Aqabah, came to him and told him of a dream in which a man taught him the manner in which he was to call others to prayer. The Prophet listened to him and immediately recognized that the vision was genuine. He sent for the former slave Bilal, whose voice was extraordinarily beautiful, and had him stand on top of the highest house near the mosque and call the people to prayer.

This same, never-changing call, based on the affirmation of God's greatness (*"Allahu Akbar"*), the profession of faith ("I bear witness that there is no god but God and that Muhammad is God's Messenger"), and an invitation to prayer and success in this world and the next, has for almost fifteen centuries been resonating through Muslim towns and cities. In all its different intonations, rhythms, and voices, this call in its musicality expresses the union of faith and beauty, of spirituality and aesthetics—just as the Prophet had wished it when he chose Bilal as a muezzin. It is a reminder of the One God who loves beauty, and who, five times a day, welcomes those who answer the beautiful call that invites them to meet the Most Beautiful (*al-Jamil*).[29]

CHAPTER NINE

Medina, Life, and War

The Prophet and his Companions who had come from Mecca were gradually settling down in Medina, and they were beginning to find their marks in this new environment. For the first seven months, Muhammad stayed at Abu Ayyub's; he was his guest until the mosque and the two adjoining dwellings were built. The Prophet eventually moved into his own quarters and was joined by his wife Sawdah and then, a few months later, by Aishah, whose wedding was celebrated in Medina. Muhammad's daughters also arrived during the following weeks.

A society was being constituted under particularly difficult circumstances. Intertribal and power conflicts often complicated the relationships between Muslims and members of different clans, in spite of the covenants and alliances. Sometimes among the faithful themselves old reflexes acquired in pagan times would resurface and cause tensions between individuals. The Companions' religious and spiritual education nevertheless went on, and the Prophet was always available to remind them of the principles to which believers must henceforth remain faithful.

In Mecca, resentment was high, and the success of the emigration was perceived not only as a humiliation but also as a threat to the balance of power in the Arabian Peninsula as a whole. For decades, the Quraysh had been naturally acknowledged as the unchallenged leaders on account not only of their past but also of the fact that they were in charge of the city of Mecca, the idols' sanctuary and the site where all the tribes converged once a year to trade. The news of Muhammad's secession and settlement in Medina had spread all over the area, and this significantly affected the Quraysh's reputation and actual power. Muhammad and his Companions knew it and were expecting some imminent reaction from the clan and family members they knew so well.

Dispute with the Quraysh

Not all the Muslims had emigrated; those who had stayed behind were treated all the worse by the Quraysh leaders, as the latter were obviously most upset by Muhammad's success. Indeed, some had stayed in Mecca without publicizing their conversion to Islam, and they now feared the fierce reprisals that would inevitably ensue if that fact became known.

Some of the Quraysh went further and even decided, in violation of the honor code respected by all the clans in the peninsula, to seize the property and belongings the emigrants had left behind in Mecca. When they heard of this behavior, which was considered shameful and cowardly, the Prophet and the Muslims who had settled in Medina were angry. It was decided, six months after their exile, that they would attack the Meccan caravans passing near Medina in order to take back the equivalent of their belongings expropriated in Mecca.

In the months that followed, the Prophet organized no fewer than seven expeditions (in which he did not always take part).[1] These included only Muhajirun, since only they were the victims of Quraysh usurpation. The Ansar were left out, as they were not involved in the conflict. In those expeditions, no fighting or killing occurred: the merchants gave up their goods, then were free to move on. The Muhajirun occasionally arrived too late at the spot where the Meccans were supposed to have stopped; the caravans had already left, and the operation failed. Generally, however, they were successful, and the exiles managed to obtain significant compensation in the form of booty.

Over the same period, the Prophet also sent out missions whose main purpose was to gather intelligence about the Quraysh's movements and activities, their intentions (or possible war preparations), and the new alliances they might set up in the area. Watchfulness was essential, as the Quraysh's hostility was intensifying and becoming increasingly open and widespread. However, one of those missions took a bad turn: Abdullah ibn Jahsh and a small group had been ordered to get very near to the Quraysh clans in the Nakhlah valley (between Mecca and Taif) and gather intelligence about their leaders' intentions. Coming upon a caravan, Abdullah ibn Jahsh and the members of his group decided to attack it despite the fact that it was the last night of Rajab, one of the four sacred months during which all the tribes considered war to be forbidden. A Quraysh man was killed, another managed to escape, and two members of the caravan were taken prisoner. When they went back to Medina, the Prophet reacted very angrily to this action, which was totally at variance with his instructions. This event marked a turning point in the relations between Medina and Mecca.

For more than a year, the Prophet had been setting up pacts with some tribes along the Red Sea coast, on a route generally taken by Mecca caravans traveling north, beyond Medina, to Iraq or Syria. This was bound to inconvenience the Quraysh, who had to find new routes to the east. Tensions were growing steadily, and the Quraysh, who wished to tarnish the exiles' reputation and mobilize the area's tribes against them, found an excellent pretext in the attack on the caravan, which had taken place during the sacred month. The intelligence gathered here and there by Muhammad's envoys pointed to the fact that a clash was imminent.

Revelation

During this same period, the Prophet received two successive Revelations, totally different in nature, but whose consequences were equally to constitute a break with the past. For more than thirteen years, Muslims had been called upon to exercise patience and passive resistance in the face of the persecution and terror they suffered at the hands of the Quraysh leaders and other clans. They had endured, persevered, then emigrated, without responding to aggressions, avoiding confrontation.

Once the Muslims had settled in Medina, it had become obvious that the Quraysh were going to step up their opposition and find other means to put an end to the Prophet's mission, which now no longer threatened only the political balance in Mecca but also the order of powers throughout the Peninsula. What was at stake was the Quraysh's position with regard to all the other tribes and clans; their religious and military standing was at risk. *Hijrah*, which was liberation, also meant conflicts and struggles to come.

Then the Prophet received a Revelation that left no room for doubt:

> Permission [to fight] is given to those against whom war is being wrong-
> fully waged—and verily, God has the power to succor them—those who
> have been driven from their homelands unjustly for no other reason except
> that they say: "Our Lord is God!"[2]

Abu Bakr was later to say that when he heard this verse, he immediately understood that it announced impending conflict and war, and so did
the Prophet and his other Companions. Henceforth, the Muslims were no
longer required to resist passively; rather, they were to defend themselves
against enemy aggression. To the *jihad* of spirituality and intelligence,
which had consisted either in resisting the darkest attractions of the ego-
centric, greedy, or violent self or in answering the pagan contradictors'
arguments through the Quran, a new possible form of *jihad* was now
added: *al-qital*, necessary armed resistance in the face of armed aggression, self-defense against oppressors.

All the forms of *jihad* are, as can be seen, linked to the notion of resistance. On the level of *qital*, armed fighting, it is so as well. At the end of
the verse fighting is presented as a necessity in order to resist human
beings' natural propensity for expansionism and oppression:

> Had God not checked one set of people [the oppressors] by means of
> another, monasteries, churches, synagogues, and mosques, in which the
> name of God is commemorated in abundant measure, would surely have
> been destroyed. God will certainly aid those who aid His cause; for verily
> God is most powerful, almighty.[3]

The need for a balance and regulation of forces is presented as an
objective necessity given human nature. Absolute power for one individual, one nation, or one empire would result in the annihilation of diversity among people and the destruction of the various places of worship
(the list ending with mosques), which here symbolize the pluralism of religions determined and willed by God. Hence, the confrontation of forces
and resistance to human beings' temptation to war are presented, in an
apparent paradox, as the promise of peace among human beings. This is
what the other verse confirms on a more general level: "And had God not

checked one set of people [the oppressors] by means of another, the earth would indeed be full of mischief."[4]

At the origin of creation, the angels had asked God about His intentions in creating humans as His vicegerents: "Will You place therein one who will make mischief therein and shed blood . . . ?"[5] They thereby recalled that humans are, by nature, greedy for power and inclined to spread evil and to kill: the other aspect of humans, their love of good and justice, must resist and, by reaching a balance, produce the conditions for peace—the fragile fruit of a balance between opposite forces and tendencies. Thus, both *jihad* and *qital* are the ways that, by resisting the dark temptations of the inner self as well as human beings' proclivity for war, will make it possible to reach peace, the fruit of an ever-renewed effort to overcome temptations as well as oppressors. The essence of *jihad* is the quest for peace, and *qital* is, at times, the necessary path to peace.

A new era was opening for the Muslim community in Medina. They were to face the aftermath of wars, their toll of death and suffering intensified by the fact that their enemies were from the exiles' own clans, their own relatives. Such was the cost of their survival.

The Change of Qibla

The Muslims had been settled in Medina for about a year and a half when the Prophet received the second Revelation mentioned above. *Qibla*, or the direction in which Muslims had prayed, had hitherto been toward Jerusalem, but Revelation suddenly ordered:

> We see the turning of your face [for guidance] to the heavens: now shall We turn you to a *qibla* that shall please you. So turn your face in the direction of the Sacred Mosque! Wherever you are, turn your faces in that direction! The people of the Book know well that [this commandment] is the truth from their Lord, and God is not unmindful of what they do.[6]

This verse carried several messages and was to have consequences for the Prophet's relations with Jewish and Christian tribes, as this change established a distinction, and a distance, between the monotheistic traditions. Although Jerusalem's place remained essential at the heart of Muslim tradition, the new orientation of prayer restored a direct ritual and spiritual link between Abraham, who built the first house for the worship of the One, and Islamic monotheism. Muslims rejoiced in this and understood it as a return to the origin. "Turning one's face" meant turning one's being, one's heart, toward the Source, the Origin, the One God, the God of Abraham, of the universe, and of humankind. The Kaba thereby resumed its primary function: on earth, it was the House of God, the center toward which all hearts, from all peripheries, would now turn.

Jewish tribes by no means shared in this satisfaction. From the beginning of the Muslims' settlement in Medina, the Jews and the Muslims had had differences involving recognition of the One God and the signing of covenants. But also, more covertly, some Jews had doubts about the new religion and feared that its expansion constituted a threat; Muhammad had heard of contacts established between some Jewish tribes and some of the Quraysh's allies. Because of this distrust, Revelation of this verse could not have been expected to comfort Medina's Jewish dignitaries, since the monotheism professed by Muhammad now seemed to clearly stand apart from the message of Judaism.

Furthermore, the change of *qibla* sent just as strong a message to the inhabitants of Mecca. The central place that the city was acquiring in the message of the new religion led its inhabitants to fear future Muslim designs on the city and the Kaba. This the Quraysh could not accept, and it was now clear that only the termination of Muhammad's mission could protect them and ensure the continuation of historical privileges they had so arduously obtained.

A Caravan

The Prophet had just learned that a caravan led by Abu Sufyan was on its way back from Syria with a large quantity of goods and that most of the Quraysh clans had a share in this trading venture. Muhammad decided to intercept the caravan. One reason was the same as the one that had propelled him to attack the earlier caravan: the wish to recover the wealth appropriated by the Quraysh when they had usurped the exiles' belongings after their departure for Medina. The second reason was that it would serve as a show of power to impress the inhabitants of Mecca, who were increasingly plotting against Medina.

Muhammad set off at the head of 309 (or 313, according to some accounts) of his Companions, including both Muhajirun, the exiles from Mecca, and Ansar, the Muslims from Medina. They were carrying with them substantial weapons—considering the importance of the caravan they planned to attack—even though they were not really fitted out for war. The Prophet had asked Uthman ibn Affan, one of the Meccan exiles who would normally have been a part of the expedition, to stay behind to look after his wife Ruqayyah, the Prophet's daughter, who was seriously ill.[7]

The Prophet intended to intercept the caravan at Badr, but Abu Sufyan had been warned of the impending attack by his own spies; he sent an envoy to the Meccan leaders to inform them of the danger he was in and ask for help. He immediately changed his route as well, and once he was sure that he had managed to avoid the attack, he sent a new envoy to the Quraysh leaders to tell them that the danger was over and that he no longer needed help. However, by this time the Quraysh leaders had already set off with more than a thousand men, and they decided, at Abu Jahl's insistence, that the expedition must go on in spite of the apparent lack of danger. Even though the confrontation might be avoided, they in their turn intended to stage a show of strength against their enemy. The Prophet and his Companions, who had set up their camp near Badr, heard that a mighty army had set off from Mecca. This meant a total change of plans: they had left Medina intending to lay their hands on a caravan of goods (which they had failed to do), and now an army three times the size of their own force was marching toward them, with its leaders seemingly intent on fighting it out. This was war, and the Muslims were not really ready for it.

Consultations

Muhammad was wondering whether he should move forward and try to catch up with the caravan or stop and go back to Medina in order to avoid risking a clash with the mighty Quraysh army. He decided to consult his Companions and find out what they thought about the matter. Abu Bakr and Umar spoke first and confirmed their readiness to move forward and risk a full-scale confrontation. Another exile, al-Miqdad ibn Amr, spoke next: "Go ahead, you and your Lord, and fight; and with you we shall also fight, to the right and to the left, in front of you and behind you."[8]

This attitude comforted and pleased the Prophet, but this was what he could naturally have expected from the Muhajirun. It was from the Ansar that he needed explicit support, since they were not directly involved in the conflict with the Quraysh and had signed an assistance agreement binding them only in case of war in Medina, not outside the city. Sad ibn Muadh, speaking on behalf of the Ansar, said with determination: "Do what you will, and we are with you. By He who has sent you with the truth, were you to order us to cross the sea and dive into it yourself, we would dive in with you. Not one of us would stay behind."[9] Having thus obtained the assent of both groups, Muhammad decided to move forward without allowing the Quraysh's maneuvers to intimidate him.

Throughout his mission the Prophet sought his Companions' advice, encouraging them to express their opinions and paying them careful attention. Furthermore, the Prophet had evolved a genuine pedagogy through which he allowed the Muslims to develop their critical faculties, express their talents, and mature in his presence. He would often ask questions on various subjects and give the answers only after his Companions had thought by themselves and expressed different conjectures. Sometimes, more subtly, he would utter a judgment in a paradoxical form, thereby prompting his listeners to consider the matter more deeply. For example, he once said: "A strong man is not a man who overcomes his enemy!" The Companions mulled this over among themselves, then asked him: "Then who is a strong man?" The Prophet surprised his audience and led them to a deeper understanding of the question with his answer: "A strong man is a man who controls himself when he is angry!"[10] He would sometimes speak figuratively: "Wealth does not lie in the riches you possess!" After the Companions pondered this, Muhammad would elaborate: "True wealth is the wealth of the soul."[11] On occasion the Prophet's statement appeared to contradict common sense or ethics: "Help your brother, whether he is just or unjust!" The Companions could not but wonder about the nature of the help they were to give an unjust brother: how could that be? The Prophet, inverting the perspective, would add: "Prevent him [the unjust brother] from acting unjustly, such is the way for you to help him!"[12]

Both by asking questions and by formulating paradoxical or seemingly contradictory statements, the Prophet stimulated his Companions' critical sense and their ability to go beyond mere blind obedience or mechanical, mind-destroying imitation. This method developed the intellectual capacities necessary for consultations to be effective. Indeed, if they were to give useful advice, the Companions had to be intellectually awake, bold, and independent, even in the presence of a Prophet whose personality and status must have impressed them. By stimulating their intelligence and giving them opportunities to speak, he exercised a type of leadership that made it possible for his Companions to learn to assert themselves and take initiative.

Hubab ibn al-Mundhir was the most outstanding example of this at the particular time we have been discussing. When he arrived at Badr, the Prophet set up his camp near the first wells he found. Seeing this, Ibn al-Mundhir came to him and asked: "Was this place where we have stopped revealed to you by God, so that we must not move either forward or backward from it, or is it an opinion and a strategy of yours, linked to war expedients?"[13] The Prophet confirmed that it was his own personal opinion; Ibn al-Mundhir then suggested another plan that consisted of camping near the biggest well, the nearest to the way from which the enemy was to arrive, then blocking the other wells in the area so that the enemy could not get to the water. During the battle, the Muslims' opponents were thus bound to find themselves in difficulty. Muhammad carefully listened to the explanation of this strategy and accepted it straightaway: the camp was moved and Hubab's plan was implemented.

This example shows that the Companions made a distinction between Revelations the Prophet received, which they obeyed without a second thought, and the opinions of Muhammad the man, which could be debated, improved on, or even rejected outright. The Messenger's authority in human affairs was neither autocratic nor unrestricted; he allowed his Companions a substantial role in consultation, and his teaching, as we have seen, developed the conditions for acquiring those critical and creative faculties. The Prophet gave his Companions, women and men alike, the means and confidence to be autonomous, to dare to address and contradict him without his ever considering it as lack of respect for his status. Through this attitude, he showed them his deep respect for their intelligence and for their heart: as for them, they loved their Prophet, their leader, for this attention, this availability, and this demand to use their abilities to the fullest.

The Battle of Badr

When it had become clear that the caravan had escaped and that a full-scale war lay ahead, Muhammad tried to discourage the Quraysh from choosing war. He sent Umar ibn al-Khattab to suggest to the Quraysh that they should turn back and thus avoid confrontation. Among the Quraysh, some also wanted to avoid war, and Utbah, one of the Meccan leaders, even offered to pay blood money for their ally who had been killed during the sacred month. Nothing helped, however: the advocates of war among the Quraysh were determined, and they knew that the numbers were clearly in their favor. Indeed, they considered Umar's attempt a sign of weakness. This was a great opportunity for them to destroy the Muslim community and get rid of Muhammad.

The Prophet had, for his part, had a number of inspirations and dreams. He understood that war was going to result from this encounter with the Quraysh and that the outcome would be in his favor. He kept praying to God and encouraging his Companions to persevere and remain determined. He announced to them: "By He who holds Muhammad's soul between His hands, nobody will be killed today, fighting in the firm hope of a reward, going forward and not turning back, but God will directly make him enter His Paradise."[14] He again prostrated himself for a very long time, praying to God to keep His promise, protect his community, and grant the Muslims victory, until Abu Bakr invited him to stop, convinced that God could not let them down.

The battle was going to take place in the month of Ramadan, on the seventeenth, in the second year of *hijrah* (624 CE). On the road to Badr, the Prophet reminded the Muslims who wished to fast that this was not compulsory when traveling: "Piety does not consist in fasting when traveling; it is your duty to make good use of the permissions [*rukhas*, sing. *rukhsa*] granted to you by God. Accept them!"[15] Each circumstance of life was useful to remind the Muslims of their religion's teachings, and the Prophet kept insisting on the permissions granted to the faithful, who must make the practice of their religion easy and bring good news rather than cause repulsion: "Make things easy, and do not render them difficult! Bring good news [which cheers the heart], not bad news [which puts off and displeases]!"[16] The Prophet drank water conspicuously on that occasion to set an example for his Companions.

The battle began with three duels involving Hamzah, Ali, and Ubaydah ibn al-Harith: Hamzah and Ali overcame their opponents, but Ubaydah was fatally wounded. Then hostilities began, and the Muslims showed such determination that the Quraysh were fairly rapidly defeated. Although they were three times as numerous, they could not hold back the Muslims' onslaught. Revelation was later to mention God's constant protection at the heart of the fighting, His angels, and the fulfillment of His promise: "God helped you at Badr, when you were helpless. Then fear God [be intimately conscious of His presence]: thus may you show your gratitude."[17] This victory was a turning point: the Quraysh's status and supremacy had been seriously affected and the news of their defeat spread like wildfire throughout the Peninsula.

The Muslims had lost fourteen of their men, while the Meccans had lost more than seventy, including Abu Jahl, who had been one of Islam's fiercest opponents and who had been most eager for that battle to take place. Abbas, the Prophet's uncle (in whom the latter had confided in Mecca, and who had witnessed all the preparations preceding the emigration), was among the seventy Quraysh prisoners.

In Mecca, in Medina

The Quraysh's return to Mecca was painful, as most of the clans had suffered the death of a member. Some were already calling for revenge, such as Hind, who had lost her father, brother, and uncle in the battle. She swore she would drink the blood of Hamzah, who had killed her father and her uncle. The Quraysh leaders wasted no time in reacting, striving to set up alliances with neighboring cities and tribes in order to fight the Muslims, avenge their humiliation, and put an end to the Muslims' presence in the Peninsula.

Abu Lahab, whose ill health had prevented him from taking part in the fighting, had remained in Mecca. He asked Abu Sufyan to tell him what had happened and the circumstances of the defeat.[18] While the latter was giving his account, a slave who was sitting nearby, and who had so far kept his conversion to Islam secret, could not control his joy and was thus discovered. Abu Lahab sprang to him and beat him savagely while holding him down. Um al-Fadl, Abu Lahab's sister-in-law and Abbas's wife, who was also present and who had also secretly embraced Islam, rushed on her brother-in-law and gave him a violent blow with a tent post. The deep head wound became infected in the following days and the infection eventually spread to Abu Lahab's entire body; he died within a few weeks. Both Abu Lahab and his wife had always given free rein to their hatred of Islam, and in fact the Quran had, years before, announced his fate, as well as his wife's.[19] Unlike some other oppressors who eventually changed their minds, neither Abu Lahab nor his wife ever showed the least sympathy for Muhammad's message. Abu Lahab's death, which occurred in rejection and violence, confirmed what Revelation had announced: both of them would, to the end, remain among those who deny and rebel.

The Muslims had buried their dead and were preparing to go back to Medina. They had seventy prisoners, and a discussion of their fate took place between the Prophet, Abu Bakr, and Umar. Umar wanted the prisoners to be killed, while Abu Bakr disagreed. Muhammad decided to spare their lives, except for two prisoners who had been particularly cruel to the Muslims in Mecca, humiliating them and torturing them to death. Holding prisoners represented an added means of humiliating the Quraysh, who would be compelled to go to Medina and pay a heavy ransom (which would also bring the Muslims considerable profit). However, a Quranic Revelation was to reproach the Prophet for this choice, which indeed was mainly motivated by the desire to acquire wealth.[20]

Moreover, the Muslim soldiers had already quarreled over the sharing of spoils, and different opinions had been expressed as to the merits of the various groups of soldiers and the way the spoils should be divided. Pre-Islamic customs, in which the quantity of spoils gained after a war contributed to the victors' pride and honor, remained deeply rooted. A Quranic Revelation referred to this dispute and stated that the spoils must go to "God and the Messenger," which implied that the Prophet was to distribute the wealth equitably according to Quranic injunctions, thereby putting an end to such disputes.[21] Muhammad was again and again to be confronted with such disputes among his Companions, and each time, Revelation or the Prophet himself would repeat that they must ask themselves what their intentions were: did they seek wealth in this world or peace in the hereafter? They remained human beings, with their weaknesses and temptations; they needed reminders, spiritual education, and patience, as does everyone, whether near the Prophet or at any other point in human history. History teaches us, after all, that nothing and nobody should be idealized.

When they reached Medina, the Prophet was informed of the death of his daughter Ruqayyah, Uthman ibn Affan's wife. He had just lost his first Companions, and now he was given the news that his daughter was gone as he was returning from a victorious expedition. The blending of sorrow and joy reminded him of the fragility of life and, once more, of his essential relationship to the One through hardship or success. Nothing was ever acquired to last. Later on, Uthman was to marry Um Kulthum, another of the Prophet's daughters, while the Prophet was to marry Hafsah, Umar ibn al-Khattab's daughter, who came to live in one of the dwellings near the mosque.

Bargaining with the prisoners' relatives began. Some relatives came to pay their due and returned with their family member. Other prisoners were freed without any ransom, while the poorest were dealt with individually, according to their particular circumstances. For example, those of the captives who could read and write and who could not pay a ransom pledged to teach ten Medina youths to read and write in exchange for their freedom. Once more the Prophet demonstrated the importance of knowledge by means of the message he sent the members of his community: whether in peace or in war, knowledge—learning, reading, and writing—provides people with essential skills and gives them dignity. The knowledge some captives possessed was their wealth and became their ransom.

Banu Qaynuqa

The months that followed the return from Badr brought difficulties on the regional level. Only a few days after returning from Badr, the Prophet had been compelled to lead a force of two hundred men to the villages of the Banu Salim and Banu Ghatafan in the al-Qudr area to put an end to a plot and prevent any harm. The inhabitants ran away. It was now clear that the Muslim community's status had changed. Many cities in the area, as well as those who had not concluded any pact, were afraid of the military, political, and symbolic power Muhammad was acquiring at the heart of the Arabian Peninsula.

The Prophet was constantly getting intelligence about the initiatives and alliance attempts carried out by the Quraysh leaders in order to quench their thirst for revenge. An inspired dream had enabled him to foil an assassination attempt by Umayr ibn Wahb, who, astonished by how much the Prophet knew about the attempt, converted on the spot. Muhammad knew, however, that the Quraysh would soon undertake a large-scale action with the help of as many tribes as they could mobilize.

After his return from Badr, the Prophet noticed that a number of Medinans were disappointed or worried by the Muslims' success. He had identified a number of hypocrites who had converted to Islam out of self-interest and political calculation. He also knew that some of the signatories to the alliance agreement drawn up when he had first arrived in Medina could not be relied on and would not hesitate to turn against him when the opportunity arose. Muhammad had just received a Revelation inviting him to be watchful: "And if you fear treachery from any group [with whom you made a covenant], cast it back at them in an equitable manner, for God does not love the treacherous."[22] For the time being, the Prophet simply kept an eye on the activities of the various groups, while taking the hypocrites' pledges at face value and strictly respecting the terms of the agreement, since Revelation advised him to show prudence and wisdom: "But if they incline toward peace, do you [also] incline toward peace, and trust in God."[23]

The Jewish tribe of Banu Qaynuqa was the only one of the three Jewish tribes settled in the Medina area who lived inside the city. They were a signatory to the covenant. Yet alarming news of treason and a possible plot came to the Prophet from within their ranks. To determine the truth of what was going on, and to avoid letting the Banu Qaynuqa think that they could act as they pleased, Muhammad paid them a visit and invited them to ponder the Quraysh's defeat. The Banu Qaynuqa leaders retorted haughtily that if they were to go to war against him, things would not turn out in that way; they would certainly win. This threatening answer was confirmation of Muhammad's suspicions: they had become hostile to the Muslims.

A few days later, a Muslim woman went, as usual, to the Banu Qaynuqa market; there, she was mocked and humiliated by a merchant who tied her garment in her back while she was seated, so that the lower part of her body was exposed when she stood up. A Muslim man who had witnessed the scene wanted to intervene: a fight followed, and both the merchant and the Muslim died as a result of their injuries. According to the terms of the covenant, such a case should have been dealt with by the Prophet and resolved peacefully according to the principles of justice and honor codes. But the Banu Qaynuqa betrayed the covenant by trying to ally themselves with Ibn Ubayy, a hypocrite with whom they had already been bargaining for some time and who they hoped would help them mobilize their allies in the area in order to fight the Muslims.

Muhammad reacted quickly, gathering an army and immediately besieging the fortress to which the Banu Qaynuqa had rushed to protect themselves. They hoped to receive outside support from Muslim ranks through the hypocrites who had converted to Islam in name only and who had always assured the Banu Qaynuqa that they too hoped for the Muslim community to be wiped out. No support came, however, and after a two-week siege the Banu Qaynuqa surrendered.

The Prophet remembered the Revelation that "it is not fitting for a prophet that he should have prisoners of war" out of a desire for profit.[24] He had the option of killing the men of the tribe who had betrayed the covenant and banishing their women and children, as was the usual practice after victory in war. This would have enabled him to send a strong message to neighboring tribes about the fate awaiting whoever betrayed or attacked the Muslim community. He had received a Revelation pointing to this: "If you gain mastery over them in war, deal with them so as to strike fear in those who follow them, that they may remember."[25] Muhammad nevertheless received Ibn Ubayy—whose hypocrisy and secret dealings he was aware of—when he came to intercede for the Banu Qaynuqa. Once again, he decided to spare his prisoners' lives, but he demanded that their belongings be confiscated and that they move out of the city. They took refuge with some of the other tribes and colonies in the area, but this did not stop them from plotting against the Prophet. On the contrary, their recent humiliation increased their hatred: the number of Muhammad's enemies kept growing and their resentment deepened. He knew it and kept inviting his Companions to wisdom and patience, as well as watchfulness.

CHAPTER TEN

Teachings and Defeat

Life went on in Medina. In spite of the complexity of relations between tribes and the need to remain watchful, Muhammad went on dispensing his teachings in the light of Revelations he received. Always his distinctive feature was the combination of strict faithfulness to his principles and human warmth constantly radiating from his presence. The Companions were so eager for his company that they would take turns with him, in order to spend as much time as possible with him, listening and learning. Their love for him was deep, respectful, and faithful, and the Prophet kept inviting them to further deepen that affection and to love him in the superior light of God's love.

Gentleness, Caring, and Love

In his daily life, though he was preoccupied by attacks, treachery, and his enemies' thirst for revenge, Muhammad remained mindful of the small details of life and of the expectations of those around him, constantly allying rigor and the generosity of fraternity and forgiveness. His Companions and his wives saw him pray for hours during the night, away from the others, alone with the whispered prayers and invocations that nurtured his dialogue with the One. Aishah, his wife, was impressed and surprised: "Don't you take on too much [worship] while God has already forgiven all your past and future sins?" The Prophet answered: "How could I but be a thankful servant?"[1] He did not demand of his Companions the worship, fasting, and meditations that he exacted of himself.

On the contrary, he required that they ease their burden and avoid excess; to some Companions who wanted to put an end to their sexual life, pray all night long, or fast continuously (such as Uthman ibn Mazun or Abdullah ibn Amr ibn al-As), he said: "Do not do that! Fast on some days and eat on others. Sleep part of the night, and stand in prayer another part. For your body has rights upon you, your eyes have a right upon you, your wife has a right upon you, your guest has a right upon you."[2] He once exclaimed, repeating it three times: "Woe to those who exaggerate [who are too strict]!"[3] And on another occasion, he said: "Moderation, moderation! For only with moderation will you succeed."[4]

He kept striving to soothe the consciences of believers who were afraid of their own weaknesses and failings. One day, the Companion Hanzalah al-Usaydi met Abu Bakr and confessed to him that he was convinced of his own deep hypocrisy because he felt divided between contradictory feelings: in the Prophet's presence, he almost saw paradise and hell, but when he was away from him, his wife and children and daily affairs caused him to forget. Abu Bakr in his turn admitted that he experienced similar tensions. They both went to the Prophet to question him about the seemingly dismal state of their spirituality. Hanzalah explained the nature of his doubts, and Muhammad answered: "By He who holds my soul in His hands, if you were able to remain in the [spiritual] state in which you are when in my company, and remember God permanently, the angels would shake your hands in your beds and along your paths. But it is not so, Hanzalah: there is a time for this [devotion, remembrance] and a time for that [rest, amusement]."[5] Their situation had nothing to do with hypocrisy: it was merely the reality of human nature, which remembers and forgets, and which needs to remember precisely because it forgets, because human beings are not angels.

In other circumstances, he would surprise them by stating that the sincerity of a prayer, an act of charity, or an act of worship found expression at the very heart of their most human needs, in the humble acknowledgment of their humanity: "Enjoining good is charity, forbidding evil is charity. In having sexual intercourse with your spouses there is charity." The Companions, surprised, asked: "O Messenger of God, when one of us satisfies his [sexual] desire, does he also get a reward?" Muhammad replied: "Tell me, if one of you had had illicit intercourse, would he not have committed a sin? That is why he is rewarded for having lawful intercourse."[6] He thus invited them to deny or despise nothing in their humanity and taught them that the core of the matter was achieving self-control. Spirituality means both accepting and mastering one's instincts: living one's natural desires in the light of one's principles is a prayer. It is never a misdeed, nor is it hypocrisy.

The Prophet hated to let his Companions nurture a pointless feeling of guilt. He kept telling them that they must never stop conversing with the One, the Most Kind, the Most Merciful, who welcomes everyone in His grace and benevolence and who loves the sincerity of hearts that regret their misdeeds and return to Him. This is the profound meaning of *at-tawbah*, offered to everyone: sincerely returning to God after a slip, a mistake, a sin. God loves that sincere return to Him and He forgives and purifies. The Prophet himself exemplified that in many circumstances. On one occasion a Bedouin came and urinated in the mosque; the Companions rushed on him and wanted to beat him up. The Prophet stopped them and said: "Leave him alone, and just throw a bucketful of water on his urine. God has only sent you to make obligations easy, and not to make them difficult."[7]

Aishah reports that once a man came to the Prophet and told him: "I am lost!" When the Prophet asked why, the man confessed: "I had intercourse with my wife during the fasting hours of Ramadan." Muhammad answered, "Give charity!" The man replied, "I own nothing!" Then he sat down a short distance from the Prophet. Some time later, a man arrived, bringing a dish of food as a gift for Muhammad.[8] The Prophet called out: "Where is the man who is lost?" "Here," answered the first man, the one who had confessed his transgression. Muhammad told him, "Take this food and give it away in charity." In astonishment, the man cried, "To one poorer than myself? My family has nothing to eat!" "Well, then, eat it yourselves," the Prophet replied with a smile.[9]

That gentleness and kindness were the very essence of his teaching. He kept saying: "God is gentle [*rafiq*] and he loves gentleness [*ar-rifq*] in everything."[10] He also said: "He gives for gentleness what He does not give for violence or anything else."[11] He declared to one of his Companions: "There are in you two qualities that God loves: clemency [*al-hilm*] and forbearance [*al-ana*, "nobleness," "tolerance"]."[12] He invited all his Companions to that constant effort of gentleness and forgiveness: "If you hear about your brother something of which you disapprove, seek from one to seventy excuses for him. If you cannot find any, convince yourselves that it is an excuse you do not know."[13]

A number of new converts to Islam who had no home and often nothing to eat had settled around the mosque, near the Prophet's dwelling. They were destitute (sometimes intentionally, since some of them wished to lead an ascetic life detached from worldly possessions), and their subsistence depended on the Muslims' charity and gifts. Their number kept increasing, and they were soon called *ahl as-suffah* (the people of the bench).[14] The Prophet was most concerned by their situation and showed them continuous solidarity. He would listen to them, answer their questions, and look after their needs. One of the characteristics of his personality and of his teachings, as much in regard to the people of the bench as to the rest of his community, was that when he was asked about matters of spirituality, faith, education, or doubt, he would often offer different answers to the same questions, taking into account the psychological makeup, experience, and intelligence of the questioner.

The faithful felt that he saw, respected, understood, and loved them. Indeed, he did love them, and he told them so. Moreover, he advised them to remember to tell one another of their mutual love: "When someone loves their brother [or sister] let them tell them that they love them."[15] He once took young Muadh ibn Jabal by the hand and whispered: "O Muadh, by God, I love you. And I advise you, O Muadh, never to forget to say, after each ritual prayer: 'O God, help me remember You, thank You, and perfect my worship of You.'"[16] Thus the young man was offered both love and spiritual teaching, and the teaching was all the more deeply assimilated because it was wrapped in that love.

The Najran Christians

The date of the Najran Christians' visit to Muhammad is not precisely known. Some sources, such as Ibn Hisham, situate it even before the Battle of Badr, while others have it take place, according to a text attributed to Ibn Ishaq (and also in reference to some hadiths and the chronology of some verses of the Quran related to the episode), between the Battle of Badr and the Battle of Uhud. The exact date matters little in the end; what remains essential is the nature and objective of the encounter.

A delegation of fourteen religious leaders from Najran (Yemen) had visited the Prophet in order to question him about the new religion, about his faith, and of course about the status of Jesus in Islam.[17] Numerous Christian tribes lived in the Arabian Peninsula, and it seems that most of the Yemeni Christians followed the Melchite Orthodox rite, whose center was in Constantinople. The Prophet answered their questions, pointing out the link between the two traditions, Islam being the continuation of the prophet Jesus's message, but he categorically rejected the dogma of the Trinity. He invited them to worship the One God and accept Islam as the last Revelation. The Quran gives a lengthy account of that encounter as well as of the similarities and differences between Christian and Islamic teachings.[18] The beginning of the third surah, "Ala Imran" (The Family of Imran), establishes the Islamic frame of reference:

> *Alif, lâm, mîm.* God! There is no god but Him, the Ever-Living, the Self-Subsisting by whom all things subsist. It is He who sent down to you step by step, in truth, the Book, confirming what went before it; and He sent down the Torah and the Gospel before this, as a guide to humankind. And He sent down the Criterion [the Quran].[19]

Revelation confirms the recognition of the previous Books that came down to humankind through Moses and Jesus, and adds that the Quran is part of the same monotheistic tradition. Further on, the text details the terms of the invitation made to the Christians:

> Say: "O People of the Book! Come to common terms between us and you: that we shall worship none but God; that we shall associate no partners with Him; that we shall not erect, from among ourselves, lords and patrons other than God." If then they turn back, say: "Bear witness that we have surrendered ourselves unto Him."[20]

Along with the affirmation of God's oneness and the rejection of the Trinity, this verse also denounces the status and role of priests in Christian tradition. Here, as in other verses or Prophetic traditions, the reference to potential "masters" (lords, authorities) indicates those who place themselves between God and people and might thus claim illegitimate or inordinate religious powers.

The Najran delegation refused to accept the Prophet's message. Before they left, the members of the delegation wanted to perform their prayers inside the mosque. The Companions present thought it fit to oppose them, but the Prophet intervened: "Let them pray!"[21] They prayed in the mosque, facing east. When they were about to leave, they invited the Prophet to send with them an envoy who would live with them, answer their questions, and, if needed, judge some of their affairs. Abu Ubaydah ibn al-Jarrah was chosen; later Umar ibn al-Khattab was to admit that he unsuccessfully tried to attract the Prophet's attention so that he would name him for the task.

The delegation went home. The Christians had come to Medina, inquired about the message, listened to the contents of the new religion, put forward their arguments, prayed inside the mosque itself, then gone back without suffering any harm, remaining Christians and perfectly free. The first Companions were not to forget the Prophet's attitude. They were to draw from it the substance of the respect that Islam demands of its faithful, whom it invites to go beyond tolerance, to learn, listen, and recognize others' dignity. The command "No compulsion in religion" is in keeping with this respectful approach to diversity:[22]

> O humankind! We created you from a male and a female, and made you into nations and tribes, that you may know each other. Verily the most honored among you in the sight of God is the most righteous of you [the most deeply aware of God's presence]. And God has full knowledge and is well acquainted [with all things].[23]

More than tolerance (which smacks of condescension within a power relationship), the respect required by God is based on an egalitarian relationship of mutual knowledge.[24] God alone knows what hearts contain and how deep is the piety of one or another individual. Elsewhere, the Quran mentions and acknowledges the sincerity of their humble quest for the divine, even though it criticizes and rejects the status of priests and religious dignitaries:

> You will find the nearest among men in love to the believers [the Muslims] those who say, "We are Christians," because among these are priests and monks, and they are not arrogant.[25]

This verse from the fifth surah (the last injunction to be revealed) states the terms of a privileged relationship between Muslims and Christians, based on two essential qualities: sincerity and humility. With Christians, as with all other spiritual or religious traditions, the invitation to meet, share, and live together fruitfully will always remain based on these three conditions: trying to get to know the other, remaining sincere (hence honest) during the encounter and the debates, and, finally, learning humility in regard to one's claim to possess the truth. Such is the message the Prophet bore in his relationship with the faithful of other religions. As can be seen, he did not hesitate to question and even contradict the Christians' beliefs (such as the Trinity or the role of priests), but in the end his attitude was based on knowledge, sincerity, and humility, which are the three conditions of respect. They were free to leave, and the dialogue went on with the Prophet's envoy.

A Daughter, a Wife

The Prophet lived very modestly: his dwelling was particularly bare, and he often had nothing but a few dates left to eat. Yet he kept helping the destitute around him, especially *ahl as-suffah*, the people of the bench, who lived near his home. When he received presents, he had them given out, and he immediately freed the slaves who were sometimes sent to him as gifts: he did so with the slave Abu Rafi, whom his uncle Abbas had sent him when he had returned to Mecca after his release. In spite of his increasingly important role in Medinan society and of his many responsibilities, he kept this simplicity in his life and in the way he allowed the members of his community to approach him. He owned nothing, and he let himself be accosted by women, children, slaves, and the poorest people. He lived among them; he was one of them.

His daughter Fatimah was very close to her father. Married to Ali ibn Abi Talib, the Prophet's cousin, she had eventually moved near her father's dwelling and she was most devoted to the cause of the poor, including *ahl as-suffah*. When the Prophet was at home or in public and his daughter came to him or entered the room, he would stand up and greet her, publicly showing her great respect and tenderness. Both the people of Medina and the Meccans were surprised at this behavior toward a daughter, who in their respective customs did not usually receive such treatment. The Prophet would kiss his daughter, talk to her, confide in her, and have her sit by his side, without paying attention to the remarks or even the criticisms that his behavior could give rise to. Once he kissed his grandson, al-Hassan, Fatimah's son, in front of a group of Bedouins, who were startled. One of them, al-Aqra ibn Habis, expressed his shock and said: "I have ten children and I have never kissed any one of them!" The Prophet answered: "He who is not generous [loving, benevolent], God is not generous [loving, benevolent] to him."[26] In the light of his silent example and his remarks, the Prophet taught his people good manners, kindness, gentleness, respect for children, and regard for and attentiveness toward women. He was later to say: "I have only been sent to perfect noble manners."[27]

Fatimah received that love and the teachings of faith and tenderness from her father and spread them around her through her activities with the poor. One day, however, she told her husband about her difficulties: like her father, they owned nothing, and she felt it increasingly difficult to manage her daily life, her family, and her children. Her husband advised her to go to her father and ask for his help; perhaps he might supply her with one of the slaves he had received as gifts. She went to see him, but she dared not express her request, so deep was her respect for her father. When she came back, silent and empty-handed, Ali decided to go with her and ask for the Prophet's help himself. The Prophet listened to them and informed them that he could do nothing for them, that their situation was far better than that of the *ahl as-suffah*, who urgently needed his help. They had to endure and be patient. They left, sad and disappointed: although they were the Prophet's daughter and cousin, they could not claim any social privilege.

Late in the evening, the Prophet came to their door. They wanted to get up to receive him, but Muhammad entered and sat at their bedside. He whispered: "Shall I offer you something better than what you asked me for?" They assented, and the Prophet told them: "They are words Gabriel has taught me, and that you should repeat ten times after each prayer: 'Glory to God' [*subhan Allah*], then 'Praise be to God' [*al-hamdu liLLah*], then 'God is the Most Great' [*Allahu Akbar*]. Before going to bed, you should repeat each of those phrases thirty-three times.'"[28] Sitting at his daughter's bedside late at night, deeply attentive to her needs, he answered his daughter's material request by granting her the privilege of a confidence from the divine: a spiritual teaching that has come down to us through the ages and that each Muslim now adopts as his own at the heart of his daily life. Fatimah, like her husband, Ali, was a model of piety, generosity, and love. She lived in the light of her father's spiritual teachings: getting by on little, asking everything of the One, and giving everything of herself to others.

Years later, by her dying father's side, she was to weep intensely when he whispered in her ear that God was going to call him back to Him, that it was time for him to depart. She smiled happily when, a few minutes later, he told her in confidence—loving confidence seems to reveal the essence of this father-daughter relationship—that she was to be the first in her family to join him.

Aishah, the Prophet's wife, was also nurtured by Muhammad's example and conversation. Everything led to spiritual edification, and she was later to be an invaluable source of information about the Messenger's personality, attitude in private life, and public commitments. She has told how Muhammad was attentive to her expectations and wishes when, while still quite young, she arrived in his home in Medina. Play was part of their lives, and Muhammad never refrained from sharing in it or allowing her to satisfy her curiosity, as for instance when a delegation from Abyssinia visited him. The Abyssinians performed various games and traditional dances in the courtyard of the Prophet's house, and the Prophet stood on the doorstep of his dwelling, thus allowing his wife to watch the performance discreetly from behind his shoulder.[29] Time and time again, she spoke of the particular nature of his attentiveness to her, of his expressions of tenderness, and of the freedom he allowed her in her daily life. The contents of the Prophetic traditions she later reported shows to what extent Muhammad spoke to her, conversed with her, and expressed his love and tenderness. In her presence, through the example of his behavior toward his wife, he reformed the Muhajirun's and the Ansar's customs.

The two Quranic verses dealing with women's dress were revealed around the second year of *hijrah*.[30] The *khimar* was a piece of cloth women wore on their heads, throwing its ends on their backs: the Quran ordered Muslim women to draw the ends forward over their chests, covering their throats. The Prophet's wives, like all other women, respected that injunction; not until two years later was their specific status as "the

Prophet's wives" established, so that they could no longer address men except from behind a protective screen (*al-hijab*). Before Revelation of the verses enjoining the Prophet's wives to remain hidden from men's sight, Aishah behaved like all other women and was most present in Medina's public life.[31] The Prophet involved her and wished his Companions to understand, through her example, the role that women, and particularly their wives, were to assume in their daily and public lives.

A Persian neighbor once invited the Prophet to a meal. The Prophet answered: "What about her?" pointing to his wife Aishah. The man replied negatively, implying that the invitation was meant for him alone. Muhammad then refused the offer. The neighbor invited him again some time later. The Prophet again asked: "What about her?" The Persian answered negatively, and Muhammad once more refused. The Persian invited him a third time, and when the Prophet asked, "What about her?" he answered in the affirmative. The Prophet accepted the invitation and went to the neighbor's with Aishah.[32] Through steadfastly maintaining a position, the Prophet was reforming customs and practices among the Arabs and Bedouins in the Peninsula without attacking their conventions. Aishah, as well as Khadijah before her, and indeed all of his wives and daughters, were present in his life, were active in public life, and never confused modesty with disappearing from the social, political, economic, or even military sphere.

The Messenger had granted them the means to be and develop, to express themselves and be critical, and to avoid false modesty and speak of delicate subjects linked to their womanhood, their bodies, their desires and expectations. Years later, Aishah was to recall with respect and admiration that intellectual boldness characteristic of Ansar women who, unlike most Meccan women, dared to speak out and ask direct questions: "Blessed be [what excellent women were] the Ansar women: modesty did not prevent them from seeking instruction [regarding their religion]."[33] She herself had been trained in the same way by the Prophet: she was present when Revelations took place, and she remained by the Prophet's side when he conveyed the message or gave recommendations and advice, or simply when he was alone and lived his religion in private. She would listen, question, and attempt to understand the reasons and meaning of her husband's choices and attitudes. Thanks to her memory, intelligence, and critical mind, more than two thousand hadiths (Prophetic traditions) have come down to us through her, and she also repeatedly corrected the accounts given by other Companions.

The love the Prophet and Aishah showed each other was powerful and intense. Aishah has not hesitated to tell of his tender and loving attitude in their daily life and of his warmth and attentiveness, even during the month of Ramadan. She has also told of her questions to the Prophet about the depth of his love, of her jealousy of the deceased Khadijah, and of the Prophet's way of always finding the means to reassure her. Aishah's loving, attentive, and intelligent presence is largely what has made it possible to draw a subtle, in-depth portrait of the Messenger.

Later, in the fifth or sixth year of *hijrah*, she was to experience the most difficult trial in her life. On the way back from an expedition to the Banu al-Mustaliq, noticing that she had lost her necklace, she went to look for it. In the meantime, the convoy moved on without noticing the absence of Aishah, who normally rode in a howdah, hidden from sight. She was eventually taken home by a man, Safwan ibn al-Muattal, who was traveling behind the army. Rumors began to spread about her relations with Safwan, and she was eventually accused of having betrayed and deceived the Prophet. Muhammad was greatly affected, all the more so as some Companions were waging a campaign against his wife, spreading calumny (*ifk*) about her. He kept away from her for more than a month, but Aishah stood firm and repeatedly protested her innocence. Verses were eventually revealed not only establishing her innocence but also condemning slander and slanderers and setting very strict conditions as to the evidence that must be brought in order to judge the behavior of a woman or a man in an ambiguous or doubtful situation.[34]

This trial at first upset both Aishah and the Prophet, but it eventually reinforced their love and trust. On a broader level, the Muslim community realized that misfortune could strike the best among them, and Revelation most firmly condemned calumny, slander, and libel, reminding the Muslims to "hold their tongues," as the Prophet was later to put it.[35] Aishah recovered her position and became a reference as far as Islamic knowledge and science are concerned. The Prophet advised his Companions: "Seek science from this red-colored young woman."[36] Beyond doubts and suspicion, beyond calumny, Aishah remained sincere in her faith and in her love for the Prophet, and she became a model, as much in her piety and devotion as in her intellectual and social commitment. She was a model in the light of the love shown to her by the Prophet: it was in her apartment that the Prophet wanted to breathe his last, and there he was buried.

Uhud

Beyond his private affairs and his spiritual and social teaching, the Prophet remained watchful of the Medina Muslims' security, and he knew that the Quraysh were preparing their revenge. He received a letter from his uncle Abbas informing him that an army of more than three thousand men had set out toward Medina. Muhammad had only about a week to think up his strategy and organize the resistance. He very quickly decided to organize a consultation meeting (*shura*) to get his Companions' opinions about the matter. They could choose between remaining inside the city and waiting for the enemy to enter, so as to ambush them, and marching out of the city and directly facing the enemy in a nearby plain. The Prophet, like many of his Companions, including the unreliable Abdullah ibn Ubayy, felt that they should wait for the enemy inside the city. Nevertheless, during the debates, his opinion was defeated, particularly through the opposition of the younger Companions and those who had not taken part in the Battle of Badr: they hoped to acquire merit similar to that of the Badr fighters in the impending battle.

The majority had voted in favor of marching out of the city and confronting the enemy face-to-face. Muhammad accepted the decision and promptly went home to put on his battle gear, for they had no time to waste. Feeling guilty and thinking that perhaps it would be better for them to obey the Prophet, some Companions came to him as he was walking out of his home and suggested the decision should be reconsidered and they should act according to his opinion. He refused categorically: the decision had been taken collectively, he had dressed for battle, and turning back was out of the question.

They set out toward Uhud. The army was a thousand strong, about to face an enemy of three thousand. As they were marching on, Abdullah ibn Ubayy decided to desert, followed by three hundred of his men. Ibn Ubayy reproached the Prophet for having allowed young, inexperienced people to influence him, instead of taking the decision—which had been his own as well—to remain in Medina and wait for the enemy. His desertion was a serious matter, since it reduced to seven hundred the Muslim army, which could no longer change their strategy or turn back. Ibn Ubayy's hypocrisy was well known, and he was suspected of multiple betrayals: that decision, just before the showdown, was additional evidence of his duplicity.

The Muslims moved on, although they were now considerably weakened. On the way, the Prophet noticed that six youths, between the ages of thirteen and sixteen, had mingled with the army. He immediately sent back four of them, who were too young, but agreed to keep two boys of fifteen and sixteen who proved to him on the spot that they were better marksmen and fighters than many grown men. The choice, in such a situation, was a difficult one, but the Prophet repeatedly insisted that children be kept away from battle areas, both as soldiers and as potential victims. He reiterated it forcefully, as we shall see, before one of the last expeditions, and this teaching, pertaining to the ethics of war, always remained uncompromising in his message.

The Muslim army had to find an inconspicuous route to Uhud that would enable the army to approach the battleground without its movements being anticipated or discovered. Once again, the Prophet trusted a non-Muslim guide who answered his call: his abilities were widely known, and he led the army to their destination. They took up their position, and the Prophet explained his fighting strategy to his troops. The archers were to stay on the hillside, while the horsemen and soldiers directly confronted the enemy in the plain. The archers were not to leave their posts under any circumstance, whether the troops below might seem to be winning or losing, in order to prevent the Quraysh from coming round the hill and attacking the troops from behind. This was in fact what one of the Quraysh divisions tried to do at the very beginning of the battle, but they were greeted with a shower of arrows that compelled them to move back. The strategy was working perfectly.

The fighting began and, down in the plain, the Muslim troops were gradually taking control. The Quraysh were losing ground and suffering many losses, while the Muhajirun and the Ansar displayed remarkable courage. Among those fighters, two women stood out for their energy and vigor: Um Sulaym and especially an Ansar woman called Nusaybah bint Kab, who had initially come to carry water and aid the wounded, and who eventually stepped into the battle, took a sword, and fought the Quraysh.[37] The Prophet had never invited or advised women to fight, but when he saw Nusaybah's spirit and energy in the battle, he praised her behavior and prayed to God to protect her and grant her victory and success.

It was becoming clear that the Muslims were winning, in spite of setbacks and the death of some Companions. Hamzah, the Prophet's uncle, had been the target of Hind's vengeance since the defeat at Badr. Wahshi, an Abyssinian spearman, had been set the single task of killing Hamzah, and this was what he concentrated on doing: while Muhammad's uncle was fighting, Wahshi drew near to him and threw his spear with utmost precision, hitting him and killing him instantly. Later on, Hind sought out Hamzah's body on the battlefield, and after chewing on his liver, thereby fulfilling her promise to drink his blood in revenge for her relatives' deaths, she disfigured him, cutting off his ears and nose and hanging them around her neck.[38]

Nevertheless, as the battle progressed it seemed that victory could not escape the Muslims, who kept pressing forward while the Quraysh pulled back, leaving their mounts and belongings behind them. The archers, posted on the hillside, looked on the favorable turn of events, on victory close at hand, and especially on the booty that lay within reach of the soldiers who were, unlike them, fighting at the front. They forgot the Prophet's orders and the injunctions of their leader, Abdullah ibn Jubayr: only a few archers stayed on the hillside, while about forty of them ran down the hill, convinced that victory was achieved and that they too were entitled to a share in the booty. Khalid ibn al-Walid, a fine tactician who led one of the three Quraysh divisions, noticed the archers' move and immediately decided to sweep round the hill and attack the Muslim troops from behind. He succeeded in launching a pincer attack on the Prophet's Companions that resulted in total confusion, and the Muslim fighters scattered in utter disorder. Some were killed and some ran away, while others kept fighting without really knowing where to strike. The Prophet was attacked and fell off his mount: one of his teeth was broken and the rings of his helmet were driven into the bloody flesh of his cheek. A rumor spread that the Prophet had been killed, which increased the chaos among Muslims. Eventually, some Companions carried him to his mount and protected him, thus enabling him to escape his assailants. The Muslims managed to pull out of the battlefield, where it was getting increasingly difficult to see what was going on, and gathered to face the enemy again if needed. When the fighting ended, there were only twenty-two dead among the Quraysh, while there were seventy dead among the Muslims, who had clearly been beaten, both on the battlefield and symbolically.

The archers' disobedience had had dramatic consequences. Attracted by wealth and profit, the archers had succumbed to old practices from their pagan past. Despite being nurtured with the message of faith in the One, justice, and detachment from worldly goods, they had suddenly forgotten everything when seeing riches within their reach. War victories were measured, in their ancient pagan tradition, by the amount of booty gained, and that past, that part of themselves and of their culture, had gotten the better of their spiritual education. Consequently, the Muslims had been trapped by the strategy of a formidable man, Khalid ibn al-Walid, who a few years later was to convert to Islam and become the Muslim community's warrior hero. That particular moment of the Uhud encounter is rich with a profound teaching: human beings can never completely overcome the culture and experiences that have fashioned their past, and no final judgment can ever be expressed as to the future of their choices and orientations. The Muslims were caught up by an unfortunate feature of their past customs; Khalid ibn al-Walid was to undergo a future conversion that would wipe out whatever judgments had been pronounced about his past. "Nothing is ever final" is a lesson in humility; "no final judgment should be passed" is a promise of hope.

The Quraysh carried away their dead and all their belongings. Abu Sufyan asked Umar about the Prophet's fate and received confirmation that he was still alive. When the Muslims, in their turn, went back to the battlefield, they saw that the corpses had been mutilated; the Prophet was most affected at the sight of his uncle Hamzah. In his anger, he expressed the wish to take revenge and mutilate thirty enemy corpses in the next confrontation, but Revelation reminded him of order, measure, and patience: "But if you show patience, that is indeed the best [course] for those who are patient."[39] The Prophet was to require that the bodies of the living as well as the dead be respected, that no torture or mutilation be ever accepted or promoted, in the name of respect for creation and for human beings' dignity and integrity.[40]

A Defeat, a Principle

The Muslims had gone back to Medina, wounded, disappointed, and deeply distressed by the turn of events: their dead were many, their defeat was due to disobedience motivated by the lust for profit, the Prophet was wounded, and the Quraysh were of course going to regain their dignity and their status in the Peninsula. Arriving in Medina, the Prophet lost no time asking all the men who had taken part in the Battle of Uhud—even the wounded soldiers—to prepare for another expedition. He refused Abdullah ibn Ubayy's offer to join them, for he had deserted the army just before the battle. But the Prophet had informed nobody of his real intentions. He went to Hamra, camped there, and asked each of his men to prepare ten fires and light them during the night. From a distance, those fires gave the impression that a huge army was on the move.

Muhammad had staged that maneuver to lead the Quraysh to believe that he was preparing immediate retaliation and that it would be dangerous to attack Medina. He sent an envoy (again a pagan) to Abu Sufyan to inform him of this extraordinary deployment of Muslim troops. Abu Sufyan was impressed; though he had initially planned to take advantage of the Muslims' weakness and deal them a final blow at the very heart of Medina, he changed his mind and decided not to attack the city. Things went no further: Muhammad's expedition left Hamra three days later, and life resumed its course.

During the days that followed, the Prophet received a Revelation that returned to the subject of the Battle of Uhud, and in particular the disagreements about strategic choices, the disobedience, the defeat, and then the Prophet's attitude. The Prophet had remained composed and understanding toward the Companions who had been carried away by their desire for wealth and had disobeyed him. Revelation relates the event and confirms what we said at the beginning of the present chapter, about the constant blending of respect for principles and the strength of gentleness in the Prophet's personality:

> It was by the mercy of God that you were lenient [gentle] with them, for if you had been severe or harsh-hearted, they would have broken away from about you. So pardon them and ask for God's forgiveness for them; and consult them upon the conduct of affairs. Then, when you have taken

a decision, put your trust in God. For God loves those who put their trust in Him.[41]

The string of events leading to defeat had started with the decision taken against the Prophet's opinion; then, of course, there had been the archers' disobedience. The Quran here confirms the principle of *shura*, consultation, whatever the result: this Revelation is of crucial importance and states that the principle of deliberation, of majority decision making, is not to be negotiated and must be respected beyond historical contingencies and human mistakes in decisions. Muslims are, therefore, those who "conduct their affairs by mutual consultation," and that principle must remain even though the ways in which it is implemented cannot fail to change over time and from place to place.[42]

As far as the archers' disobedience is concerned, Revelation points out that the Prophet's qualities of heart were what enabled him to overcome the situation and keep his Companions around him. He was neither brutal nor stern, and he did not condemn them for being carried away by the reflexive greed stemming from their past customs. His gentleness soothed their pain and enabled them to draw many lessons from that setback: God accompanied their fate insofar as they themselves felt responsible for it. Just as there was no room for fatalism in revealed teachings, there was no room either for the airy optimism that their path would be easy just because they struggled for God's sake. On the contrary, faith required additional rigor in terms of respect for principles, additional feeling in human relations, and additional caution about the risk of complacency. Uhud had been that lesson in fragility, and the wounded Prophet, after the battle, reminded everyone that anything could happen: his blood expressed and recalled his blatant humanity.

CHAPTER ELEVEN

Tricks and Treason

The situation had become difficult for the Muslim community in Medina. The defeat at Uhud had had manifold consequences, not the least of which was their loss of prestige in the sight of the neighboring tribes, who now viewed them differently and thought them vulnerable. The Muslims were seen as weakened, and many expeditions were being organized against them to try to take advantage of that situation. As for Muhammad, who was sometimes warned of planned attacks on Medina, he would send his men—in groups of 100 to 150—to the various tribes to pacify them or prevent an aggression. The fourth year after *hijrah* (626 CE) was largely taken up with such low-intensity local conflicts, which nevertheless served to modify (and sometimes maintain) the alliances or the balance of power in the area. This amounted to a kind of chess game between the Quraysh and the Medina Muslims, and both parties knew that a full-scale confrontation lay ahead. The people of Mecca did not conceal their desire to eradicate the Muslim community from the Peninsula, and to that end, they kept making pacts with the neighboring tribes. Their situation was all the more difficult because the most direct commercial routes to the north, leading to Syria and Iraq by the coast, were still watched over and controlled by Medina. The Quraysh therefore felt that they had to take swift and radical action in order both to take advantage of the Muslims' fragility after defeat and to liberate the routes that their caravans needed to take to go north.

Banu Nadir

Many Muslims were taken prisoner during those years after falling into ambushes or simply being outnumbered by their enemies. They were often tortured and dreadfully put to death, and tradition reports their courage, patience, and dignity in the face of death. Most of the time they asked, like Khubayb, to be allowed to perform two cycles of prayer before they were executed, and they prolonged them with invocations to God, the One, for Whom they had given their possessions and their lives.

One day, a man from the Banu Amir tribe called Abu Bara came to the Prophet and asked him to send back with him a group of about forty Muslims to teach his whole tribe Islam. Muhammad, who was apprised of local alliances, expressed his fear that they might be attacked by other tribes who were hostile to Islam or had entered into pacts with the Quraysh. He received the pledge that his men would be protected by the Banu Amir, who enjoyed unchallenged prestige and could also rely on many alliances. However, he had not taken into account the internal rivalries in the Banu Amir clan. Abu Bara's own nephew caused the Muslim group's scout (who carried a letter from the Prophet) to be killed; then, when he saw that his clan wanted to remain faithful to the protection pact offered by his uncle, he commissioned two other clans to kill the whole Muslim group near Bir al-Maunah, apart from two men who escaped because they had gone to fetch water.[1] One of them preferred to die fighting the enemy, while the other, Amr ibn Umayyah, went back to Medina to inform the Prophet that his men had been slaughtered. On his way there, he met two members of the Banu Amir, whom he thought to be responsible for the ambush, and he killed them in revenge.

The Prophet was shocked, worried, and deeply grieved by what had happened to his men. It indicated that the situation was getting more and more dangerous and that alliances as well as betrayals were taking on complex and subtle features. The Banu Amir had been faithful to Abu Bara's pledges and were therefore not responsible for his men's death; the Prophet, scrupulously respectful of the terms of his pacts, immediately decided that blood money must be paid for the two men whom Amr had mistakenly killed. He decided to go to the Banu Nadir Jews and ask for their help in paying the blood debt, since this was part of the terms of their mutual assistance agreement. Muhammad knew that since the Banu Qaynuqa's forced exile, the Banu Nadir had become suspicious, if not hostile to him, and that they had established ties with tribes hostile to the Muslims. He was therefore extremely cautious.

He visited them with his closest Companions, including Abu Bakr, Umar, and Ali. The Banu Nadir's behavior was strange and their chiefs, among them Huyay, suggested no concrete steps to help pay the blood debt; they suddenly disappeared under the pretext of preparing a meal and gathering the sum needed. The Prophet had the intuition that the Banu Nadir leaders were planning some mischief, so he rose and left discreetly, his Companions thinking he was going to come back. When he did not, they also left and followed him to his home, where he told them of his intuitions and disclosed to them that Gabriel had informed him that the Banu Nadir wanted to kill him, which indeed their strange behavior in the delegation's presence confirmed. A betrayal by the Banu Nadir, who lived inside Medina itself, made it impossible for the Muslims to set up a defense strategy. The Prophet had to act fast. He sent Muhammad ibn Maslamah to the Banu Nadir to inform them that they had betrayed the mutual assistance agreement and that they had ten days to leave the place with their women and children and their belongings, or else they would be put to death. The Banu Nadir were afraid and began to prepare to leave, but Abdullah ibn Ubayy, the hypocrite, came to them and advised them not to leave the city, pledging to give them his unfailing support from within. The Banu Nadir chiefs listened to him and informed Muhammad that they would not leave. In effect, this was a declaration of war.

The Prophet immediately decided to besiege the fortress where the Banu Nadir had sought refuge. They were at first surprised at such a rapid response, but they hoped that Ibn Ubayy or their own allies, especially the Jewish tribe of Banu Qurayzah, would come to their rescue. They did not, and after ten days the situation had become quite unbearable for them. This was when the Prophet decided to cut the tallest palm trees, those that were visible from inside, beyond the fortifications; the palm trees were the city's most valuable resource, and in cutting them down Muhammad was trying to convince the Banu Nadir that if they kept up their resistance, nothing of value would be left in the city. Only that once did Muhammad ever damage trees or another part of nature, whether in war or in peace.

The situation was so exceptional that Revelation made express mention of it: "Whatever palm trees you cut down or left standing on their roots, it was by leave of God."[2] Never again would the Prophet act in disrespect of creation, and he was to repeat again and again, as we shall see, that such respect must be complete, even in wartime. The Revelation of the abovementioned verse is in itself the confirmation of the rule set by that single exception.

The strategy turned out to be most successful. The Banu Nadir, besieged and penurious, surrendered and tried to negotiate the terms of their exile. Before the siege the Prophet had offered to let them leave with all their wealth, but the Banu Nadir had refused, and now they were in a weak position. According to the terms of the Prophet's threat, they ought to have been executed. In any case, allowing them to take away their possessions was now out of the question. Forgetting his threat to execute them, the Prophet demanded that they leave the city, taking only their women and children with them. Banu Nadir's chief, Huyay, nonetheless tried to negotiate, and the Prophet eventually allowed them to leave with all the goods and belongings their camels could carry; they eventually found refuge at Khaybar.[3] He not only did not carry out his threat, sparing their lives, but he also allowed them to take away a considerable amount of wealth. Muhammad had always been generous and lenient after battles, despite his enemies' betrayals and ungratefulness; he had found some of the captives he had spared after Badr among his fiercest enemies at Uhud. The same thing would happen this time too: several months after allowing the Banu Nadir to flee, he would find some of the tribe's leaders and other members among the Confederates (al-Ahzab), who were to join against him a few months later.

The Muslims' situation had marginally improved, but the dangers remained considerable and manifold. After Uhud, Abu Sufyan had told Umar and the Prophet that they would meet the following year at Badr. The Prophet had accepted the challenge. He did not want to go back on his word, and he therefore went to Badr with an army of fifteen hundred men. Abu Sufyan set out with two thousand soldiers, but he stopped on the way and turned back. The Muslims stayed on the spot for eight days, waiting for the Quraysh, who did not appear. They had been true to their word, and this display of fidelity to their promise and confidence in the face of challenge both reassured them and reinforced their prestige.

Excellence and Singularity

The Prophet held one of his Companions, called Abu Lubabah, in great esteem, so much so that he had left him in charge of Medina when he had left for the first Badr expedition. Some time later, a young orphan came to Muhammad to complain that Abu Lubabah had taken from him a palm tree that had long been his. The Prophet summoned Abu Lubabah and asked him to explain. Investigations showed that the palm tree did belong to Abu Lubabah, and the Prophet judged in the latter's favor, greatly disappointing the young orphan, who thereby lost his most precious belonging. Muhammad privately asked Abu Lubabah, justice having now been rendered, to give the tree to the young orphan, for whom it was so important. Abu Lubabah adamantly refused: he had gone to such lengths to assert his right of ownership that to concede to this request was inconceivable. This obsession veiled his heart and compassion. Revelation was to recall, on both the individual and collective levels, the singular nature of the spiritual elevation that makes it possible to reach beyond the consciousness of justice, that demands right, to the excellence of the heart, that offers forgiveness or gives people more than their due: "God commands justice and excellence."[4]

It was not a question of giving up one's right (and Abu Lubabah had been justified in requiring it to be acknowledged); rather, it involved learning to sometimes reach beyond, for the sake of those reasons of the heart that teach the mind to forgive, to let go, and to give from oneself and from one's belongings, moved by shared humanity or love. The Prophet was saddened by the reaction of his Companion, whom he held in great esteem: he realized that Abu Lubabah's almost blind attachment to one of Islam's recommendations, justice, prevented him from reaching the superior level of justness of the heart: excellence, generosity, giving. Eventually, another Companion, Thabit ibn Dahdanah, who had witnessed the scene, offered Abu Lubabah an entire orchard in exchange for that single palm tree, which he then gave away to the young orphan. Muhammad rejoiced at that outcome and did not resent Abu Lubabah's attitude. He later entrusted him with other missions, such as conveying to the Banu Qurayzah the terms of their surrender. Abu Lubabah carried out his mission but could not resist speaking too much; ashamed of his behavior, he eventually tied himself to a tree for six days, hoping that God and His Prophet would forgive him his lapse and his lack of steadfastness. Forgiveness came, and the Prophet himself unfastened Abu Lubabah's ties. This individual experience shows that spiritual edification was never totally accomplished, that consciences were constantly being tried, and that the Prophet accompanied his teaching with strictness but also with benevolence.

Muhammad had, some time before, married a widow named Zaynab, of the Banu Amir clan, who was esteemed for her generosity and her love for the poor. It was through that marriage that he had set up ties with her tribe, which was to remain faithful to him in spite of pressures from both inside and outside the clan. Zaynab, known as *um al-masakin* (the mother of the poor), was most devoted, and she came to live in a dwelling that had been arranged for her near the mosque. However, she died only eight months after her wedding, and she was buried near Ruqayyah, the Prophet's daughter. A few months later, Um Salamah, the widow of Abu Salamah, with whom she had exiled herself in Abyssinia, married the Prophet and settled in the dwelling left empty by Zaynab. Pious, enterprising, and particularly beautiful, she enjoyed a considerable position and role at the Prophet's side, and Aishah confessed that she felt jealous of Um Salamah, both, it seems, because of her beauty and because the Prophet listened to her and was greatly influenced by her opinions.

The Messenger continued, as circumstances warranted and in spite of difficulties, to spread Islam's teachings and illustrate them through his example. A Companion had once taken a fledgling from a nest and suddenly been attacked by the parent bird, which wanted to defend its offspring; the Prophet asked him to put the fledgling back in the nest and told those who were present, "God's goodness [mercy] to you is superior to that of this bird for its offspring."[5] He taught them to observe the elements, to marvel at and draw teachings from the nature around them and the smallest parts of life. Revelation had repeatedly expressed this invitation:

Whatever is in the heavens and on earth, declares the praises [and glory] of God. For He is the Almighty, the Wise.[6]

Or again:

The seven heavens and the earth, and all beings therein, extol His limitless glory: there is not a thing but celebrates His praise; and yet you do not understand how they glorify Him. Verily He is Oft-Forbearing, Most Forgiving![7]

And the bird in the sky elicits this meditative observation:

> Do they not observe the birds above them, spreading their wings and fold-ing them in? None can uphold them except the Most Gracious [the Merciful]. Truly it is He who watches over all things.[8]

Revelation was later to confirm the importance of such spirituality, act-ing through observation, contemplation, and remembrance of God, and linked to the constant reminder of God's infinite goodness toward human hearts. "The sun and the moon follow courses exactly computed," the Quran tells the physical eye and the mind, "and the stars and the trees both alike bow in adoration," it goes on, addressing the heart's eye and faith.[9] Those two teachings fashioned and molded the Prophet's spiritual strength; he knew where both his vulnerability and his power came from, when so many enemies tried to deceive, lure, or destroy him. God had already reminded him of His goodness and protection in the face of his weaknesses: "And had We not given you strength, you would nearly have inclined to them [those who wish to negate you, your enemies] a little."[10] The signs in creation, his ability to marvel at events or at the seemingly slight details of life, to recognize the heart's charity in a person's generous word ("A benevolent word is charity")[11] or through a fellow being's smile ("The smile you offer your brother [your sister] is charity"),[12] gave him that strength to resist and persevere. Being constantly with the One, and remembering His presence through a look or a gesture as the presence of the Friend and Protector rather than that of a judge or a censor—such is the meaning of excellence (*al-ihsan*), of the power of the heart and of faith: "Excellence is worshiping God as though you see Him, for if you do not see Him, He indeed sees you."[13]

His Companions recognized those qualities in him, loved him, and drew their spiritual energy from his presence among them. He taught them to constantly deepen that love: "None of you believes [perfectly, completely] until I am dearer to him than his father, his son, and all humankind."[14] They had to carry on their spiritual and loving quest, love the Prophet, and love one another in God, while the Prophet himself was reminded that such communion was beyond his own human power: "Not if you had spent all that is in the earth, could you have put affection between their hearts, but God has put affection between their hearts."[15] He was the example, the model, who lived among them and offered his love to them all, to the poor, to the old; he showed courteous regard for women and was attentive to children. He was a grandfather and would carry his grandchildren while praying in the mosque, thus conveying through his daily example that one cannot remember and be close to God without generosity and human attention.

Revelation was to establish his singularity in many spheres. The One demanded of him more rigorous practice, particularly concerning night prayers, and his obligations toward the Angel Gabriel and toward God were equal to none. On another level, the Quran had restricted the number of wives to four for the believers at large, but it had established the Prophet's singularity in this respect; moreover, his wives were reminded that they were "not like any of the other women."[16] Henceforth, they were to cover their faces and speak to men from behind a screen (*hijab*), and they were informed that they could not marry again after the Prophet's death. In the light of the Quran's prescriptions, Muhammad married another woman named Zaynab; she was the divorced wife of Muhammad's former slave Zayd, who had become known as Zayd ibn Muhammad after being adopted by the Prophet, but who had eventually resumed his former name, Zayd ibn Harithah, since he was not the Prophet's biological son. The Quran commented: "Muhammad is not the father of any of your men, but [he is] the Messenger of God and the Seal of the Prophets."[17]

The Confederates

A great number of the Banu Nadir people went to settle in Khaybar after their exile from Medina. They nurtured deep resentment toward the Prophet and hoped for quick revenge. They knew, as did all the tribes in the Peninsula, that the Quraysh were preparing a full-scale attack to crush the Muslim community and finally put an end to Muhammad's mission. The Banu Nadir chief, Huyay, went to Mecca with Jewish leaders from Khaybar to seal an alliance with the Quraysh that left no room for doubt:

Muhammad and his community must be attacked and eliminated. To this end, they contacted other tribes to integrate them into the pact; the Banu Asad, Banu Ghatafan, and Banu Sulaym joined in. Only the Banu Amir, one of whose women the Prophet had married, and who had already shown unfailing fidelity (apart from a few individuals who had betrayed their word), refused to be part of the new coalition because they had previously entered into a pact with Muhammad.

The forces assembled were considerable, and when the armies marched off toward Medina, it seemed that the Muslims were no match for them. The Quraysh army and their allies from the south were more than four thousand strong, and another army, coming from Najd in the east, and made up of various tribes, brought together more than six thousand men. The city of Medina was going to be attacked from two sides, then encircled, by ten thousand warriors: one could hardly imagine its inhabitants coming out unharmed. When the armies set out, the Prophet's uncle, Abbas, secretly sent a delegation to Medina to warn the Prophet of the attack. When the delegation reached Medina, the people of Medina had only a week or less left to draw up a resistance strategy. They could not hope to muster more than three thousand soldiers, less than a third of the enemy force.

True to his custom, the Prophet gathered his Companions and consulted them about the situation and the plan of action they should adopt. Some felt that they must go out and meet the enemy, as they had done at Badr. Others thought that only by waiting inside the city would they have a chance to succeed, and that lessons must be drawn from the Uhud defeat. Among the Companions present was a Persian named Salman (Salman al-Farisi), whose story was singular in many ways. He had long been in quest of the truth and of God, and he had traveled toward Mecca in the hope of living in proximity to the Prophet. Circumstances had not been favorable, and he had eventually been sold as a slave in the Banu Qurayzah tribe. The Prophet and his Companions had gathered the amount needed to set him free, and he had for some time been a free Companion. He took part in their meetings and stood out by his fervor and devotion. When he rose to speak, he suggested a strategy hitherto unknown to the Arabs: "O Messenger of God, in Persia, when we feared an attack from a cavalry, we used to dig a moat around the city. Let us dig a moat around us!"[18] The idea was unexpected, but all the Companions liked it and they decided to implement it. They had to act fast, having only a week to dig a moat sufficiently wide and deep to prevent horses from jumping over it.

This was the third major confrontation with the Quraysh, and it was also, in effect, the third strategy the Muslims adopted. Badr, with the gathering around the wells, and Uhud, with the strategic use of the hill, had nothing to do with the present technique of waiting and keeping the enemy at a distance, which seemed to be the only means available to withstand the attack and possibly, if the siege lasted, to give those sheltered inside the city a chance to resist. Such inventiveness in military strategy is revealing of the manner in which the Prophet taught his Companions both deep faith and the exploitation of intellectual creativity in all circumstances: they had not hesitated to borrow a foreign war technique, suggested by a Persian, and adapt it to their situation in Medina. The genius of peoples, the wisdom of nations, and healthy human creativity were integrated into their mode of thinking, without hesitation or timidity. As the Prophet forcefully stated: "[Human] wisdom is the believer's lost belonging; he is the most worthy of it wherever he finds it."[19] This was an invitation to study the best human thoughts and products and adopt them as part of humankind's positive heritage (*maruf*, what is acknowledged as the common good). On a broader level, it meant showing curiosity, inventiveness, and creativity in the management of human affairs, and this appeared not only through his approach to war and its strategies but also, as we have seen, through his way of considering the world of ideas and culture.

The Moat

Work started immediately, and the whole city joined in. They determined where the moat was to be dug, and where rocks or the topography of the area would prevent the enemy from getting through and so a moat was unnecessary. Working days were long, and the Companions labored from dawn prayer to sunset.

Muhammad took part in the work, and his Companions would hear him sometimes invoking God, sometimes reciting poems, sometimes singing songs in which they would all join. Such moments of communion through work molded their fraternity and sense of belonging, and also made it possible to give collective expression to feelings, aspirations, and hopes. Through his invocations, poems, and songs, the Prophet enabled the women and men in his community—beyond their communion in faith and ritual prayer—to commune through the voicing of emotions and the musicality of hearts articulating their belonging to a common expression of the self, a collective imagination, a culture. They were united not only by what they received from the One—and in which they had faith—but also in their manner of speaking about themselves, of articulating their feelings and of considering their place in the universe. Communion in faith, in the intimacy of meaning, cannot remain purely conceptual; it can maintain its vivifying energy only if it associates with communion in speech and action within a common space of social and cultural references. Faith needs culture. Thus, when he needed to unite his Companions' energies, Muhammad summoned up all the levels of their being in the world in order to perfect the unity of his community: deep faith in the One, the poetic phrasing of feelings, the musicality of the song of emotions. From within his community, sharing their daily lives, he attested that while he was indeed at the One's service, beyond time and space, he also experienced their history and partake of their culture: he was one of them.

The moat that was emerging as the work progressed was a great success: it would be impossible for enemy horsemen to cross it in any spot, and the Muslim archers would without difficulty be able to prevent them from undertaking any bold attempt. Before settling inside the city, the Medina people gathered all the crops in the oasis so that the enemy would have to rely on their own food reserves. The enemy armies were now approaching, and the Muslims hurried back inside the city, behind the moat, to wait for them.

The Siege

To the south and east of Medina, the armies arrived and settled around the city. They were surprised to see the moat, which thwarted their plan to encircle the city and invade it in a joint attack from all sides. The moat was indeed a war technique unknown to the Arabs, and the Confederates therefore had to find another plan of action to defeat the Muslims.

Consultations began between the various tribes to find the best means of shortening the siege and taking possession of the city: without any other provisions than their own, protracted hostilities could not be considered. They decided that a majority of forces would gather to the north in order to mobilize the Medina forces on that side, while the rest tried to cross the moat from the hence unguarded south, where access seemed easier near the rocks. The Jewish tribe of Banu Qurayzah mainly lived in that area; they had signed an assistance agreement with Muhammad, but they might constitute the weak point in Medina's unity. Huyay, the chief of the Banu Nadir clan, insisted on going to the Banu Qurayzah fortress to speak to their chief, Kab ibn Asad, and try to convince him to break his alliance with Muhammad. Kab ibn Asad initially refused to receive Huyay, but the latter insisted so strongly that the Banu Qurayzah chief let himself be convinced, first to listen to him, then to betray the covenant. This defection meant that the whole strategy of the Medina people collapsed, since the Banu Qurayzah's alliance with the enemy opened a breach from inside and gave the enemy access to the city, which meant certain defeat and no less certain extermination for the Muslims.

By no means were all the Banu Qurayzah satisfied with their chief's decision, and tensions developed within the group, but the vast majority agreed to join forces with the Quraysh and their allies. In the meantime, the Prophet's observations of the movements of enemy troops in the north led him to anticipate a trick, so he decided to check the reliability of his alliances in the south, for he knew the Banu Qurayzah were far from being all favorably inclined toward him. Meanwhile, he heard rumors that the Banu Qurayzah chiefs had one-sidedly broken the covenant. If the news turned out to be true, not only would the Muslim army's morale collapse, but they would have little chance of winning the battle. He sent two scouts whom he asked to gather intelligence and act judiciously: if the rumor was groundless, they were to announce it loud and clear to reassure the troops and restore their courage; if it was true, they were to let him know discreetly. The news was true, the scouts reported, and Muhammad had to react immediately. He sent Zayd to the southern front with three hundred men in order to prevent any enemy attempt to get through with the Banu Qurayzah's support.

The siege was getting increasingly difficult to bear, and the Muslims had to be constantly on alert. One day, the attacks were so numerous and came from so many fronts that the Muslims could not perform the early afternoon and midafternoon prayers (*az-zuhr* and *al-asr*) at their respective times, nor after that the sunset prayer (*al-maghrib*). The Prophet was annoyed, and the siege was beginning to affect the Companions' morale. Revelation tells of their feelings:

> When they came on you from above you and from below you [from all sides], and when the eyes swerved and the hearts gaped up to the throats, and you imagined various thoughts about God! In that situation, the Believers were tried: they were shaken as by a tremendous shaking.[20]

The trial was a difficult one, and it also revealed the sincerity and fidelity of tribes as well as individuals. Not only had the war brought to light the Banu Qurayzah clan's double-dealing, but it had also, once again, exposed the hypocrites, who were quick to think of reconsidering their commitment or even surrendering. The Quran says: "And when the hypocrites and those in whose heart is a disease [doubt] say: 'God and His Messenger promised us nothing but delusions!'"[21] Some wanted to return to their families, saying, "Truly our houses are bare and exposed."[22] Others merely wanted to escape the fighting and protect themselves, since it seemed obvious to them that the Muslims' defense would shortly give way. Resisting for days in this manner appeared impossible.

The majority of Muslims, however, were faithful to the Prophet and his example and shared his determination. It is in relation to this crisis, which brought to light the depth and sincerity of faith and of commitment to the One, that the verse about the Prophet's exemplarity was revealed: "You have indeed in the Messenger of God an excellent example for he who hopes in [aspires to get close to] God and the Final Day and who remembers God intensely."[23]

The meaning of the verse far transcends the circumstances of that battle. It tells of the Prophet's role and status in and for the life of every Muslim individual, but it takes on an even more powerful dimension when one remembers the circumstances of its Revelation: a besieged community, shaken, unable within the scope of human sight and intelligence to see any way out of the impending disaster, whose ranks dwindle away through desertion and treason, and who unite around the Messenger, his faith, and his trust. Revelation confirms this:

When the Believers saw the Confederate forces, they said: "This is what God and His Messenger had promised us, and God and His Messenger told us what was true." And it only added to their faith and their zeal in obedience.[24]

At the heart of the turmoil, the Prophet had been most upset at not being able to perform the various prayers at their appointed times. That consciousness of discipline in prayer never left the Messenger; he was scrupulous about his daily religious worship. "Prayer is enjoined on believers at stated times."[25] Neglecting the time of a prayer had touched his heart and bred deep resentment against those who had compelled him to such a lapse. All his Companions had witnessed, in all the circumstances of his life, that seemingly surprising blend of infinite generosity of heart, unambiguous determination in adversity, and strict management of time. At another time Ibn Abbas was to report seeing the Prophet join the two afternoon prayers and the two evening prayers for no obvious reason, and Muslim scholars have recognized the lawfulness of such arrangements on a journey or in an exceptional situation, but the teaching that remains, in the light of the Prophet's life, is the need for strict respect of prayer, which is both a reminder of a privileged relationship with the One and the experience of that relationship.[26] This is what the Quran confirms when it tells of God's call to Moses: "Verily, I am God: there is no god but I: so worship Me [only], and establish regular prayer for My remembrance."[27]

A Trick

The Muslims were in serious difficulty, but as the days went by the Confederates also found themselves in a difficult position, since they did not have much food left and the nights were bitterly cold. The Prophet tried to negotiate the defection of two Ghatafan clans by offering them a third of Medina's date crop; they informed his envoy that they wanted half, but the Prophet kept to his offer and they eventually accepted. Before sending Uthman to seal the deal, the Prophet consulted the leaders of the two main Medina clans, the Aws and the Khazraj, because of their knowledge of the neighboring clans. They asked whether his action was the result of Revelation or personal choice. When they heard that it was a personal initiative meant to protect them, they refused the terms of that treaty and informed the Messenger that in view of the situation, the only way out was to fight.

At that moment, the Prophet received a visit from Nuaym ibn Masud, a prominent elder from the Quraysh who was well respected by all the tribes in the Peninsula, who came to tell Muhammad that he had converted to Islam but that nobody knew it so far. He placed himself at the Prophet's disposal. Nuaym was well known and respected by all the chiefs who were besieging Medina. Muhammad knew it and told him, "Do what is necessary to stir up discord among them!" Nuaym asked if he could lie, and the Prophet answered: "Do what you want to loosen the grip on us; war is deceit!"[28] Nuaym came up with an efficient stratagem. He first went to the Banu Qurayzah and warned them about their new allies' intentions. If things took a bad turn, he said, the Confederates would not hesitate to let them down, and they would be given over to Muhammad without any protection. He advised them to demand that the other tribes send some of their men as hostages, as a guarantee that they would not forsake the Banu Qurayzah. They liked the idea and decided to send an envoy to the Quraysh leaders to explain their request. Nuaym then hurried to Abu Sufyan to warn him that the Banu Qurayzah were deceiving him and were in fact Muhammad's allies. He declared that they were going to ask him for men as a pledge of his fidelity, but that in reality they intended to give them up to Muhammad as evidence of their good faith. When the Banu Qurayzah envoy came to Abu Sufyan and told him about the request for hostages, Abu Sufyan was convinced that Nuaym had spoken the truth and that the Banu Qurayzah were indeed deceiving him. He immediately summoned Huyay, the Banu Nadir chief, and questioned him about that betrayal. Huyay, surprised and taken aback, at first did not know what to say, and Abu Sufyan thought he could see in this an acknowledgment of treachery.

The first signs of division were appearing in the Confederate camp. Mutual trust reigned among some clans, while others were wary of each other. The news greatly weakened the resolution of the fighters in league with the Quraysh. Weariness and lack of food only heightened the atmosphere of discouragement. Then a strong, bitter wind beset the plain and convinced them that it had become impossible to overcome Medina's resistance. Muhammad had been informed of the enemy troops' morale, and so he sent Hudhayfah to gather intelligence during the night. Hudhayfah came back with the good news of their total disarray: chaos reigned in the enemy ranks, and the cold had paralyzed them. The men were breaking camp, and many fighters had already left. The Prophet told his Companions the good news after morning prayer, when daylight confirmed that the enemy was gone. The siege, which had taken place in the fifth year of *hijrah* (627 CE), had lasted twenty-five days, and the Confederates were going home beaten without having fought, bearing the burden of a real as well as symbolic defeat.

The Banu Qurayzah

The Prophet released his men and allowed them to visit their homes. The enemy was gone and the siege had been lifted; the exhausted Medina people, who had lost hope and reached the limits of their resistance, rejoiced at the outcome. Muhammad went home immediately and rested until the first afternoon prayer. After he had prayed, the Angel Gabriel came to him and informed him that God commanded him to go immediately to the Banu Qurayzah, whose betrayal had almost led to the extermination of the Muslim community, and besiege their fortress.

The Prophet at once addressed his Companions and the whole audience present in the mosque, requesting them to get ready immediately in order to go to the Banu Qurayzah. As the Muslims set off in groups, the Prophet ordered: "Let none of you perform the second afternoon prayer [*al-asr*] until you reach Qurayzah territory."[29] Time was short, and the Muslims, who had hoped to have some rest at last, had only enough time to gather their equipment, put on their battle gear, and start out. In one of the groups heading toward the Banu Qurayzah, an argument took place. It was time to pray *al-asr*, and some of them, literally repeating the Prophet's order, maintained that they must not pray on the way but must wait until they reached the Banu Qurayzah.[30] The others argued that the Prophet's intention was that they must hurry there, but that when prayer time came they must of course pray on time. So part of the group did not pray, keeping to the literal meaning of the Prophet's words, while the other part prayed, referring to the spirit of the recommendation. Later on, they asked the Prophet which was the correct interpretation, and he accepted both. This attitude was to have major consequences for the future of the Muslim community, as after the Prophet's death two main schools of thought appeared: the *ahl al-hadith*, who after Abdullah ibn Umar and in the spirit of the first group mentioned above kept to the literal meaning of the sayings reported in Prophetic tradition (*sunnah*), and the *ahl ar-ray*, who with Abdullah ibn Masud tried to understand the purpose of the saying, its spirit, and its occasionally figurative meaning. Both approaches had been accepted by the Prophet, and both were therefore correct and legitimate ways of remaining faithful to the message.

About three thousand men now encircled the Banu Qurayzah fortresses. Trapped, with little food, the Banu Qurayzah nevertheless resisted for twenty-five days, so strong was their fear of the fate they expected them after such serious treason. The Prophet sent Abu Lubabah, a man from the Aws (who had formerly sealed a pact with the Banu Nadir and had in effect remained close to the Banu Qurayzah), to discuss the terms of their surrender. At the sight of the desolation inside the fortress walls, Abu Lubabah could not help hinting to the Banu Qurayzah that death would be their fate if they surrendered. He later bitterly regretted his attitude, which could have led the Banu Qurayzah not to surrender or to seek a way out through other alliances. However, they decided to open the doors of their fortresses and acknowledge their defeat.

The women and children were placed in the custody of a former rabbi, Abdullah ibn Sallam, and the seven hundred men were tied up and kept aside in a field. Their belongings, riches, and weapons were collected to be taken back to Medina. The Aws immediately sent a delegation to the Prophet requesting him to deal with the Banu Qurayzah with the same clemency he had shown so far to the other groups that had joined against him. Muhammad asked the Aws: "Would you be satisfied if I asked one of you to pronounce the judgment about them?"[31] They answered most positively, convinced that one of their own could not forget past alliances, and the Prophet sent for Sad ibn Muadh, who was still wounded and was being nursed in the Medina mosque. A delegation went to fetch him.

The Prophet had so far spared his prisoners' lives. As previously noted, he had found some of the Badr captives among his fiercest enemies at Uhud, and the same had happened with the Banu Nadir: he had allowed them to leave with their women and children and their wealth, and later their chief, Huyay, led the Confederate plot. Among the Banu Qurayzah prisoners, many had also been exiled from the Banu Nadir. Thus, his clemency had had no effect on most of those who had enjoyed it, and it sent a confusing message throughout the Peninsula: Muhammad, people thought, never killed his prisoners, contrary to Arab or even Jewish customs.[32] His clemency, repeatedly betrayed, was seen as a sign of weakness, if not madness. Besides, the Banu Qurayzah's treason was so serious that if their plans had been successful, it would have led to the extermination of the Muslims, betrayed from within and crushed by an army of more than ten thousand.

Sad ibn Muadh eventually arrived among the Banu Qurayzah. He first wanted to make sure his verdict would be respected by all. He turned to the leaders of the various groups, who one by one pledged to abide by his decision. He finally addressed the Prophet, who confirmed that he would not oppose the judgment. Ibn Muadh judged that the men were to be executed while the women and children were to be considered as war captives. Muhammad accepted the sentence, which was carried out during the following days. A number of captives were ransomed by the Banu Nadir, and Rayhanah, a Banu Qurayzah captive originally from the Banu Nadir, became the Prophet's slave. She embraced Islam, but accounts differ as to what became of her. According to some sources, the Prophet set her free and married her; others merely report that he married her, while some have it that she refused marriage and remained his servant for five years, until he died.[33]

The news of the Muslims' twofold victory spread through the Peninsula and radically transformed perceptions and power balances. Not only had the Muslims resisted an army more than ten thousand strong, but they had also shown unfailing determination. The fate meted out to the Banu Qurayzah men delivered a powerful message to all the neighboring tribes that betrayals and aggressions would henceforth be severely punished. The message had been heard: such a situation never occurred again while the Prophet was alive.

Zaynab and Abu al-As

The Prophet's daughter Zaynab had been married to Abu al-As, who had not accepted Islam. She had initially stayed with him in Mecca, until the

Prophet asked her to join him in Medina with her small daughter Umamah. Zaynab deeply loved her husband, but their different life choices had eventually caused them to part. However, neither of them had remarried.

A few months after the Battle of the Moat, the Prophet sent an expedition to stop a rich Quraysh caravan coming from the north. Zayd, who commanded the Muslim horsemen, seized the caravan's goods and captured most of the men, while others managed to get away. Among the latter was Abu al-As, who decided on his journey back to Mecca to stop at Medina and pay a secret visit to his wife and daughter. This in itself was madness, but his desire to see his wife and child was stronger than his awareness of the risks incurred. He knocked on his wife's door in the dead of night, and Zaynab let him in. He stayed with her, and when dawn drew near, she went to the mosque for prayer as she usually did. She entered the mosque and stood in the first line of women, just behind the men. When the Prophet said the formula announcing the beginning of prayer, she took advantage of the short pause to exclaim in a very loud voice: "O you people! I grant my protection to Abu al-As, son of Rabi!" When prayer was over, the Prophet, who had had no prior knowledge of what had happened between his daughter and her husband, had the audience confirm that they had heard the proclamation as well. He insisted that the protection granted—whether by his daughter or by any other ordinary Muslim—must be respected. He then went to his daughter, who told him about the situation facing Abu al-As, whose goods had all been taken during the recent expedition in the north and who was therefore in debt, for the said goods had been entrusted to him by people in Mecca. Muhammad suggested that the people who had those goods in their possession might give them back to Abu al-As if they wished to, and all of them complied. Some Companions advised Abu al-As to convert to Islam and keep those belongings for himself. He refused, saying that becoming a Muslim and beginning by betraying people's trust would not have been suitable. He took all the goods, went back to Mecca, and gave each owner his due. He then came back to Medina, converted to Islam, and was reunited with Zaynab and their daughter Umamah.

Thus, the first Muslims' generosity and open-handedness were plain for all to see. Like the Prophet, they had required nothing of Abu al-As: he was not a Muslim, he belonged to an enemy clan, and he refused to convert, but they let him go anyway, allowing him the freedom to choose and the time needed for his spiritual development. He even received—at a critical time in interclan relations—the Muslim community's protection, and it was a woman who spoke out publicly and forcefully on his behalf. Zaynab often went to the mosque, which was a space open to both men and women, and nobody objected to her making a statement there, among men; in fact, it was not at all uncommon for Muslim women to speak up publicly in such a manner. Later, in one such instance that is particularly famous in Muslim history, a woman would address Umar ibn al-Khattab, who had become the Muslims' caliph, and point out an error of judgment that he immediately acknowledged.

Inside the mosque, the women would line up behind the men's ranks, as the postures of prayer, in its various stages, require an arrangement that preserves modesty, decency, and respect. Women prayed, studied, and expressed themselves in that space. Moreover, they found in the Prophet's attitude the epitome of courtesy and regard: he demanded that men remain seated in order to let women leave first and without inconvenience. There was always gentleness and dignity in his behavior toward women, whom he listened to, and whose right to express themselves and set forth their opinions and arguments he acknowledged, protected, and promoted.

CHAPTER TWELVE

A Dream, Peace

The victory over the Confederates and then the expedition against the Banu Qurayzah had changed the situation in the Peninsula, with the power of the Prophet and his Companions acknowledged. Some, such as the Persian and Byzantine empires, were even beginning to speak of Muhammad as the "powerful King of the Arabs," since they saw him as an unchallenged regional power. As soon as he had intelligence of danger, Muhammad did not hesitate to send expeditions to the nearby tribes in order to forestall any attempt at rebellion or attack and thus make it clear to all neighboring clans that the Medina Muslims remained on alert and were ready to defend themselves.

It was during one such expedition, against the Banu al-Mustaliq, in the fifth or sixth year of *hijrah*, that the episode of Aishah's necklace took place. That event reminds us, like many others, that life and teachings went on as circumstances warranted and that religious practice was being clarified while the social dimension of Islamic ethics grew in depth. Internal difficulties also remained, particularly because of the actions of a number of hypocrites who tried to take advantage of any situation to cause Muhammad trouble.

A Dream

The month of Ramadan[1] had begun, and the Prophet, as he usually did, intensified night worship and was even more attentive to the well-being of the poor and needy. This was a month of intense spirituality, when

Muhammad recited back to Angel Gabriel all that had been revealed of the Quran, and during which he lengthened ritual prayers and performed the additional prayers of *tarawih*.[2] Invocations (*dua*) were also constant, while women and men were requested to fast during the day, liberating themselves from the characteristics that most directly defined their humanity: drinking, eating, and satisfying their sexual desire. By controlling their natural needs, believers were to strive to get closer to the qualities of the divine and experience His presence through meditation. Beyond the body's fast, Muslims were also expected to "fast" with their tongues (avoiding lies, vulgarity, and indecent remarks) and their hearts (avoiding bad feelings or thoughts). That spiritual discipline, as we have said, went along with additional demands as to the care and attention the poor must receive: the month of Ramadan was both the month of the Quran and that of generosity, giving, and solidarity. Believers, whether women, men, or children, were strongly advised to pay special alms at the end of the fasting month in order to take care of the needs of all the members of the community during the days of celebration they observed. The quest for proximity to the One can only be experienced and perfected through proximity to the poor: respecting, caring for, and serving them bring one closer to God.

During that month, the Prophet had a surprising dream, both perplexing and gratifying. He dreamed that he entered the Kaba sanctuary, his head shaved, holding the key to the sanctuary in his right hand. The vision was powerful, and the Prophet, as he usually did in such circumstances, interpreted it as a sign and a message. The next day, he told his Companions about it and invited them to get ready to go and perform the lesser pilgrimage (*umrah*) in Mecca.[3] They were both happy and surprised: how could they enter the Mecca territory, how would the Quraysh allow them to, how were they to avoid a conflict? The Prophet's obvious confidence nevertheless soothed them: the journey was to take place during the month of Dhu al-Qidah, which was one of the sacred months during which the Arabs never fought. Moreover, the Prophet's visions had up till then proved truthful: he had so far led them quietly and confidently. They got ready for departure.

Between twelve hundred and fourteen hundred faithful undertook the journey. The danger was considerable, but the Prophet did not allow the pilgrims to carry weapons (apart from the equipment necessary for hunting and other needs of the journey) and took with him his wife Um Salamah as well as Nusaybah and Um Mani, two women who had been present at the first covenant of al-Aqabah. They set out and, at the first halt, the Prophet himself consecrated the camels that were to be sacrificed during the pilgrimage. As for the Meccans, they very soon heard that a convoy of Muslims was heading for Mecca, intending to visit the Kaba. Visiting the sanctuary had, for decades, been the Peninsula tribes' most legitimate right, but with the Muslims, the Quraysh were faced with an irresolvable dilemma: they did not see how they could either justify barring them from entering (and how could they compel them to comply in the sacred month of Dhu al-Qidah, during which war was prohibited) or, on the other hand, allow their enemy into the city, which would endow the Muslims with unacceptable prestige. Quraysh decided to send Khalid ibn al-Walid with two hundred men to stop the pilgrims from getting near Mecca. The Muslims' scout came to inform them of the fact, and they decided to change their route in order to avoid a situation that would inevitably lead to a clash. The Prophet relied on a Companion's knowledge of the area, and they took a route through which they arrived south of Mecca, on the edge of the sacred territory, in the plain of al-Hudaybiyyah. At that point, the Prophet's camel, Qaswa, halted and refused to go on. As had been the case when he had arrived in Medina seven years before, the Prophet saw this as a sign. He had to stop and negotiate the pilgrims' entry into Mecca with the Quraysh.

The Quraysh were once more totally taken aback by the Prophet's attitude, which did not fit with any of their religious, cultural, or warfare traditions. At the height of his new power, he was coming to Mecca unarmed, and thus in effect vulnerable, even though circumstances could have enabled him to attain even greater supremacy over his enemies. Moreover, he called people to a new religion but did not hesitate to rely on respect of the rules of Arab traditions to protect himself from their attacks, and in doing so he put the Quraysh into a dilemma, since they had to choose between their honor (respecting the rules) and the loss of their prestige (allowing the Muslims to enter Mecca). Muhammad's tactical choices proved rewarding.

Negotiations

The Quraysh were determined not to allow the Muslims to perform the pilgrimage, because of the crucial symbolic stakes involved but also, of course, because they did not know what Muhammad's actual intentions were. They decided to send an envoy from the Banu Khuzaah clan, Budayl ibn Warqa, who had no quarrel with any of the clans present and could therefore act as a mediator. He went to the Prophet, who assured him that he had no intention of waging war, but only wanted to perform the lesser pilgrimage with his Companions and go home. He added, however, that he was ready to fight anyone who opposed their right to enter the sanctuary freely, like all the other clans and tribes. If, nevertheless, the Quraysh needed time to get ready to let the pilgrims in, they would wait at al-Hudaybiyyah until the Quraysh had finished their preparations. Budayl returned to Mecca and suggested that the Quraysh should let the Muslims in, but his proposal got a chilly reception; in particular, it was flatly reject-ed by Ikrimah, Abu Jahl's son.

A chief named Urwah decided to meet Muhammad and negotiate, while at the same time taking a closer look at the people with him and the nature of the expedition. He went to the Prophet and began talking with him according to the customs habitual among Arab clans: he addressed him familiarly, on an equal footing, and took hold of his beard, as was usual among tribal chiefs. For this he was firmly taken to task by Mug-hirah, one of the exiles from Mecca, who threatened to beat him up if he went on behaving like that. Urwah was surprised, but before he left, he stopped to observe and visit the Muslims' camp, and was amazed at the respect and devotion the believers showed their leader, Muhammad. He went back to the Quraysh and told them, as Budayl had done, that it would be wiser to let the Muslims in, since they obviously had no inten-tion of fighting. However, the Quraysh's leaders refused again.

While Urwah was on his mission, two other negotiation attempts had taken place. Hulays, of the Banu al-Harith, had also come to speak with the Prophet. The latter recognized him from a distance and, knowing how much Hulays and his clan respected religious and sacred matters, had the herd of camels consecrated for sacrifice sent out to meet him. When Hulays saw the camels, he understood the message and decided to turn back immediately, certain that Muhammad indeed had no intention other than peacefully performing a pilgrimage. The Prophet himself had not remained inactive: he had sent the Quraysh an envoy named Khirash, but Ikrimah refused to listen to him, cut his camel's legs, and was about to strike him too when Hulays stepped in to protect him and request that he be allowed to return to the Prophet unharmed.

Four attempts at negotiation had failed, then, and the Quraysh seemed more unyielding than ever. The Prophet decided he must make a last attempt, sending an envoy who enjoyed sufficient respect and protection in Mecca that he would meet another fate than Khirash's and be listened to. He eventually chose Uthman ibn Affan, his son-in-law, who had solid clan connections in Mecca and whom nobody would dare attack. Uthman went and was indeed well received, but met with the same refusal: the Quraysh would not allow the Muslims to perform the pilgrimage. He himself could, if he wished to, perform the circumambulations around the Kaba, but letting in Muhammad and his men was out of the question. Uthman refused the offer. His mission had taken longer than expected, and for three days the Prophet had no news of him. The rumor spread that Uthman had been killed, and this caused the Prophet deep sorrow. Such an action on the part of the Quraysh—killing an envoy during the sacred month and opposing the Muslims' legitimate right to visit the Kaba, as all other tribes were allowed to—could only be seen by the Muslims as a new declaration of war. From then on, they had to prepare for the worst.

The Pledge of Allegiance

The Prophet had all the Companions summoned, and they hurried to him. He sat at the foot of an acacia tree and asked each of the Muslims to pledge allegiance (*bayat ar-ridwan*), swearing him obedience and fidelity. Through that gesture, they explicitly stated that they would remain by the Prophet's side whatever the outcome might be. They had come to perform a pilgrimage, they were unarmed, and now they faced the very high probability of a conflict for which they were not prepared. The affirmation of their fidelity to the Prophet meant to them that they pledged not to run away and to go so far as accepting death, since the balance of forces was heavily against them. The Prophet himself put his left hand in his right hand and told the assembled faithful that this represented Uthman's pledge, since the latter had not given any sign of life and he considered him dead.[4]

However, just as the last Companions had finished giving their pledge, Uthman suddenly reappeared. The Prophet rejoiced at this: not only was Uthman, his son-in-law, alive, but the Quraysh had not been so rash as to act in disrespect of the custom of nonviolence during the sacred months. A conflict with the Quraysh thus seemed to be less likely, and the Prophet was informed that they had finally sent a new envoy, Suhayl ibn Amr, to seal a formal agreement with the Muslims. He decided to receive him and examine their proposals.

Uthman too had pledged allegiance to the Prophet. Like all the others, he had understood that this expression of faithfulness would be required in a potential war situation. However, the circumstances were now completely different, with Muhammad about to start negotiations on the terms of peace between his community and the Quraysh. They had all pledged allegiance thinking that they were expressing their fidelity in a situation of conflict, and moreover one in which they were in a weak position. Now their fidelity was going to be tested through the implementation and terms of a truce in which they held a strong position. Revelation relates that pledge: "God's good pleasure was on the believers when they swore fealty to you under the tree."[5] The Muslims were demanding their right, they bore a message that they were certain was true, and they had acquired great prestige after the latest battles, so keeping a low profile was out of the question.

The Covenant of al-Hudaybiyyah

The Prophet received the Quraysh envoy, Suhayl ibn Amr, who came with two other men, Mikraz and Huwaytib. The negotiations began at some distance from the Companions, and each element in the agreement was discussed, sometimes sharply. When the terms of the covenant were at last settled, the Prophet asked his cousin Ali ibn Abi Talib to write them down. The latter naturally began the writing of the text with the usual formula "In the name of God, the Most Gracious, the Most Merciful" (*BismiLLah ar-Rahman ar-Rahim*), but Suhayl opposed the phrase, saying that he did not know *ar-Rahman* and that they should use the formula "In Your name, O God" (*Bismika Allahumma*), the only one all the Arabs knew (even polytheists used it to address their main god). Some Companions immediately retorted that changing the formula was out of the question, but the Prophet intervened and told Ali to write "In Your name, O God."[6] Then he instructed him to write on: "These are the terms of the truce signed between Muhammad, God's Messenger, and Suhayl ibn Amr." Suhayl again disagreed: "If we had known you to be God's Messenger, we would not have fought you. Write instead: 'Muhammad ibn Abdullah.'" Ali, who had already written the usual formula, refused to give in and maintained that he could do no such thing. The Prophet asked him to show him where the phrase was written, wiped it out himself, then asked him to add what Suhayl had requested, which meant "Muhammad, son of Abdullah." Ali and the other Companions were shocked and could not understand the Prophet's attitude. The terms of the agreement were to alarm them even more, as they looked like a series of compromises highly unfavorable to the Muslims. The treaty was based on four essential points: (1) The Muslims could not perform their pilgrimage that year, but they would be allowed to stay three days the following year. (2) A ten-year truce was to be observed by both sides, and all their members would be free to travel safely in the region. (3) The terms of the agreement would immediately apply to any clan or tribe that entered into a covenant with either side. (4) Any Muslim leaving Mecca for Medina would immediately be delivered to the Meccan leaders, whereas anyone fleeing Medina and seeking protection in Mecca would be granted asylum.[7]

The Companions were beginning to realize that after the signing of a covenant that appeared to them to be a swindle, they would have to return without visiting the Kaba. Their disappointment reached its peak when they witnessed the arrival of Abu Jandal, the youngest son of Suhayl, who had just signed the pact. Abu Jandal had converted to Islam and had run away, his feet still in shackles, after his father had imprisoned him to prevent him from joining the Muslims. When Suhayl saw his escaped son, he reminded the Prophet that according to the agreement he had just signed, he could not keep him and had to give him back. The Prophet admitted this, and Abu Jandal, although he appealed to the Companions for help, was delivered into his father's hands while Muhammad enjoined him to remain patient. His elder brother Abdullah, who had been a Muslim for a long time and was among the pilgrims who witnessed the scene, was revolted by the situation. Another Companion, Umar, could not control himself when Suhayl struck his son's face with his chains. He rushed to the Prophet and remonstrated sharply, firing at him a series of questions that expressed his total disapproval: "Are you not God's Prophet? Are we not right, and are our enemies not wrong? Why should we so shamefully give in against our religion's honor?"[8] Each time, the Prophet answered sedately, but that was not enough to satisfy Umar, who, now seething with intense anger, turned to Abu Bakr for help. Abu Bakr advised him to calm down, as he believed the Prophet was right. Umar controlled himself and kept quiet, even though he clearly remained convinced that the agreement was a humiliation.

Suhayl and the other two envoys left the camp, taking with them Abu Jandal, who had collapsed into tears. The Muslims observing the scene felt intense sorrow and deep revulsion: they could not understand the Prophet's attitude. He had taught them courage and dignity, and now he was accepting an unfair deal obliging them to look on helplessly as one of them received degrading, humiliating treatment. When the Prophet asked them to sacrifice the camels that had been consecrated for the pilgrimage, none of the Companions could bring themselves to comply, for the wounds and the bitterness were too deep. The Prophet repeated his order three times, but nobody responded. This was the first time he was faced with disobedience in such a collective, determined manner. The Prophet, startled and saddened, retired into his tent and told his wife Um Salamah about what had just happened and the Companions' refusal to sacrifice the beasts. She listened, then suggested he should act wisely and silently: she advised him to go out without saying a word and sacrifice his own camel, merely setting the example. Muhammad listened to her advice, which turned out to be judicious. He went to his camel, pronounced the ritual formula, and sacrificed it. When they saw this, the Companions rose one after another and did the same. Then the Prophet shaved his head, and some of the Companions did too, while others cut their hair or just a lock of it.

Spirituality and Understanding Victory

The Companions were soon to realize that their first judgments about the treaty had been completely wrong and that they had not sufficiently appreciated the Prophet's deep spirituality, strict rational coherence, extraordinary intelligence, and strategic genius. He listened for signs, and when his camel had stopped and refused to budge, he had the intuition that the Muslims would not move any further than the plain of al-Hudaybiyyah that year. The failure of the first four negotiations and the Quraysh's obstinacy convinced him that he must be patient. He was deeply confident: in his dream, he had seen himself entering the sanctuary, and this would not fail to happen, although for the moment he could not say when. The pledge of allegiance that had initially seemed to unite the Muslims against the enemy was thus, as we have seen, to turn into a pledge of fidelity requiring them to bear with dignity the conditions of a covenant for peace.

Moreover, when Suhayl refused the Muslims' two habitual formulas referring to God and to Muhammad's status as God's Messenger, the Prophet heard his point of view and was able, at that particular moment, to shift his perspective and see things from his interlocutor's standpoint. What Suhayl was saying was perfectly true according to his outlook. It was indeed obvious that if the Quraysh had acknowledged his status as God's Messenger, they would not have fought against him; therefore, an agreement on an equal footing could not possibly state an element that would in effect acknowledge what one side held as truth while contradicting the other's position. The Companions, whose respect for the Prophet was so deep, had been unable to immediately hear the other's truth, but the Prophet's attitude and his reasonable approach to the terms of the covenant were pregnant with spiritual and intellectual teaching. The point was that the heart's relation to the truth—deep spirituality—must never be allowed to turn into emotional, passionate blindness: reason must always be called upon to analyze the situation, temper one's reaction, and help establish an attentive, coherent relation to the other's truth. What appeared as an unacceptable compromise from the sole viewpoint of the believers' faith was fair and equitable from the double viewpoint of the respective rationalities of each of the parties drawing up the peace treaty.

Muhammad could not humiliate the Quraysh in order to save the Muslims' honor and prestige, or even to take advantage of the new political situation after the moat victory. Agreeing not to enter the sanctuary that year took into account the Quraysh's vulnerability and protected their prestige, and this contributed toward long-term peace. Such peace, which considered the general interests of both camps, was soon to turn to the

Muslims' advantage. The clauses stating that emigrants to Medina should be sent back and Muslims leaving Medina for Mecca given asylum only marginally affected the Muslims' interests: a believer leaving Medina was of no use to the Muslim community, and the Muslim faith of a Meccan sent back to his clan ought not—despite the suffering—to be shaken by this forced exile. Contrary to appearances, which Abu Jandal's plight reinforced, Muhammad had not made any serious concessions on this point.

Trust in God, allied to strict intellectual coherence and an exceptionally acute mind, had enabled the Prophet to establish a ten-year truce with the prospect of a visit to the sanctuary the following year. Most of the Companions, and particularly Umar ibn al-Khattab, considered only immediate results, however, and felt this was a humiliation that could amount to nothing but a defeat. Like many others, he regretted his violent reaction against the Prophet, but he remained convinced that the covenant was a capitulation. On the way back, he was told that Muhammad had sent for him; he was afraid the Prophet was going to blame him for his inappropriate attitude or, worse still, tell him that verses had been revealed disapproving his behavior. He found the Prophet with a beaming face, and Muhammad told him about Revelation of verses quite different from what he might have expected. The Divine Word announced: "Verily We have granted you a manifest victory."[9] Then it mentioned the pledge of allegiance, saying: "He knew what was in their hearts, and He sent down tranquility [as-sakinah] to them; and He rewarded them with a victory near at hand."[10] All this was recalled in the light of Muhammad's initial dream, which was therefore truthful: "Truly did God fulfill the vision for His Messenger: you shall enter the Sacred Mosque, if God wills, with minds secure, heads shaved or hair cut short, and without fear. For He knows what you do not know, and he has granted you, besides this, a victory near at hand."[11]

The events of the recent past were presented in a manner totally at odds with the Companions' perception of them: the pledge of allegiance to prepare for war was in reality a pledge of fidelity for peace, the apparent defeat was presented as "a manifest victory," and a seemingly aborted dream was announced as a certainty in the future: "you shall enter the Sacred Mosque." The vast majority of Muslims had not understood, had not seen, or had been unable to perceive the prospects and hopes the covenant allowed. The signing of the pact was therefore, once again, a privileged moment of spiritual edification with, moreover, an exceptional lesson about the value of intelligence and perspicacity. Listening, the ability to shift one's point of view, sensitivity to the other's dignity, and foresight were some of the qualities showed by the Prophet, contributing to fashion his role as a model.

He was an example too in another dimension of his life: when his Companions refused to sacrifice the camels, he went back to his wife Um Salamah, who listened to him and comforted him. She showed him her trust and suggested the solution to his problem. That dialogue, that understanding and listening, expresses the very essence of the Prophet's attitude toward his wives. As with Khadijah so many years before, he never hesitated to take the time to confide in the women around him, to consult them, talk with them, and adopt their opinions. At a time when the future of the whole community was playing out through visions, pledges of allegiance, and peace covenants, he returned to his wife's side and, like a simple human being, told her of his need for love, trust, and advice—an example for all human beings.

Respecting Covenants

The Muslims had returned to Medina and daily life had resumed its course, in a far less tense atmosphere than before. The truce allowed them to lower their guard against the outside and give more attention to the community's internal affairs. The number of converts kept growing, and their integration and Islamic education had to be constantly planned and organized. Powerful figures in the Peninsula were to join the anonymous hundreds who accepted Islam in Medina or came to settle in the city. For instance, Aishah's brother Abd al-Kaba emigrated after the death of his mother, Um Ruman, which deeply affected her husband, Abu Bakr. The Prophet changed Abd al-Kaba's name to Abd ar-Rahman: his practice was to modify a name when the original one could have an unpleasant meaning or refer to an attitude Islam considered unlawful. Thus, the name Abd al-Kaba (worshiper of the Kaba) had a meaning opposed to Islam's principle of worshiping God alone. In other situations, the Muslims could decide whether to keep their original name, which the vast majority chose to do. Never did the first Muslims imagine there could be such a thing as

"Islamic names," of exclusively Arab origin. Indeed, what preoccupied them was the opposite: they were to avoid the few names with a meaning clearly contrary to Islamic teachings, and allow an unrestricted choice of all sorts of different names, from all languages and origins. They had extremely varied names, of Arab, Persian, or Byzantine origin, and this was no problem at all for the Prophet and his Companions.

During those months of internal management and organization, the Muslims were faced with a new extradition case. Abu Basir came to Medina from Mecca and asked Muhammad for asylum. The Prophet, scrupulously faithful to the terms of the covenants he signed, could not allow him to stay, and when a Quraysh envoy, accompanied by a slave called Kawthar, came to demand Abu Basir back, Muhammad could not but comply. They left, taking Abu Basir as a prisoner, while Muhammad and the Companions exhorted Abu Basir to be patient. Early during the journey back, Abu Basir took advantage of his guards' momentary inattention and killed the Quraysh envoy. The slave ran away in terror and returned to Medina, where his former prisoner soon joined him. Muhammad wanted to send them back to Mecca again, but Kawthar was so afraid that the Prophet had no solution that would allow him to keep his word other than to send Abu Basir away from Medina (since the pact forbade him to stay). However, he did not have to make sure he actually went to Mecca, since there was now no guard to take him there. The Prophet ordered him to leave as the treaty required, and addressed an elliptical remark to his Companions: "Would that he had other Companions with him!"[12] Of course, Abu Basir did not go back to Mecca: he settled on one of the roads to the north, frequently used by caravans, especially the Quraysh's. Other Muslims who had escaped Mecca and had heard about his story soon joined him, and they decided to attack the Meccan caravans traveling on the northern route.[13] The group of Muslims became so numerous and the attacks so frequent and efficient that the Quraysh themselves eventually asked the Prophet to take in Abu Basir and his men as well as all future emigrants from Mecca. Their stratagem had been successful, and the Prophet received them, according to the Quraysh's wish to suspend the enforcement of that clause. It should be noted that Muhammad refused to send back women (for instance, Um Kulthum bint Uqbah) under any circumstances, because the treaty mentioned only men: to this the Quraysh raised no objection.

To All Rulers

In the course of the year following the treaty, the number of Muslims was to double. During those months of truce, the Prophet decided to send letters to all the rulers of the neighboring empires, kingdoms, or nations.

Thus, the Negus of Abyssinia received a new letter from the Prophet before he converted to Islam, and he agreed to represent the Prophet at his proxy wedding with Um Habibah, who, as mentioned earlier, had been abandoned by her husband in Abyssinia. Muhammad also wrote to Chosroes, the king of Persia; to Heraclius, the Byzantine emperor; to Muqawqis, the ruler of Egypt (who sent the Prophet a Coptic slave girl, Mariyah, as a gift);[14] to Mundhir ibn Sawa, king of Bahrain; and to al-Harith ibn Abi Shimr al-Ghassani, who reigned over part of Arabia up to the outskirts of Syria. The content of the letters was always more or less the same: the Prophet introduced himself as "God's Messenger" to the recipients of the various letters, reminded them of God's Oneness, and called on them to accept Islam. If they refused, he held them responsible before God for keeping their whole people in error.

The kings and rulers reacted differently to those various letters: some (the Negus, Mundhir ibn Sawa) accepted the message, some (Muqawqis, Heraclius) showed respect with no wish to either fight or convert, and others (al-Harith ibn Abi Shimr al-Ghassani, for instance) rejected the message and threatened to attack. Nevertheless, the message was known to all and the Muslim community was henceforth settled in Medina, acknowledged in its religious identity, and respected as a regional power. Its leader, Muhammad ibn Abdullah, was considered either as a prophet whose reign was destined by God to inevitable expansion or as a powerful and fearsome king who was to be respected and dreaded.

The truce of al-Hudaybiyyah was indeed a victory and an opening (*fath*) to the world: the warring had taken up all the energy of the community, who sought to protect themselves, resist, and survive. Things had now changed, and in that peaceful situation, the Prophet was at last able to convey the contents of Islam's message: the principle of God's Oneness (*at-tawhid*), which liberates human beings from possible alienation to temporal interests or powers, in order to direct them toward the respect of a spiritual teaching, an ethic, and values to which they must remain faithful. Colonized by the need to defend themselves, hampered by the imperative to react, the Muslims had defended their lives and their integrity, but they had not had the means to express the contents and meaning of what they believed. Peace, which now reigned over the whole Peninsula, had transformed the situation: more and more clans could now grasp the essence of Islam's message. Some converted; others respected Islam without embracing it; others fought it but with full awareness, and not merely for matters of domination, wealth, and power relations.

Khaybar

One last stronghold, however, seriously threatened the Muslim community's security after the signing of the al-Hudaybiyyah covenant. This was the city of Khaybar, which had received many refugees from the Muslims' previous conquests. Khaybar was a regional power feared by all, and attacking it seemed unthinkable because its fortresses, weaponry, and riches were far superior to what their enemies, including Medina, could ever hope to fight and overpower. The Khaybar leaders, advised by members of the Banu Qaynuqa, Banu Nadir, and Banu Qurayzah, were hostile to Muhammad's presence in the region and never failed to show it and to harm the interests of his community or of isolated individuals whenever they had a chance.

The Prophet decided to organize an expedition against Khaybar, but he determined to keep it secret until the very last moment, so as not to alert the enemy. While Khaybar and its allies could rely on nearly fourteen thousand men, Muhammad decided to go there with an army of only fourteen hundred (though he could have mobilized more). Nearing the city at night, he called upon a guide who knew the area well, and made his camp between two of the Khaybar fortresses: in that way, he could cut off all communication between the Khaybar people and their Ghatafan allies. When day broke, the inhabitants of the two forts were surprised and impressed, and fear immediately invaded their ranks. The siege lasted several days, during which Muhammad and his men gathered information enabling them to use the best strategy to compel their enemy to give in. They decided to attack the citadels one by one, beginning with the most exposed and vulnerable. The method worked very well, and it was not long before the first fortresses fell. The surrender conditions were discussed for each individual case, but most of the time the vanquished were required to leave their possessions and exile themselves with their women and children.

The last major fortress, Qamus, resisted for fourteen days but eventually gave in, for the Muslims' siege was choking it and left no hope of victory. Then the last two forts also surrendered and they, in their turn, negotiated the terms of their capitulation. The Prophet agreed to allow the inhabitants to stay and manage their farms and orchards, provided they paid the Muslims a regular tax on their products. With all the fortresses conquered, the Prophet had neutralized his last major enemy in the area.

Among the war captives was Huyay's daughter (Huyay had been responsible for the Banu Qurayzah's treason). Safiyyah in no way resembled her father, and she had long been trying to learn the contents of the Prophet's message. She was pious and did not share her people's animosity toward him. The Prophet had heard of that woman and of her spirituality, and she did not hesitate to tell him about one of her dreams, associating her fate with that of the city of Medina. Muhammad listened to her, then gave her a choice: remain a Jew and return to her people, or become a Muslim and marry him. She exclaimed: "I choose God and His Messenger!" and the wedding was celebrated a short time later.

A new stage was reached in that seventh year of *hijrah* (628 CE). Peace now reigned over the area, and the Muslims no longer had to fear attacks from the north. Agreements regulating tribe or clan relationships, or trade in general, enabled the Muslim community to settle down with maximum security. The Prophet's marriages also had to do with that situation: some of his wives came from clans that had, in effect, become family to Muhammad and so considered themselves his natural allies. Hence, the Muslim community itself seemed to have become invulnerable and unassailable: in the space of eight years, it had not only settled in a new city, Medina, but had secured unparalleled status and regional prestige.

CHAPTER THIRTEEN

Coming Home

The Muslim community in Medina welcomed the women and men who had emigrated to Abyssinia and who had lived there for almost fifteen years, such as Jafar ibn Abi Talib (who came back married to Asma bint Umays and a father to three children). Um Habibah bint Abi Sufyan, whose wedding to the Prophet had been celebrated with the Negus standing in for Muhammad, also came back and settled in her apartment near the mosque. Daily life went on, and the number of Muslims increased constantly, compelling the Prophet to multiply teaching opportunities and to delegate that task to his most faithful and competent Companions.

Hostility was expressed here and there, and Muhammad was still sending small groups of scouts to settle matters, but it was sometimes necessary to fight tribes that remained determined to challenge Medina's supremacy.

Usamah ibn Zayd

Muhammad had sent an expedition to the northern Bedouin tribes, particularly the Banu Murra, who kept attacking the Jewish farmers working on the Fadak oasis, which was under the Prophet's authority. The Muslims met with strong opposition, and all thirty men sent on that expedition were killed. The Prophet decided to send another troop of two hundred men, including Usamah ibn Zayd, who was only seventeen years old.[1]

The battle was difficult, since numerous tribes had joined together, hoping to defeat the Muslim troops and take over the Fadak oasis and its riches. The situation nevertheless turned to the Muslims' advantage. A member of the Banu Murra tribe mocked Usamah and his young age. Unable to control himself, Usamah decided to fight it out then and there with the man who insulted him. In a weak position, the Bedouin chose to run away. Usamah, in his anger, pursued him, ignoring the expedition leader's order to stay together at all times. He managed to catch up with his enemy, threw him down, and wounded him. The Bedouin cried: "I bear witness that there is no god but God!" (*la ilaha illa Allah*), but Usamah ignored this and killed the man. When he returned to the camp and told his story, the troop leader and all the other soldiers were shocked at his behavior. Usamah realized how serious his mistake was and isolated himself until they returned to Medina.

He promptly went to see the Prophet, who first greeted him most warmly, happy to learn about the victory. When Usamah told him about the duel, however, the Prophet expressed severe disapproval and asked: "Usamah, did you kill him after he had said 'There is no god but God'?" Usamah replied that the Bedouin had only uttered the words to avoid being killed, and the Prophet retorted: "Did you split his heart open to know whether he was saying the truth or lying?" Usamah was horrified and feared his mistake would never be forgiven. The Prophet nevertheless forgave him, after conveying to him an essential teaching about the way one should deal with people and the secrets of their hearts, whether in war or in peace.

The Bedouin's profession of faith required that Usamah should not kill him. If he was sincere, his life should obviously have been spared. If he was not, his exclamation amounted to an appeal for peace and clemency. In such a case, Revelation had already enjoined the Muslims to show discernment and restraint and to seek peace:

> O you who believe! When you go out in the cause of God, investigate carefully, and do not say to anyone who offers you peace: "You are not a believer!"—coveting the perishable goods of this life: with God there are abundant gains. You yourselves were thus before, till God conferred on you His favors: therefore carefully investigate. For God is aware of all that you do.[2]

The Bedouin, when he saw death coming, had appealed for peace, but Usamah, blinded by his determination to defend his honor in this world (since he had been mocked), had reverted to tribal practices, which his understanding of Islam ought to have reformed. Whatever his interpretation of the intentions behind his enemy's profession of faith, nothing could justify his actions or his attitude. Usamah promised himself he would never again be carried away in this manner and he would henceforth act with discernment and respect. It is to him, as we shall see, that three years later—when he was about to leave this world—the Prophet was to entrust the recommendations and teachings that constitute Islamic war ethics.

What hearts contain lies beyond the limits of men's knowledge, and the Prophet himself was an example of prudence and humility when it came to judging individuals whose sincerity or intentions were doubtful. He was well aware of the presence of many hypocrites around him, but he took no particular action about them. He remained cautious, sometimes wary, but he avoided any final judgment. The most edifying example was that of Abdullah ibn Ubayy, who had lied several times, then had deserted just before the battle of Uhud, and continued to maintain relations with enemies of the Muslim community. The Prophet took no retaliatory measures against him and his friends, except leaving him out of delicate situations or expeditions. He even led the funeral prayer when ibn Ubayy died shortly after returning from the Tabuk expedition, in spite of Umar's strong disapproval. Furthermore, Revelation enjoined him not to pray for notorious hypocrites: "Never pray for any of them who die, nor stand at their grave; for they rejected God and His Messenger, and died in a state of perverse rebellion."[3]

This verse, seemingly firm and clear-cut as to the attitude one is expected to show hypocrites when they die, conversely conveys a very demanding message as to the way one should deal with them in daily life and until the last moments of their lives. Nothing warrants passing a final judgment on their hypocrisy while they are still alive, and the only suitable behavior is that exemplified by the Prophet, who never allowed himself to utter a judgment about a hypocrite while that individual was still alive, since to the very end everything remained possible as far as conversion and sincerity of heart were concerned. God only enjoined him not to pray for them after they died, when the situation could no longer be reversed and it had become clear that they had lived and died in hypocrisy, treason, and lies.[4]

Mariyah

The Prophet continued to lead a private life that required him to be particularly attentive to his wives, for sharp and troublesome tensions sometimes occurred between the women or with their respective families. He himself remained most conciliating, and he hated to cross one or another of his wives. Aishah reported that the Prophet was very present and engaged in his household, that he was very thoughtful, helped with the housework, "sewed his clothes, [and] repaired his shoes," stopping only when he heard the call to prayer and had to leave for the mosque.[5] In all circumstances, even during the month of Ramadan, he was gentle, tender, and particularly affectionate. Many accounts, narrated especially by Aishah, stress this aspect of his character, which his wives greatly appreciated and praised.

Life in Medina, where women were far more present and spirited than in Mecca, and the improving economic situation resulted in many changes in the behavior of the Prophet's wives. Umar was concerned by this; he himself, as we have seen, had to face the reproaches of his wife, who did not hesitate to answer back to him, in contrast with the habits of Meccan women. When Umar remonstrated with his wife, she replied that their own daughter, Hafsah, answered in the same way to the Prophet, her husband, who accepted it, and that Umar would have to accept a similar attitude. Umar was shocked and went to inquire of his daughter, who confirmed that she and the other wives never hesitated to express their opinions and argue with the Prophet, that they answered him freely, and that he accepted the situation. Umar went to the Prophet to advise him to set his private affairs right immediately. The Prophet listened to him and smiled but did not react.

Muhammad had accustomed his wives to attention and dialogue; he listened to their advice, and throughout his life he kept the same respectful attitude he had already displayed with Khadijah. His wives could differentiate between Muhammad's role as a prophet and his life as an ordinary husband and human being. Even Aishah, after the calumny affair, had resented the Prophet and his doubts, and when her mother told her to thank the Prophet for obtaining God's forgiveness, she refused and said that she would thank God but not the Prophet, who after all had doubted her. Muhammad had never demanded to be treated in any specific way, and he tried to respond to his wives' many expectations. With time, the situation changed, because the various victories, the truce, and the accumulating booty had brought some degree of wealth into the Prophet's household, and his wives were beginning to ask for more goods, which seemed to them fair compensation for the restrictions on their public appearance and movements that their status entailed.

Events were to accelerate with the arrival of the slave girl Mariyah, gifted to the Prophet by Muqawqis.[6] Mariyah was exceptionally beautiful, and the Prophet visited her frequently. Jealousy took hold of the Prophet's wives, and Aishah and Hafsah did not hesitate to criticize Mariyah and the Prophet's attitude when they talked together in his absence. The Prophet first decided to move Mariyah's dwelling further away, since those attacks were painful to her. Some time later, with the situation worsening, he promised to part from her. But Revelation contradicted the decision the Prophet had forced himself to take, and demanded that the women choose whether they wanted to stay with him or wished to divorce.[7] This crisis situation alarmed the wives, as well as many Companions, including Umar, as the Prophet isolated himself and refused to see his wives for nearly a month, until they had made their choice, as the Quran ordered. They all chose "God and His Messenger," according to the formula Aishah had used when the Prophet questioned her (quoting the Quranic verses that had been revealed to him about his wives and their future).[8]

The slave girl Mariyah had been a trial for all the Prophet's wives. In private life, as noted, they could differentiate between Muhammad's status as a prophet and the fact that he remained a human being who could be advised and with whom they could debate or even argue. But they could not try to use his status as a prophet in public life to obtain special rights or treatment from the community. Revelation moreover reminded them that being the wife of a prophet or of a pious man was not enough to claim to have acquired the qualities of faith and implicitly consider oneself as elect: thus, Noah's and Lot's respective wives were lost, whereas Pharaoh's wife was saved for her piety, even though she had lived with an arrogant, prideful man who denied God.[9] Within a couple, each spouse's responsibility, choices, and behavior determine his or her fate. In this respect, the Prophet's wives could claim no privilege, and humility was required. The wives' trial was to be intensified by the fact that Mariyah became the mother of the only boy born to the Prophet after Qasim and

Abdullah (Khadijah's sons, who had died at a very young age). The Prophet called his son Ibrahim, after the prophet Abraham, whom the Coptic tradition of Mariyah also recognized as the father of monotheism.

The Lesser Pilgrimage (Umrah)

One year had elapsed since the covenant of al-Hudaybiyyah, and it was now time to prepare for the visit to Mecca mentioned in the agreement. Two thousand Muslims accordingly set off with the Prophet with the intention of performing *umrah*, the lesser pilgrimage.[10] Among them was a poor man who had arrived from Mecca shortly after the Muslims' return from Khaybar and had settled with the *ahl as-suffah* (the people of the bench). He was poor and humble, and the Prophet called him "the father of the kitten," so much did he love kittens. This was Abu Hurayrah, who had converted to Islam rather late and who was to become one of the most reliable and respected narrators of Prophetic traditions (*ahadith*).

The pilgrims went to Mecca and stopped on the edge of the sacred territory to wait for the Quraysh to move out of the area, allowing the Muslims to perform their rites freely. The Muslims were wearing the humble garments consecrated for pilgrimage, and they entered Mecca while the Quraysh people watched them from the surrounding hills. The Prophet performed the seven circumambulations around the Kaba, then the same number of comings and goings between the hills of as-Safa and al-Marwa. After that, he sacrificed a camel and had his head shaved: he had thus completed the rites of the lesser pilgrimage, followed by all the other pilgrims. He wanted to get into the Kaba itself, but the Quraysh refused, arguing that this was not part of their agreement. The Prophet did not challenge them, and throughout his stay he remained in the enclosure of the House of God (*bayt Allah*), from which Bilal called the pilgrims to prayer five times a day in his beautiful, powerful voice. From the hills where they looked on, many Quraysh people were impressed, as they were later to confess, by the simplicity and dignity of the Muslims' religious practice and behavior.

Around this time the Prophet's uncle, Abbas, publicly declared his conversion to Islam. He offered the Prophet the opportunity to marry his sister-in-law Maymunah, who had become a widow, and the Prophet accepted. He would have liked to celebrate his wedding in Mecca, but the Quraysh were adamant: the three nights were over, and the pilgrims were to leave the city according to the terms of the treaty signed a year earlier. The Prophet complied: he forbade his Companions to say anything inappropriate about the Quraysh and promptly left Mecca for Medina. By marrying the widow Maymunah, the Prophet also established a kinship relationship with his fierce opponents the Makhzum, who were henceforth bound to him.

When the Prophet was back in Medina and daily life had resumed its course, he heard of the unexpected arrival of three men who had met on the way and who were arriving together to meet him. Uthman ibn Talhah, Khalid ibn al-Walid, and Amr ibn al-As were all coming to convert to Islam and pledge allegiance to the Prophet, whom they had fought so fiercely for so many years. The Prophet was very happy about that, and so were all the Companions, who were aware of the three men's qualities: their commitment was sincere and unreserved, and the future was not to disappoint them, as it was to be strewn with success. Those conversions, like Abu Hurayrah's some time before, were pregnant with teachings, for not only was the past of Islam's worst enemies forgotten as soon as they recognized God's oneness, but the time these people had needed in order to follow the path of this recognition said nothing about their sincerity, their moral qualities, and their future status within the community of faith. After being hostile to the Prophet and his message for almost twenty years, they had undergone a profound conversion, and during the last two years of the Prophet's life they were to become epitomes of faith, self-abnegation, and integrity for the Companions as well as for all Muslims through the ages. Thus faith—its intensity and its power to convert and transform hearts—cannot be measured on the basis of time or rationality; its very sincerity and intensity attest to its nature, and this is why a recent convert can attain a deeper, more complete inner illumination than someone else can reach after years of religious practice. The opposite is also true, and again, this requires people to refrain from judging others' hearts.

Mutah

A few months later the Prophet decided to send envoys to the north, to ensure the solidity of existing alliances and the ability of Muslims to travel to Syria for their trade. Fifteen men were sent out, but fourteen of them were killed; at the same time another envoy, who had been sent to Busra, was also stopped and killed by a leader of the Ghassan tribe. The threat from Syria was clearly intensifying, and those murders of peaceful envoys had to be redressed. The Prophet decided to send an army of three thousand men, and he placed the former slave Zayd ibn Harithah in command—which greatly surprised many Companions. He added that if Zayd was killed, Jafar, who had recently returned from Abyssinia, would take over the command, and if Jafar died too, he would be replaced by Abdullah ibn Rawahah.

They marched out, and when they arrived near Syria, they heard that a majority of Arab tribes had banded together and that they had managed to obtain the support of the Byzantine imperial troops, which made them more than a hundred thousand strong. Having only three thousand men, the Muslims had no chance: a meeting took place to decide whether they should return to Medina, send an envoy to ask for reinforcements, or simply go ahead and fight in spite of the vast disparity between the two armies. Driven by the confidence and ardor of some Companions (including especially Abdullah ibn Rawahah, who on the way had disclosed that he sensed he was going to die as a martyr), they decided to go ahead according to the initial plans and say nothing to the Prophet. They arrived near the enemy, spent a while observing them, then suddenly shifted their route toward Mutah; the Arab and Byzantine troops pursued them, thinking they were retreating. Once they reached Mutah, where the topography was more favorable, Zayd ordered his troops to launch a sudden attack, seeking to create a surprise. The strategy momentarily staggered the enemy, but it was not sufficient to tip the scales in favor of the Muslims, who were so heavily outnumbered. Zayd was killed, then Jafar, his successor, then Abdullah; the Muslim troops were in disarray until eventually Khalid ibn al-Walid took command, gathered the men, and enabled them to protect themselves from a new attack. They had lost only eight men, but they had had to retreat, and this was plainly a defeat; however, Khalid ibn al-Walid had managed to avoid a confrontation that could have ended up in a slaughter.[11]

At that point, the Companions who had stayed in Medina with the Prophet underwent a most peculiar experience. They knew the Prophet had dreams and visions that very often came true; they knew he was inspired, and they had followed him as Revelations came to him in fragments. They were therefore accustomed to the strange, surreal dimensions of his life among them. One day, Muhammad came to them and, though no envoy had come from the north and they had received no information about the expedition, started to recount the battle as if he had been present among the fighters. With tears in his eyes and painful emotion, he told them about the deaths of Zayd, Jafar, and Abdullah. He praised Khalid's feat and called him "*sayf al-islam*" (the sword of Islam), but he could not conceal his deep sorrow when mentioning the dead who were so dear to him. He went to Asma, Jafar's wife, and her children to tell them the news and comfort them; he began to weep before he could speak, and Asma burst into tears when she heard of her husband's death. The Prophet then went to Um Ayman and Usamah and told them about Zayd's death, his eyes full of tears: he had loved him like a son, and his family was particularly dear to him. Just after he left their dwelling, Zayd's youngest daughter came out of her home and rushed into the Prophet's arms; he tried to comfort her while tears were streaming down his face and he was sobbing. One of the Companions who was passing by, Sad ibn Ubadah, was surprised at this scene and particularly at the Prophet's tears, and asked him for an explanation. The Prophet answered that this was "someone who loves weeping for his beloved."[12] The Prophet had taught his Companions to express love and tenderness, and at that moment, when faced with the final parting of death, he taught them about human fragility and the dignity of tears expressing love and the suffering of those who love.

The Companions returned from Mutah under Khalid's leadership and confirmed the Prophet's vision: things had happened precisely as he had told them, and the three Companions had been killed fighting. For the whole community, those visions and that knowledge were additional signs of Muhammad's prophethood. He was singular, he acted singularly, his intelligence and qualities did not resemble anyone else's, and yet he remained humble and fragile, and like them, he wept.

The situation remained difficult in the north, and the Arab tribes certainly thought they could use the Muslims' defeat in Mutah to their own advantage. Muhammad received intelligence that some tribes were preparing a full-scale expedition against Medina. He decided to mobilize three hundred men under the command of Amr ibn al-As, who had family ties with some northern tribes; the Prophet asked him to study the situation and let him know how things stood, and he ordered him to draw up alliances with as many clans as possible. He sent him another two hundred men because opposition seemed to be stronger than he had anticipated: however, it was not, and the Muslim force was able to proceed into Syrian territory, consolidate existing alliances, and establish new ones, which made it possible to secure that hitherto unsafe front.

The Covenant Is Broken

As previously noted, the covenant of al-Hudaybiyyah applied not just to the Medina community and the Quraysh but to all their allies as well. The Khuzaah were Muhammad's allies, and one of their clans, the Banu Kab, was treacherously attacked one night by the Banu Bakr, the Quraysh's allies, who killed one of their men. The Banu Kab promptly sent the Prophet an envoy to inform him of that treason. It constituted a breach of the covenant, and Muhammad decided the crime must not go unpunished: he had to help his Khuzaah allies.

As for the Quraysh, they understood how serious the situation was, and they decided to send their most influential man to persuade Muhammad not to respond to that isolated action. Yet, ever since the covenant had been signed, the Quraysh had kept encroaching on the terms and limits of the treaty, and they never hesitated to prompt other clans to set upon the Muslim community to weaken or even attack them. This time, however, things had gone too far, and this was why Abu Sufyan himself went to Medina to confer with the Prophet. The latter was curt and aloof: Abu Sufyan tried to enlist the support first of his daughter Um Habibah, the Prophet's wife, then of Ali, but he found no means to negotiate. The Prophet remained silent, as did his Companions, and Abu Sufyan did not know what to think of the situation.

During the weeks that followed, the Prophet asked his Companions to get ready for an expedition, though he kept its objective secret. Only a few close Companions knew what was coming, and he asked them to initiate several contradictory rumors. They were to suggest that the army would march toward Syria, or toward Thaqif, or against the Hawazin, so as to spread uncertainty over the whole Peninsula.

Yet, after an invocation in the mosque, the Prophet had a vision informing him that the secret was going to be betrayed and that a woman was taking a letter to the Quraysh warning them of an impending attack. He had the woman stopped as she was heading toward Mecca, and she gave up the letter to Muhammad's envoys. The Prophet decided to forgive the traitor who had written the letter, Hatib, in spite of Umar's wish to execute him. Hatib, whose behavior had been prompted by family motives, remained free, and Muhammad concentrated on preparing for war, sending envoys to all allied clans so that they could prepare to join the Muslims in an expedition of which they did not know the exact destination.

The expedition set off during the month of Ramadan, and the Prophet at first let the Muslims decide whether or not they wanted to fast. He himself fasted until they reached Marr az-Zahran; when they camped there, he required the Muslims to stop fasting, for they would need all their energy. On the way, he also asked a Muslim to see to it that a litter of puppies that he saw on the roadside were not trampled by the Muslim army; he thereby expressed his care for life, of whatever sort, and even though the survival of a few dogs might have seemed trifling to the Muslims at that particular time, he was keen to protect the puppies from the soldiers' recklessness.

The Marr az-Zahran camp lay at a crossroad: their destination might be Najd, to the east, or Taif, or Mecca. Abbas, who had left Mecca to settle in Medina, heard about the Muslims' movements and joined them. When they established their camp, the Prophet asked every soldier to light a fire in order to impress the enemy: ten thousand fires were lit, suggesting a huge army was on the move, since each fire was supposed to provide for the needs of five to ten soldiers. The Quraysh, as well as the other tribes who feared an attack, decided to send envoys to find out about the Prophet's intentions.

Once again it was Abu Sufyan who came to the Prophet from the Quraysh, along with two other envoys, Hakim and Budayl, to persuade him not to attack Mecca. They parleyed for a long time, but they eventually understood that the Prophet's determination was inflexible. They also observed the Companions, their behavior, and the serene atmosphere emanating from the camp. Hakim and Budayl decided to convert to Islam, and Abu Sufyan declared that he accepted the first part of the profession of faith ("There is no god but God") but that he retained some doubts as to Muhammad's status; he needed some more time before he pronounced the second part of the profession of faith ("Muhammad is His Messenger").[13] He spent the night at the camp, and after early morning prayer, after observing the Muslims' devotion and their behavior with the Prophet, he decided, following Abbas's advice, to say the whole profession of faith. The Prophet knew that this change of heart remained very fragile, and he asked Abbas to go with Abu Sufyan to the edge of the valley so that he could watch the Muslim army marching by. That produced the desired effect, as Abu Sufyan was greatly impressed. Before that, Abbas had, in a whisper, reminded the Prophet that Abu Sufyan loved to be honored and advised him not to forget that; Muhammad, a good psychologist, did not forget the advice and sent word that anyone in Mecca who sought refuge at Abu Sufyan's, or in the Kaba sanctuary, or simply remained inside their home, would have nothing to fear and would be spared. Abu Sufyan hurried back to Mecca before the Muslim army got there and (jeered at by his own wife Hind, who called him a madman and a coward, and by other leaders such as Ikrimah ibn Abi Jahl, who insulted him) advised everybody to surrender and offer no resistance to the Prophet's extraordinary army.

Muhammad had turned Abu Sufyan into an ally, not only because Abu Sufyan had converted to Islam but also because the Prophet had heeded his character and personality. Abu Sufyan had first recognized God but found it difficult to confer special status on a man he had fought and considered his equal; Muhammad had understood this and had not rushed him, giving him time to observe and understand by himself. Even after Abu Sufyan had embraced Islam, the Prophet was aware that he retained an attraction for power and glory, and he took this into account when he exposed him to the strength of his army and conferred on him a specific role in the possible resolution of the conflict. Though Muhammad insisted on common principles, he was able to take particular traits into account; his mission was to reform the latter through the former, but he never neglected the character, aspirations, and specific features that made up each individual's personality. His message insisted on the principle of equality for all in justice, as well as the psychology of differences and of each person's singularity in faith.

Coming Back

Most traditionists report that the Prophet entered Mecca on the twentieth or twenty-first of Ramadan of the eighth year of *hijrah* (630 CE).

Muhammad had segmented his army into divisions that encircled the city and closed in on the center together. A few Quraysh groups posted themselves on the hills, led by Suhayl, Ikrimah, and Safwan, but after the first confrontations, they realized that resisting was pointless. Suhayl sought refuge in his home, and Ikrimah and Safwan ran away. The Prophet had demanded that no fighting or battle should take place on that day, which he called "the day of mercy."[14]

Some eight years before, the Prophet had left Mecca secretly, but with dignity and with his head held high. The Prophet now came back to Mecca in broad daylight, victorious, but this time he prostrated himself on his mount in thankfulness to the One as he recited the verses from the surah "Al-Fath" (The Victory):

> Verily We have granted you a manifest victory, that God may forgive you your faults of the past and those to follow, fulfill His favor to you, and guide you on the straight path, and that God may aid you with powerful help. It is He Who sent down tranquility into the hearts of the believers, that they may add faith to their faith.[15]

He entered Mecca expressing the deepest humility, and he required that the greatest kindness should be shown to the Muslims' former foes. He performed the greater ablution and prayed eight cycles of voluntary ritual prayer before resting for a few hours. After that, he mounted his camel, Qaswa, and went to the Kaba sanctuary, where he performed the seven rounds of circumambulation. Then, with his stick, he pulled down the idols and destroyed them while repeating the Quranic verse "Truth has arrived, and falsehood perished: for falsehood is bound to perish."[16] He had the keys to the sanctuary brought to him and required that all religious images be obliterated, in order to reconcile the House of God with its essence, which was to celebrate the worship of the One, Who cannot be represented and must not be associated with any image: "There is nothing whatever like Him, and He is the One that hears and sees."[17]

This gesture of destruction by the Prophet was, in appearance, the exact antithesis of all that he had usually been doing since leaving Mecca, as he had had mosques (devoid of any image) built to mark the sacred space of worship of the One God. On the level of the spiritual message, however, this gesture was exactly of the same essence, since by breaking the idols that lay inside and near the Kaba he was destroying what had, in the course of centuries, perverted the cult of the Transcendent. With this act Muhammad turned the Kaba into a real mosque, in which henceforth only the One was to be worshiped.

The Quraysh people were gradually coming out of their homes and gathering inside the sanctuary enclosure. After destroying the idols, the Prophet exclaimed: "There is no god but God, the One, Who has no partner. He has fulfilled His promise, supported His servant, and routed the enemy clans; He alone [has done that]."[18] Then he turned toward the Quraysh, told them about the rules of Islam, and recited this verse:

O humankind! We created you from a male and a female, and made you into nations and tribes, that you may know each other. Verily the most honored among you in the sight of God is the most righteous of you [the most deeply aware of God's presence]. And God has full knowledge and is well acquainted [with all things].[19]

After that, he asked them "how they thought he was going to deal with them."[20] They replied that as a "noble brother, son of a noble brother," he would certainly deal with them kindly.[21] At that point, the Prophet recited the verse that punctuates the story of Joseph when he was reunited with his brothers, who had wanted to kill him: "This day let no reproach be [cast] on you: God will forgive you, and He is the Most Merciful of those who show mercy."[22] Then he exclaimed: "Go on, you are free!"[23] The Prophet granted his forgiveness to all the women and men who came to him or to a Companion. Wahshi ibn Harb, who had killed Hamzah, was also forgiven, but the Prophet asked him to refrain from appearing in his presence in the future. Many Quraysh converted to Islam on Mount as-Safa in front of Umar; some years before, the Prophet had been called a liar on that same spot. When Ikrimah ibn Abi Jahl came to the Prophet, the latter warned his Companions: "Ikrimah, Abu Jahl's son, is coming to you as a believer. Do not insult his father, for insulting the dead hurts the living without reaching the dead." He thus reminded them not only to forgive but also to always remember that nobody can be held responsible for someone else's mistakes, not even their father's, according to the meaning of the Quranic verse "No bearer of burdens can bear the burden of another."[24] Prudence was required, as well as nobleness of soul.

The Prophet stayed in Mecca for two weeks, and the situation began to settle down. He sent expeditions to make sure that his alliances with the nearby tribes were solid and that those who had announced they accepted Islam had given up all idol worship. Khalid ibn al-Walid had been entrusted with such a mission among the Banu Jadhimah, who eventually surrendered, but Khalid decided, against Abd ar-Rahman ibn Awf's advice, to execute the prisoners toward whom he harbored particular resentment. After executing some of them, he stopped at Abd ar-Rahman's insistence, the latter having made it clear to him that his behavior was motivated by other intentions than faith in God and justice. The Prophet got very angry when he heard of Khalid's behavior; he decided to pay blood money for all the dead, and he kept repeating aloud: "O God, I am innocent of what Khalid ibn al-Walid has done!"[25]

The path to the education of hearts and consciences of the Medina and Mecca Muslims was still long. Deeply rooted habits and old feelings continued to rise to the surface and manifest as behaviors contrary to Islam's precepts. Moreover, the Meccans' mass entry into Islam required additional efforts in religious education. The Prophet asked Muadh ibn Jabal to make this a priority: the new converts had to be educated and taught the principles of their new religion. The unity in adversity that had prevailed so far had paradoxically been easier to achieve than the unity in faith, love, and respect that must henceforth be established now that there were no major enemies left in the region.

The Prophet had come back to the place of origin of his mission. He had experienced persecution, then exile, then war, and he was returning to the source in peace, with the aura of victory. More than the physical path of a life, this was the initiatory journey of a heart and conscience going through the stages of the great *jihad* that takes people from the natural tension of passions to the peace of spiritual education. He had come back different in the intensity of his efforts and patience, and yet similar to himself in his faithfulness to the message. When he had left, he had prayed to the One, confident that he could not but come home one day to pray at the foot of the House of God. Thus, he had left Mecca as a human being undertaking the journey of his life, intimately convinced that someday he would have to come back to the origin, the center, close to his heart, and return to the source of Life, the pulse of the divine.

CHAPTER FOURTEEN

At Home, Over There

The Prophet had come back to Mecca as a victor, and the generosity he had shown had surprised even his fiercest opponents. While many had insulted him, fought against him, and even killed members of his family and his dearest Companions, he offered them forgiveness, oblivion of the past, and protection. The Quran had mentioned those "who have been expelled from their homes in defiance of right, [for no cause] except that they say: 'Our Lord is God.'"[1] Also, Revelation had already announced that when those persecuted people were victorious, they would stand out by their human dignity and their behavior, for they are "those who, if We establish them in the land, establish regular prayer and give zakat [the purifying social tax], enjoin the right and forbid wrong."[2]

The Messenger was the living example of such nobleness. He showed no interest in revenge, wealth, or power. He entered Mecca prostrated, went to pray and prostrate himself in the Kaba sanctuary, destroyed the idols (in a gesture that recalled Abraham's), spoke numerous invocations expressing his trust in the One God and his thankfulness, and then at last established peace in the city of Mecca.

Hunayn

Muhammad realized that he still had to face a number of dangers threatening the Muslim community. All the tribes had not acknowledged the Prophet's authority, and some thought the time had come to overthrow him. Persistent rumors indicated that the Hawazin tribes and their allies had mobilized more than twenty thousand men east of Mecca and that they were preparing to attack the Muslims. The Prophet sent scouts who confirmed the rumors: the Muslims had to ready themselves quickly. All the Muslims who had come from Medina were mobilized, and they were joined by two thousand from the Quraysh.[3] Muhammad thus set off with an army of twelve thousand men, the biggest he had ever led. Some, such as Abu Bakr, expressed proud confidence as to their number and probable victory, which displeased the Prophet.[4]

The Hawazin army was led by a young warrior named Malik ibn Awf an-Nasri, who had acquired a solid reputation in the Peninsula. He had ordered his soldiers to take their women and children with them in order to impress the enemy with their number and to stir up the troops. He went to the Hunayn valley, which the Muslims coming from Mecca must necessarily cross, and under cover of nightfall he posted a great number of his soldiers in the ravines on either side of the valley. Those men were invisible from the valley. He deployed the rest of the army opposite the gorge so that they faced the Muslims arriving from the bottom of the valley and were thus deliberately visible. The Muslims were advancing in the light of early morning when suddenly Malik ordered the soldiers hiding in the ravines to attack the Prophet's army from both flanks. The surprise was total, and Khalid ibn al-Walid, who marched ahead, could not contain the charge: a general rout ensued, with Muslim warriors trying to protect themselves and retreating in total confusion. Caught in the narrow parts of the gorge, they became increasingly panicked. The Prophet, who was some distance behind in a more open space, witnessed what was happening; he immediately gathered his closest Companions and began to call the Muslims with the help of Abbas, whose voice was more resounding than his own. They both shouted: "O Companions of the tree, O Companions of the acacia!" in order to remind the fighters of their pledge of allegiance at the time of the covenant of al-Hudaybiyyah. The latter gradually realized what was going on and responded to the Prophet's call, shouting back: *"Labbayk! Labbayk!"* ("Here we are! Here we are!").[5] More and more came to join him and reorganized to launch a counterattack.

The Prophet asked for some stones and, as he had done at Badr, threw them toward the Hawazin as he prayed to God: "O God, I beg You to keep Your promise." The Muslims then began to march on the enemy

with such ardor that Malik's soldiers were totally astonished; they could
not have expected such a sudden and massive counterattack. Among the
Muslims was a woman, Um Sulaym ar-Rumaysa, who took part in the
fighting with her husband and who showed a determination shared by all.[6]
It was now their enemies' turn to be compelled to draw back, then run
away, with the Muslim troops following them. Malik eventually found
refuge in the city of Taif with the Banu Thaqif, while others had to hide
in the mountains. They had lost many men and suffered a bitter defeat
after a most unexpected and extraordinary reversal. Revelation was later
to remind the believers of the different factual, emotional, and spiritual
aspects of that fight:

> Assuredly God helped you in many battlefields, and [remember] on the day
> of Hunayn: your great numbers elated you, but they availed you nothing.
> The land, vast as it is, constrained you, and you turned back in retreat. But
> God poured His calm [*sakinah*, His Spirit] on the Messenger and on the
> believers.[7]

Although many men had been killed, the victory was total, and the
spoils gathered were considerable. For the surrender the Prophet placed
the women and children together and ordered them to be guarded and fed
in the best possible manner. He also had the mounts and riches guarded
without immediately distributing them. Wasting no time, he mobilized his
men to go to Taif, where Malik had sought refuge; this seemed to be the
last serious stronghold of resistance in the region. The Banu Thaqif, however, were well equipped with food and weapons; the Muslim army
besieged their fortress, but it soon became clear that they would not be
able to force them out by this means. After two weeks, the Muslims decided to break camp and go back to Jiranah, where the Hunayn prisoners and
booty were kept.

Spoils of War

The women and children who had been captured had been placed in a vast
enclosure, sheltered from the sun, and properly fed until the Prophet's
return. When he came back and saw that most of the captives were rather

poorly dressed, he demanded that money be taken from the booty to buy a new garment from the market for each prisoner. He then decided to share out the spoils, but he did not hand out the prisoners, who had become war captives, for he thought the Hawazin would surely send a delegation to ask for them.

He began sharing out the goods, and to the Ansar's surprise, he gave the Quraysh, and particularly Abu Sufyan and Hakim (Khadijah's nephew, who had just converted to Islam), an important part of the captured treasure. He did the same with Safwan and Suhayl, both of whom had both fought at Hunayn but still hesitated to embrace Islam. Revelation had ordered the Prophet to keep part of the booty for "those whose hearts are to be reconciled [to faith]"; this was not a means to convert people but rather was intended to strengthen, by a material gift, a faith that had already more or less expressed itself but remained fragile.[8] The Prophet knew that Safwan and Suhayl were sensitive to faith and that they had fought bravely along with the Muslims, so he gave them large amounts of goods and did not require them to convert. His forgiving attitude at the time of the conquest of Mecca, then his courage and determination during war, and finally his generosity after the battle eventually convinced them that he was indeed a prophet. As for Abu Sufyan, the Prophet knew, as we have seen, how important social recognition and honors were to him, and Muhammad confirmed his status. For his part, Hakim expressed some pride when he received his share of the spoils: it was considerable, and he seemed to rejoice at the material gain more than anything else. Muhammad accompanied that gift with an essential spiritual teaching, reminding Hakim to resist the pride of possessing wealth and adding: "The upper hand is better than the lower hand."[9] He thereby reminded him that those who are generous with their wealth and care for the poor, making gifts of both themselves and their possessions, are spiritually endowed with a far higher status than those who simply receive or beg. He also advised him to give some of his belongings to his family and all those who depended on him. Furthermore, he taught Hakim to receive in a more dignified manner, so as to give more humbly.

Seven days had elapsed since the surrender, and the Hawazin had not appeared to ask for their women and children back. Now thinking that they would not come, Muhammad decided to share out the captives between the Quraysh Muslims (who once again received a more important share) and the Ansar. He had only just finished the distribution when a Hawazin delegation arrived. The Prophet explained to them that he had waited for them, but since they had not arrived he had already shared out the captives; he said that he would intercede for them and ask people to give back their prisoners if they wanted to. After some hesitation, all the fighters gave up their captives to the Hawazin delegation. Before they left, the Prophet asked about Malik, their chief, and he was told that he had sought refuge with the Banu Thaqif. He entrusted them with a message for him: if Malik came to him as a Muslim, his family would be given back to him as well as all his goods and a hundred camels.[10] Everything happened as if the Prophet had already fathomed Malik's heart when he faced him at Hunayn, for as soon as Malik heard the Prophet's offer, he escaped from the Taif fortress by night, came to Muhammad, and immediately made the profession of faith. He had only just embraced Islam when the Prophet showed him incredible trust: he placed him in command of all the Hawazin who had already become Muslims and ordered them to go to Taif and put an end to the Banu Thaqif's resistance. The Hawazin set off immediately. Malik, who less than a month before had almost caused the ruin of Muhammad's army, was now a Muslim, in command of a Muslim expedition aiming to overthrow his former allies. The trust the Prophet had shown in him was incredible, but the following days and years confirmed his intuition: Malik not only successfully carried out his mission but also remained faithful and deeply spiritual in his commitment to Islam.

The Ansar had watched the Prophet's attitude with astonishment, since in the end almost all of the booty had been shared out among the Quraysh. Some began to give public expression to their disappointment or even disapproval, as it seemed to them that Muhammad was privileging his kin, despite all that the people of Medina had done for him when he needed them. When Sad ibn Ubadah came to him as the Ansar's envoy and voiced their complaints, the Prophet listened to him, then asked him to gather all the Medina Muslims so that he could speak to them.[11] He talked to them about their respective debts, for, he said, they owed him for his guidance and he owed them for having provided a refuge from persecution. Muhammad declared he had forgotten none of that, and he asked them not to be upset by the way he had shared out the booty, which, after all, was meant to reinforce some people's faith, no more and no less. They should certainly not measure his love for them through the amount of booty they had received. Their love of the possessions of this world had led them to forget the meaning of true love for God, in God, beyond the riches and life of this world. The Quraysh people were leaving with sheep and camels, while the Ansar would go home with the Prophet, who had decided to settle with them in Medina, his adoptive city. He added: "Should all people take one path and the Ansar take another, I would take the Ansar's path."[12] The emotions in the group were intense, and many of the Ansar began to weep, for they understood how wrong they had been in their interpretation of the Prophet's attitude and of the signs of his loyalty. His presence was the sign of his love, while the goods he had distributed were simply evidence that he knew some hearts were still attached to the illusions of this world.

He decided to leave Jiranah and perform the lesser pilgrimage before returning to Medina. He had come to that city seeking refuge, but now he felt at home there, even though its culture and habits were so different from those of Mecca, where he had lived for more than half a century before being compelled to leave. He had settled into his new environment by observing the inhabitants' customs and traditions, their psychological makeup and their hopes, and then gradually integrating many of these dimensions into his own personality. He loved the Ansar with a deep, spiritual love that transcended tribe, clan, or cultural ties.

Back in Medina the Prophet was carrying on with his teachings when he was surprised to see the poet Kab ibn Zuhayr, who had formerly used his poetic gift to mock him and ridicule his claims to be God's Messenger. Kab had for some time been secretly staying with a Medina acquaintance and observing the Muslims' daily life. He knew his life could be at risk, for if certain Companions identified him they would not hesitate to kill him. He had heard that the Prophet forgave those who came to him, whatever their past or their behavior might have been. One morning, after dawn prayer, he went to the Prophet and asked him whether he would forgive Kab ibn Zuhayr if he came to him. The Prophet answered that he would, and Kab then gave his name. One of the Ansar rushed on him to kill him, but the Prophet stopped him and told him that Kab, who had come in repentance, was no longer the same. The poet then recited for the Prophet some verses expressing respect and love and asking for forgiveness. Muhammad was deeply moved, and when Kab had finished reciting, he covered him with his garment to show not only that he had forgiven him but also that he praised his mastery of poetic language. Muhammad had a finely developed aesthetic sense and loved eloquence as well as the musicality of speech. Poetic verse expressing beauty, conveying the depth of feelings and spirituality, and highlighting the grace of the One as well as the love of beings was part of his natural universe, of his deepest cultural background. That art, that spirituality of speech, was throughout his life a means to express the depths of the self in the hope of rising naturally toward God.

Tabuk

When Mariyah gave birth to Ibrahim, the Prophet expressed particular joy at the news of the child's arrival. He organized a meal in celebration, and then the child was put to nurse north of Medina, as was usually done. During this time, the Prophet paid regular visits to his son. Life in Medina had become far more peaceful, even though a few expeditions still had to be organized in the region, especially in order to see to it that newly converted tribes did not maintain the idols' sanctuaries and lapse into syncretism, which the Prophet had always opposed—in particular, as we have seen, since Revelation had ordered him to tell his opponents and those who denied the truth of Islam: "To you be your religion, and to me mine."[13]

The news of the Byzantines' victory over the Persians some months later had a significant impact on the Muslims, for Revelation had foretold that victory some years before the event. The surah "Ar-Rum" (The Romans) mentions a defeat (which took place before the Muslims left Mecca), then a victory that was to occur in a few years (*fi bidi sinin*):[14]

> The Byzantines have been defeated, in a land close by: but they, after this defeat of theirs, will be victorious in a few years. With God is the command in the past and in the future: on that day shall the believers rejoice in God's help. He gives victory to whom He will, and He is Almighty, Most Merciful.[15]

Not only was Quranic Revelation confirmed by the events, but the news of the Persians' decline also augured possible agreements with the

Christians in the north. The Muslims were not to find this out until a few weeks later; for the moment, the news from the north was rather alarming. Everything suggested that Heraclius's Byzantine armies had allied with the Arab tribes and that together they were preparing a full-scale attack against Muhammad, "the new Emperor of the Arabs." An immediate reaction was required, and the stakes were so important and the expedition so dangerous that for the first time the Prophet informed all his Companions of his destination. They were to march to the north preventively, in order to anticipate the advance of enemy troops and if necessary surprise them on their own territory. The season was not favorable and the army was going to face intense heat until they reached the north. Mobilization was general, and the Prophet asked the Companions to contribute as much as they could to defray the cost of the expedition. Umar gave half his fortune and understood as a lesson in self-abnegation the behavior of Abu Bakr, who put everything he had at the Prophet's disposal. Uthman similarly stood out by supplying mounts for half the army. All the camels and horses in the area were requisitioned, but they did not suffice to provide for the needs of all the soldiers; as a result, the Prophet had to refuse some Companions' requests to participate in the expedition, and some of them wept, so crucial did they know the expedition to be. The expected might of the enemy was such that the community's future was clearly at stake. The army set out at the end of the year 630 (the ninth year of *hijrah*); there were thirty thousand men, and the Prophet was in command. He asked Ali to stay behind with his family. Ali was mocked by the hypocrites: he could not bear it and eventually caught up with the army at their first camp. However, the Prophet sent him back and asked him to be as Aaron had been for his brother Moses, the guardian of his people while he was away.

The heat was intense, as expected, and the march to the north was difficult. Four of the Prophet's faithful Companions had preferred to stay in Medina, aware that the journey would be difficult. One of them, Abu Khaythamah, felt deep remorse and after about ten days decided to catch up with the expedition. He arrived when they had already encamped at Tabuk. The Prophet was particularly happy to see him arrive, so saddened had he been by the four Companions' defection, which could only be interpreted as cowardice or treason. Abu Khaythamah was forgiven when he explained his remorse and the imperative need he had felt to catch up with the army. This was not the case for the other three believers, who included the faithful Kab ibn Malik: they chose to stay in Medina and manage their affairs there.[16]

The Muslim army stayed at Tabuk for twenty days, but it gradually became clear that the rumors of attacks from the north were groundless. No tribe was ready for war, and there was no sign of Byzantine presence in the area. Although it had been very trying, the expedition did not turn out to be useless. The considerable number of soldiers produced an impression all over the Peninsula, forcing the northern tribes to realize the extent of the Prophet's capacity to raise troops and his forces' incredible mobility. From Tabuk, the Prophet managed to set up alliances with a Christian tribe and a Jewish one: they kept their respective religions and accepted to pay a tax (*jizyah*) in exchange for their protection by the Muslim community against attack. Thus, the *jizyah* was understood as a collective military tax paid by tribes who did not have to share in the Muslims' military engagements, but in exchange for which the Muslim authority was to ensure their defense, their protection, and their survival if necessary.[17] From Tabuk, the Prophet sent Khalid ibn al-Walid further north to besiege a Christian fortress and draw up a similar alliance in order to secure the route leading to Iraq and Syria. All those operations were successful, and the Prophet went back to Medina with the Muslim army.

When he arrived, he was told his daughter Um Kulthum had died: he felt deep sorrow, and so did Uthman ibn Affan, who was thus losing a wife for the second time (he had married two of the Prophet's daughters). As for the three Companions who had stayed behind, the Prophet required them to keep away from him, and decreed that no Companion should speak to them until God decided their fate. Fifty days elapsed before a Revelation announced that they were forgiven: "When the earth, vast as it is, was straitened for them, and their own souls were straitened for them, and they perceived that there is no fleeing from God but toward Him; then He turned to them, that they might turn repentant to Him."[18] When he heard the news, Kab asked the Prophet, whose face was beaming with joy, if the forgiveness came from himself or from God, and the Prophet told him it was a Revelation. The news had been received happily by all the Companions, who had had to boycott their three brothers; it also delivered a profound teaching, since it showed how serious it was to selfishly prefer to manage one's own affairs rather than commit oneself, body, soul, and possessions, to the defense of the Muslim spiritual community. Another dimension of this teaching was that the weakness of a timid or lazy commitment—bordering on potential treason—can be forgiven when hearts sincerely return to the One.[19]

The Delegations

The ninth year of Hijrah was named "the year of the delegations": the Muslim community now enjoyed such power and recognition that envoys came from all over the Peninsula to draw up alliances or sign covenants.[20] The first to come to the Prophet were the Banu Thaqif, for Malik had subjected their city to such a siege that it was impossible for them to conclude any alliance with the neighboring tribes (most of whom had, anyway, either embraced Islam or established a covenant with Muhammad). They declared they wanted to become Muslims, but they wished to negotiate elements of their faith and practice: they wanted to maintain the cult of their idol al-Lat and to be exempted from prayer. The Prophet refused to negotiate about those points, as he did whenever he was asked, for accepting Islam meant worshiping none but the One God and praying to Him according to the norms established by Revelation and the Prophet's example. They eventually accepted the terms of the agreement.

Other envoys from Jewish or Christian tribes also came to the Prophet, and he did not compel them to accept Islam. For them, as he had done with the two northern tribes, he drew up an assistance pact: they would pay the collective military tax (*jizyah*), and Muhammad and his army would ensure their protection and defense. Thus, throughout the Peninsula, the message was clear: the tribes who accepted Islam were to give up any idea of syncretism, for the Prophet did not negotiate over the fundamentals of faith. As soon as the profession of faith had been pronounced, religious statues were to be destroyed, and Islamic practices were to be fully implemented, from prayer and fasting to the payment of the purifying social tax (*zakat*) and pilgrimage. When tribes wanted to remain faithful to their tradition, they drew up a pact with similarly clear terms: the payment of a tax in exchange for protection. The Prophet let the clans and chiefs choose freely between these two alternatives, which many of them did during the months that followed the return from Tabuk.

The time for pilgrimage (*hajj*) was drawing near, and Muhammad asked Abu Bakr to take the pilgrims to Mecca.[21] They set out during the following weeks, and while they were on the road, the Prophet received an important Revelation about Mecca and particularly the rites near the Kaba. He sent Ali to catch up with the pilgrims and convey the message, which consisted of the first verses of surah 9 (the only chapter in the Quran that does not begin with the ritual formula "In the name of God, the Most Gracious, the Most Merciful").[22] First, the verses announced most clearly that the rites formerly performed around the Kaba (where some pilgrims went naked) would no longer be tolerated and that idol worshipers would be allowed four months to make a choice about their future—whether to cease performing the rites near the Kaba, leave the area altogether, or accept Islam. After this period the Muslims would be free to fight them, apart from those who had either drawn up a pact (whose terms would of course be respected) or expressly asked for protection (which would then be granted to them).

The message was firm and established that the Kaba, the sacred mosque, was now exclusively devoted to the worship of the One, and that only Muslims could enter it.[23] The verse reads, "The mosques of God shall only be visited and maintained by those who believe in God and the Last Day, establish regular prayers, pay *zakat*, and fear none but God. For those, it may be that they are of the rightly guided."[24] Most of the Companions, and most scholars after them, understood this prohibition to apply only to the sacred perimeter in Mecca, not to other mosques that could receive women and men who were not Muslims.[25] What the message conveyed was the clear establishment of the worship of the One, *tawhid*, as the only possible worship in the center, near the House of God, toward which Muslims turned from all over.

Ibrahim

During the tenth year of *hijrah*, young Ibrahim, who was then about a year and a half old, fell seriously ill. At the very time when the religion of the One was being established all over the Peninsula, with adversity constantly diminishing and the number of conversions continuing to grow, the Prophet saw his only son about to leave life and to leave him. He visited him every day and spent hours by his side. When the child eventually breathed his last, the Prophet took him in his arms and held him against his breast, tears streaming down his face, so deep was his sorrow. Abd ar-Rahman ibn Awf, his faithful Companion, was surprised by those sobs, because he thought that the Prophet had previously forbidden such expressions of grief. At first, Muhammad could not speak; then he explained to him that he had forbidden excessive manifestations of distress, through wailing or hysterical behavior, but not the natural expression of sorrow and suffering. Then he gave verbal expression to his grief that, in effect, became a spiritual teaching, as he declared that his tears were "signs of tenderness and mercy." He added a comment springing from his own experience, but which was also true in every Muslim's daily life: "He who is not merciful will not be shown mercy."[26] In the difficult moments of life, kindness, clemency, mercy, and the expressions of empathy that human beings offer one another bring them closer to the One, *ar-Rahman* (the Most Gracious, the Most Merciful). Through them, God reaches closer to the believer's heart, offering the believer what the believer him- or herself has offered to a brother or sister in humanity.

The Prophet was intimately affected, and he did not hesitate to show and express his grief. He added: "The eye sheds tears, O Ibrahim, the heart is infinitely sad, and one must only utter what satisfies God."[27] God had once more tested him through his humanity and his mission. He had lost so many loved ones—Companions, his wife Khadijah, three of his daughters, and his three sons.[28] His life had been crossed with tears, but he remained both gentle with his heart and firm in his mission. It was this chemistry of gentleness and firmness that satisfied the Most Near. At the time when, in this tenth year of *hijrah*, the world seemed to open up to the Prophet's mission, Muhammad's human fate seemed reduced to that tiny grave where Ibrahim's body was laid, and over which he then led the funeral prayer. The Prophet was one of the elect; the Prophet remained a human being.

A few hours after his return from the graveyard, an eclipse of the sun occurred. The Muslims were quick to associate the eclipse with the death of the Prophet's child and see it as a miracle, a kind of message from God to His Prophet. But Muhammad put an end to all such interpretations, saying forcefully: "The sun and the moon are two of God's signs. Their light does not darken for anyone's death."[29] Muhammad was thus remind-

ing his Companions of the order of things and of the necessity to make
no mistake in interpreting signs, in order to avoid lapsing into superstition. This was, for them as well as for himself, a spiritual teaching in
restraint and humility: human beings, the Prophet among them, had to
learn how to depart, and see their loved ones depart, in silence, with discretion, and amid the indifference of the order of things. The trial of faith
and of humanity, which made the Prophet shed tears, consisted precisely
in learning how to find, at the heart of the eternity of creation and of
never-ending cycles, the strength to face the finitude of the human, sudden departures, and death. The sign of the One's Presence at the time of
a person's death lies not in the occurrence of any miracle but rather in the
permanence of the natural order, in the eternity of His creation, crossed
here and there by the passage of created beings, who come and depart.

Forgiveness and Sincerity

At the moment when the accomplishment of his mission was clearly
reaching its final stage, the Prophet continued to show a nobleness of
soul that both surprised and attracted his former enemies, whether isolated individuals or entire clans, who now came to him in large numbers.
Though he remained open, he knew he had to be wary of certain individuals or groups. His experience with the Banu Ghanam ibn Awf, and
Revelation that had ensued, had taught him prudence. The Banu Ghanam
had asked him, before he left for Tabuk, to inaugurate a mosque they
wanted to build in Quba.[30] He had been kept busy by the Tabuk expedition and decided to go to Quba after his return. He later learned that the
project had been contrived by a well-known hypocrite, Abu Amir, and
Revelation had confirmed his misgivings: "And as for those who put up a
mosque by way of mischief and infidelity—to disunite the believers—and
as an outpost for one who formerly warred against God and His
Messenger: they will surely swear that their intention is nothing but good,
but God bears witness that they verily are liars. Never stand [to pray]
there."[31] Abu Amir wanted to build a mosque in order to attract the faithful of another mosque in the area, merely to foster division and exert his
influence. Behind apparent faith and sincerity, some individuals thus tried
to obtain prerogatives and power and did not hesitate to attempt to use

the Prophet in this aim. Such situations were occurring more frequently as the community grew.

Muhammad nevertheless remained very accessible and constantly ready to receive the women and men who tried to understand Islam or were in quest of truth. He had forgiven a lot to those who had opposed him in conflict or war situations, and he was now showing great patience and deep affection to those who, in peacetime, were struggling against themselves and their own hearts to go about their spiritual quest and find the path that could lead them to the One. He observed them, answered their questions, and accompanied their progress, whether it was swift, hesitating, or sometimes even rebellious. When returning from the Hunayn expedition, the Prophet had declared: "We are back from the lesser *jihad* [effort, resistance, struggle for reform] to the greater *jihad.*" A Companion asked: "What is the greater *jihad*, Messenger of God?" He answered: "It is fighting the self [the ego]."[32] For the Muslims, as for all human beings, this inner struggle was the most difficult, the most noble, and the one that required the most understanding, forgiveness, and, of course, sincerity to oneself. War and its lesser *jihad* had shown how difficult it was to die for God; daily life and its greater *jihad* now showed Muslims that it is even more difficult to live for God, in light, transparence, coherence, spiritual demand, patience, and peace.

The Prophet asked all those around him who were not convinced of the truthfulness of his message to seek, to observe signs, to search for meaning while fighting the illusions of the self and its conceit. He taught Muslims—those who had recognized the presence of the One—to carry on their inner struggle, to remain humble and aware of their fragility, to seek to derive spiritual nourishment from *dhikr* (the remembrance of God), and, as the Quran recommended, to ask God to keep their hearts firm: "Our Lord! Do not cause our hearts to stray after You have guided us."[33] The Prophet used to pray to God and say, "O Transformer of Hearts, keep my heart firm in Your religion!"[34] Thus, in peacetime, some were searching for truth and some were searching for sincerity, while they all experienced a new form of inner conflict that required effort, patience, and a perpetually awake consciousness. At a time when the prospect of the final establishment of the last religion seemed to be opening up, each of them was sent back to his or her own inner universe to seek light or forgiveness, to find peace and the clemency of He Who constantly returns to those who come, or come back, to Him. Revelation reminded the Prophet: "When comes the help of God, and victory, and you see the people enter God's religion in crowds, celebrate the praises of your Lord, and pray for His forgiveness, for He is oft-returning [in forgiveness]."[35]

Those verses expressed the need to return to the One even when people seemed at last to recognize the message as true. Since this was an initiation to the perpetual struggle against appearances, the Prophet had, once more, to cope with contradictory tensions, which was the only way to transcend the self and reach toward the divine. While crowds were coming to him from everywhere, he was asked to return to the solitude of his heart and pursue his dialogue with the Most Near; while victory was coming to him in this world, he understood that he had to prepare to depart, to leave this life, to go home to be near the One. Abdullah ibn Masud was later to say that Revelation of that surah announced the end of the Prophet's mission and, in effect, his imminent departure.

The Farewell Pilgrimage

During the month of Ramadan of that tenth year, the Prophet received another sign from God. He told his daughter Fatimah about it: "Each year, the Angel Gabriel recites the Quran to me once, and I recite it to him once; but this year, he has recited it twice, and I think this announces my hour."[36] Only one of the five pillars of Islam had not yet been accomplished by the Prophet, and the time to prepare for it was approaching. It was widely announced that the Prophet would lead the next pilgrimage to Mecca, and in the following weeks, he set out at the head of thirty thousand Medina pilgrims, who were to be joined by three times as many from all over the Peninsula.

Once in Mecca, he performed the various rites of pilgrimage, explaining to the Companions who were with him that they were thus reviving their father Abraham's pure, monotheistic worship. The pilgrimage, like the Prophet's entire life, was a return to the Source, to the Origin: a return to God, the One, in the footsteps of His prophet Abraham, who had first built the Kaba, the House of God, to worship the One. The Companions observed every gesture done by the Prophet, who was, in effect, most precisely establishing the ritual of pilgrimage: he had told them, "Take your rites from me."[37] On the ninth day of Dhu al-Hijjah in the tenth year of *hijrah*, the Prophet addressed 144,000 pilgrims on the Mount of Mercy (*Jabal ar-Rahmah*).[38] He spoke in short portions, and men around him repeated his words so that everyone throughout the valley could hear his speech.[39]

The content of the message was powerful and intense, and the Prophet began by stating that he did not know whether he would again meet the pilgrims "in this place after this year."[40] Then he reminded them of the sacred character of the place and month, as well as of that of their lives, their honor, and their belongings. He explained that the period of ignorance had come to an end, and so had its practices, its rivalries, and its conflicts based on power and profit. Henceforth, all Muslims were united by faith, fraternity, and love, which were to transform them into witnesses of Islam's message. They must under no circumstances accept being "either oppressors or oppressed."[41] They were to learn of the equality of all people in front of God and the necessary humility because "you all descend from Adam and Adam was created from dirt. The most noble in the sight of God is the most pious. No Arab is superior to a non-Arab, except by their intimate consciousness of God [piety]."[42] The Prophet reminded all the Muslims to treat their wives gently and added: "Be intimately conscious of God as regards women, and strive to be good to them."[43] Then he added, as if to show the Way and its conditions to all the faithful present and all those who were to follow his teachings through the ages: "I have left among you what will, if you keep to it firmly, preserve you from error: clear guidance, the Book of God and His Prophet's tradition."[44] After each teaching he reminded them of, the Prophet added: "Have I conveyed the Message? O God, be my witness!" At the end of the sermon, the pilgrims answered: "We bear witness that you have faithfully conveyed the message, that you have fulfilled your mission, and that you have given your community good advice." Then the Prophet concluded: "O God, be my witness! . . . And let whoever is present convey this message to whoever is absent."

The Prophet was indeed a witness in front of the spiritual community of Muslims. In communion with them, at the heart of the pilgrimage—which itself requires simplicity and the unity of human beings before their Creator—the Messenger recalled the essential point in the One's message: the absolute equality of human beings before God, regardless of race, social class, or gender, for the only thing that distinguishes them lies in what they do with themselves, with their intelligence, their qualities, and most of all their heart. Wherever they come from, whether they are Arabs or not; whatever their color, black, white, or any other; whatever their social status, rich or poor; whether they are men or women, human beings stand out by the attention they show their heart, their spiritual education, the control of the ego, and the blossoming of faith, dignity, goodness, nobleness of soul, and, for coherence's sake, commitment among their fellow human beings in the name of their principles. In front of thousands of pilgrims of all origins, slaves as well as tribal chiefs, men as well as women, the Prophet bore witness that he had fulfilled his mission in the light of the One's message, and all the believers testified with one voice that they had received and understood its meaning and contents.

A few hours later, the Prophet received the sudden Revelation of the verse that confirmed that his mission was nearing its end: "This day have I perfected your religion for you, completed My favor upon you, and have chosen for you Islam as your religion."[45] The last cycle of prophethood was drawing to its close, and the Messenger was to return to the place of his election, his home beyond this life, in proximity to the One.

CHAPTER FIFTEEN

Debtless

The celebration that punctuated the *hajj* was over; the Prophet had performed all the rites and wanted to return to Medina, so he set out with the pilgrims who had come with him. They at last reached Medina and life resumed its course. Many Muslims taught or learned the principles of Islam and the Quran, as well as the elements of religious practice with their rules and conditions. The *zakat* was collected according to the norms that had recently been established by Revelation and the Prophet's practice.[1] Thus, all the rites of the five pillars of Islam (*arkan al-islam*) had been codified, including pilgrimage, which had just been completed, and the Muslim community had received the information necessary to live Islam in daily life and face new questions arising in the future.

The Prophet asked Muadh ibn Jabal, whom he had named as a judge in the new environment of Yemen, "Through what will you judge?" Muadh replied: "Through the Book of God." Muhammad then asked, "And if you find nothing in the Book of God?" Muadh went on: "I shall judge according to the tradition [*sunnah*] of God's Messenger." Muhammad further asked, "And if you find nothing in the Messenger's tradition?" Muadh answered confidently: "I shall not fail to make an effort [*ajtahidu*] to reach an opinion." This answer satisfied the Prophet, who concluded: "Praise be to God, who has guided His Messenger's messenger to what satisfies God's Messenger."[2] The gradation in Muadh ibn Jabal's answers contained the essence of the Prophet's teaching and offered the means for the community to follow him and to remain faithful to him through the ages: the Book of God—the Quran—and the whole body of traditions (*ahadith*) of the Prophet (collectively referred to as *as-sunnah*) were the two fundamental references, and when faced with new situations, the keepers of those teachings were to make use of their critical intelligence, their common sense, and their legal creativity to find new answers that remained faithful to Islamic principles but fit the new context. The fundamentals of Islam's creed (*al-aqidah*) and ritual practice (*al-ibadat*) were not subject to change, nor were the essential principles of ethics, but the implementation of those ethical principles and the response to new situations about which scriptural sources had remained vague or silent required answers adapted to particular circumstances. The Prophet's Companions had understood this, and he had imparted to them both the knowledge and the confidence required to go ahead and observe the world and its vicissitudes, certain that they now had the spiritual and intellectual means to remain faithful to their Creator's message.

An Expedition, and Nature

A few months after his return to Medina, in the eleventh year of *hijrah*, the Prophet decided to send an expedition to the north, near Mutah and Palestine, where a few years earlier Jafar, Abdullah, and Zayd had been killed. To everyone's surprise, he gave the command to young Usamah, Zayd's son, who was only twenty years old, though this three-thousand-strong army included such men as Umar and other experienced Companions.[3] This choice gave rise to much criticism, but the Prophet reacted very promptly and put an end to all arguments when he proclaimed: "You criticize the choice of Usamah to command the army, as you had formerly criticized that of his father Zayd. Usamah is truly worthy of the command I entrust him with, as his father was before him."[4] In the past, some Muslims had reacted to the choice of Zayd because they still considered him as a slave, though he had been freed; now some opposed the choice of his son, perhaps because of his father, but mostly because of his young age. By confirming his choice, the Prophet informed them that neither a man's social origin nor his age should prevent him from exerting authority and power if he possessed the spiritual, intellectual, and moral qualities required. One had to show discernment by offering the most destitute in society real equality of opportunity and trusting the young so that everybody could express their skills and talents. On a more general level, this was a fine lesson in humility addressed to older Companions: they were to experience the inner, greater *jihad* of obeying a man who could have been their son, and in so doing remember that their time was limited, like any man's. By that choice, the Prophet taught them that time naturally erodes one's energy, and one must be wise enough to learn to step aside, to delegate authority to those who are young and strong enough to create and build.

The Prophet gave young Usamah his recommendations and asked him to set out promptly. However, the Prophet's sudden illness was to delay that departure, and the army waited near Medina during all those days of doubt about his condition. A few weeks later, Abu Bakr was, according to the Prophet's wish, to ask Usamah to carry out the expedition. He reminded him of the Prophet's teachings concerning war ethics, for the latter had constantly insisted on the principles Muslims must respect when dealing with their enemies. "Do not kill women, children, and old people," Abu Bakr ordered him.[5] "Do not commit treacherous actions. Do not stray from the right path. Never mutilate. Do not destroy palm trees, do not burn houses and cornfields, do not cut down fruit trees, and do not kill livestock except when you are compelled to eat them. . . . As you move on, you will meet hermits who live in monasteries and serve God in seclusion. Leave them alone; do not kill them and do not destroy their monasteries."[6] Those teachings were essential, and they were conveyed to Usamah in the light of what the Prophet had said in various circumstances about warfare, respect for nature, or how to treat animals. In a few sentences, Abu Bakr was synthesizing the essence of the Messenger's teachings in this respect.

Years before, at the end of the Battle of Hunayn, the Prophet had passed by a group of people standing around a woman who lay on the ground, and heard that she had been killed by Khalid ibn al-Walid (who was then, as we have seen, a recent convert). He was deeply angered and asked that Ibn al-Walid be told: "God's Messenger forbids killing children, women, and slaves."[7] He had also blamed him when he had killed men who had already surrendered after a battle. In both cases, then, the message was the same: one should fight only enemy soldiers, while sparing all those who did not directly take part in armed conflict or could no longer cause any harm. The Prophet had clearly stated before sending the Mutah expedition: "You shall not be treacherous, you shall not deceive, you shall not mutilate, you shall not kill children nor the inhabitants of hermitages [*ashab as-sawami*]."[8] War was never desirable, but when Muslims were compelled to it because they were attacked or because their survival was threatened, they had to keep strictly to what was needed to fight enemy forces who were armed and/or determined to fight. If the latter wished for peace or surrendered, the war must be stopped, according to the Quranic injunction: "But if they incline toward peace, do you [also, in the same way] incline toward peace, and trust in God, for He is the One that hears and knows [all things]."[9]

We have seen that the Prophet made an exception when he cut down palm trees during the siege of the Banu Nadir. That exception, mentioned in Revelation, proved the rule of respect for nature, especially in wartime. Creation is filled with signs that tell of the goodness and generosity of its Creator, and it is hence a sacred space: respecting it is akin to charity (*sadaqah*) or invocation. The protection of palm trees, fruit trees, and other vegetation in wartime is the consequence of a more general teaching conveyed by the Prophet to all Muslims. One day, as he passed Sad ibn Abi Waqqas, who was performing his ritual ablutions, the Prophet said to him: "Why such waste, O Sad?" "Is there waste even when performing ablutions?" Sad asked. And the Prophet answered: "Yes, even when using the water of a running stream."[10] Water is a central element in all the teachings and ritual practices, for it represents the purification of body and heart, of physical outwardness as well as spiritual inwardness.[11] But the Prophet taught Sad and his other Companions never to consider water, or any other element of nature, as a simple means toward their spiritual edification; on the contrary, respecting nature and using it moderately was already, in itself, a spiritual exercise and elevation, a goal in their quest for the Creator.

The Prophet's insistence on not wasting any natural resource, "even when using the water of a running stream," indicates that he placed respect for nature on the level of an essential principle that must regulate behavior whatever the situation and whatever the consequences. This is not an ecology springing from the anticipation of disasters (which result from human actions) but a sort of "upstream ecology" that rests people's relation to nature on an ethical bedrock associated with an understanding of the deepest spiritual teachings.[12] The believer's relation to nature must be based on contemplation and respect. Indeed, this respect is such that the Prophet once said: "If the hour of Judgment Day comes while one of you holds a sapling in his hand, let him hurry and plant it."[13] The believing conscience must thus, to the very end, be sustained by this intimate relation with nature, to the extent that one's last gesture should be associated with the renewal of life and its cycles.

The same teaching is present throughout the Prophet's life as far as animals are concerned. We have seen that when marching toward Mecca with his army, he had expressly required that a litter of puppies lying by the wayside be protected. That the Prophet insisted that animals must be well treated even in the extreme case of war is, once again, a direct consequence of his more fundamental teachings in this respect. Muhammad particularly loved cats, but, more generally, he constantly made his Companions aware of the need to respect all animal species. He once told them this story: "A man was walking on a road in scorching heat; he saw a well and went down into it to quench his thirst. When he climbed up again, he saw a dog panting with thirst and said to himself: 'This dog is as thirsty as I was.' He went down into the well again, filled his shoe with water, and climbed up, holding it between his teeth. He gave it to the dog to drink, and God rewarded him for this and forgave his sins." The Prophet was then asked: "O Prophet, do we get a reward for being good to animals?" And the Prophet answered: "Any good done to a living creature gets a reward."[14] On another occasion, he said: "A woman was punished for a cat she had imprisoned until it died. Because of this cat, she went to hell. She did not give it food or drink while she confined it, nor did she enable it to eat its prey."[15] Through such traditions, and through his own example, the Messenger stressed that respect for animals was part of the most essential Islamic teaching. He made use of every opportunity to insist on that dimension.

Thus, concerning the sacrifice of animals for food, the Prophet did not merely order Muslims to respect the ritual and say the formula "*BismiLLah, Allahu Akbar*" (in the name of God [I begin], God is the Most Great), which made it possible to kill the animal to eat it. He required that the animal be treated in the best manner and spared any needless suffering. One day an individual had immobilized his beast and was sharpening his knife in front of it, and the Prophet intervened to say: "Do you want to make it die twice? Why did you not sharpen your knife before you laid it down?"[16] Muhammad had requested that all people strive to master their own area of competence as best they could; for someone sacrificing animals, this clearly consisted in respecting their life and their dignity as living beings, and in killing them only when necessary while sparing them any needless suffering.[17] The formula accompanying the sacrifice was to be understood as the final formula that, in effect, testified that, in its lifetime, the animal had been treated in the light of the teachings of God and His Messenger. The formula alone was by no means sufficient to prove that those teachings had been respected: properly sacrificing an animal according to Islamic ritual after ill-treating it in its lifetime was therefore, according to the Islamic principles conveyed by the Messenger, deviation and treason. The Prophet had threatened: "Whoever kills a sparrow or a bigger animal without respecting its right to exist will be accountable to God for it on the Day of Judgment."[18] Muhammad thus taught that an animal's right to be respected, to be spared suffering, to receive the food it needed, and to be treated well could not be negotiated: it was part of the duties of human beings and should be understood as one of the conditions of their spiritual elevation.

Illness

A few weeks after the month of Ramadan in the eleventh year of Hijrah, the Prophet went to Uhud, where the second battle between the Muslims and the Quraysh had taken place, and he performed a farewell prayer for the men who had been killed there. He then went back to the Medina mosque, sat on the *minbar*, and addressed the faithful.[19] First he said, "I am going ahead of you [in the hereafter] and I shall be a witness over you." Then he advised them, and concluded his speech by saying, "I do not fear your reverting to polytheism after me, but I fear you will quarrel over the riches of this world."[20] Those words clearly expressed that he felt he must get ready to leave this life. In the same breath, he expressed a fear for the future of his spiritual community: faith would not leave them, he said, but the world with its illusions would colonize them, and both would, unfortunately, coexist within them. The Prophet was in effect expressing a fear that sounded like a prediction: they would continue to pray to God, the One, but they would be divided because of honors, wealth, power, or their different affiliations, which would make them forget the fraternity that united them.

In the night following that day, the Prophet went to the Al-Baqi grave-yard, in Medina, to greet its occupants, and he punctuated his invocations with the words: "You are the first [you went ahead] and we are coming after you [we are joining you]." On the way back, the Prophet felt a violent headache, which did not leave him for almost two weeks and kept him confined to bed during the last days of his life.[21] At first, he continued to lead congregational prayer, in spite of the headache and a fever that caused him great suffering. As the days went on, the illness grew worse, and the Prophet had to lie down for longer and longer periods. He was then staying with his wife Maymunah (for his wives took turns receiving him), and he insistently asked whom he was to visit the next day, then the day after. Maymunah understood that he wished to go to Aishah's, and she spoke to the other wives about it; they decided that the Prophet would immediately be transferred to her apartment. He had become so weak that Abbas and Ali had to help him walk there.

He had been staying with Aishah for a few days when his fever increased, his head suddenly ached more intensely, and he fainted. When he recovered his senses, he requested that seven skins of water be poured over his face. After a few hours, he felt a little better and decided to go to the mosque with a bandage around his head. He sat on the *minbar*, addressed the Companions present, and spoke to them about graves, insisting that they must never turn his own grave into a place of worship: "Do not commit acts of idolatry on my grave."[22] He was the Messenger, but he remained a man: he knew how deep his Companions' love for him was, and he warned them against committing the mistakes of those who had come before them and who had idealized their Prophets and their guides to the point of worship.[23] Only God is worthy of worship.

To complete this reminder of his humanity, the Prophet rose and asked whether he owed any of his Companions anything. Did he have an unsettled debt? Had he offended or hurt anybody? If so, that person should speak out so that the situation could be settled. A man stood up and reminded the Prophet that he owed him three dirhams: the Prophet ordered that the money be given back to him immediately. The Messenger, following the injunctions of Revelation, did not pray on a believer's grave until all his earthly debts were settled, and he knew that even for one who had given up his life to God, debt remained a burden that God did not remit. He had to depart debtless, free from owing anything to any other person, taking with him no unforgiven offense, no unhealed wound, no undischarged trust, no unheard message.

The Prophet sat on the *minbar* again and confessed: "God, the Most Noble, has offered one of His servants the chance to choose between the possessions of this world and that which is near Him, and he has chosen that which is near God."[24] At those words, Abu Bakr burst into tears, for he had been the first to understand, from the depths of his love for the Prophet, that Muhammad was speaking of himself and of his own impending departure. The Messenger soothed him and, while continuing to address the congregation, directly and personally addressed Abu Bakr's heart, thus publicly settling a private love debt that was both deep and intense: "The Companion who has been the most generous to me with his company and his wealth is Abu Bakr. If I were to have an intimate friend beside God, he would be Abu Bakr; but Islamic brotherhood and affection are preferable."[25] Their communication was public, but it was in fact singular, personal, secret. Abu Bakr's tears expressed his love and cleared the debt; he loved, and at that particular moment, he understood.

Departing

The Prophet went back to Aishah's and lay down again. He intimated to the Companions who visited him later on that he wanted to have his last recommendations written down. Umar expressed reservations because of the Prophet's condition, while others backed the idea. They raised their voices in the Prophet's presence, and he asked them to withdraw, for he could not bear to hear them argue. In any case, the project was not carried out, though the Messenger gave a few more verbal recommendations about faith, practice, and maintaining the Kaba. Then he wanted to go to the mosque, but the pain was so intense that when he tried to get up he fainted. When he came to, he asked if the faithful had prayed, and Aishah informed him that they were waiting for him. He again tried to get up, but he fainted once more. When he recovered consciousness for the second time, he asked the same question and was informed that the Muslims were still waiting for him. He told Aishah to see to it that the people prayed, and that Abu Bakr was to lead the prayer.

He told her this during the following days as well, but every time he did, Aishah requested that her father be exempted from leading the prayer; she insisted that he was too sensitive and that he wept when reciting the Quran. Each time she objected, Aishah received the same firm and determined answer: Abu Bakr must lead the congregational prayer. Abu Bakr's sensitivity and tears held a secret, and the Prophet remained firm in his choice. Two days later, his illness allowing him some respite, he was able to go to the mosque while the Muslims were praying *zuhr* (the noon prayer) behind Abu Bakr. Abu Bakr wanted to step back and leave his place to the Prophet, but the latter prevented him from doing so and merely sat on his left. The Prophet led the rest of the prayer while Abu Bakr repeated, in a louder voice, the phrases that accompanied the different movements.

This was the Prophet's last appearance in the mosque. During the day that followed, he had all his belongings distributed, down to his last dirhams and his coat of mail, and he continued to give out some advice; he repeated again and again that slaves, the poor, and the lowly must be treated well. The next morning, a Monday, at the time of dawn prayer, the Prophet raised a curtain in Aishah's dwelling, enabling him to look at the Muslims in the mosque, and he was seen to give a smile. The Muslims were surprised at that gesture and thought that the Prophet was going to join them, but the curtain went down again and the Prophet did not reappear. During the hours that followed, Fatimah, his daughter, came to visit him and made a compassionate remark about the intensity of the Prophet's suffering; at this, he told her: "After this day, there will be no more suffering for your father."[26] He also whispered into her ear, as we have seen, that she would soon join him, and this made her smile through her tears. The pain was getting more and more intense, and the Prophet was soon unable to speak.

Then Aishah came to sit by the Prophet's side, pressed him against her, and laid his head on her bosom while stroking it to soothe the pain. Abd ar-Rahman, Abu Bakr's son and Aishah's brother, came into the room with a *siwak*, the small stick Muslims used to brush their teeth, in his hand, and the Prophet looked at it in such a way that Aishah understood he wanted it. She softened it in her mouth and gave it to the Prophet, who brushed his teeth with surprising vigor considering his general weakness.

Attention to hygiene thus accompanied God's Messenger until his very last moments, for he knew how important it is to keep one's body fit and in good health. Throughout life, that body has rights over the being and conscience to whom it has been offered as a gift from God, a present. One must provide for its need for tenderness, gentleness, or sexual attention, just as one must keep it fit, surround it with good hygiene, and protect it carefully from all that could affect its balance or cause it illness. Hygiene and responding to the body's needs are two dimensions and conditions of spiritual elevation, and so during the final moments of the Prophet's life he received tenderness and brushed his teeth vigorously; even though the consequences of that final attention to the body would no longer be seen by any human being on earth, God knew the intention behind the gesture. The Prophet had once declared that one of the questions believers would be asked on the Day of Judgment was what use they had made of their bodies.[27] As opposed to all the illusions of personal possession, the body is basically a trust temporarily offered to each being, and here too, one must clear one's debt before departing.

The Prophet closed his eyes. Aishah was holding him against her, and she heard him whisper: "In Paradise, in supreme union . . ." Then he recited the end of the verse: "In the company of those on whom is the Grace of God—the Prophets, the sincere, the martyrs, and the righteous; how beautiful is their company!"[28] He again repeated three times: "In supreme union!"[29] His forearm suddenly sank down and his head became heavier, and Aishah understood that the Prophet had just breathed his last. He had departed to join his Lord, his Educator, his Friend, Who had called him back to Himself to let him at last find ultimate peace, beyond the world of human beings to whom he had been sent to bring the final message from the Most Gracious. Since that day, the spiritual community of believers has never ceased, all over the world and through the ages, to salute the last Prophet and recite, with all their heart and love: "God and His angels send blessings on the Prophet. O you that believe! Send blessings on him, and salute him with all respect."[30]

Emptiness

The news of his death spread through Medina and caused infinite sorrow. Faces showed dismay; tears, sobs, and sometimes screams expressed the intensity of the pain. The Prophet had recommended that grief should be expressed but without excess, without hysteria, with restraint and dignity. Heavy silence, crossed with sighs and sobs, reigned near the Prophet's home. Umar ibn al-Khattab suddenly broke that silence and exclaimed forcefully, as we have seen, that the Prophet was not dead, that he would come back, as Moses had done, after forty days. He even threatened to kill whoever dared declare that the Prophet was dead. His love was such, and the feeling of emptiness was so intense, that Umar could not imagine the future without the man who had guided and accompanied them, and whose love and attention had been stressed by the Quran itself: "Now a Messenger has come to you from among yourselves: it grieves him that you should suffer, he is ardently anxious over you: to the believers he is most kind and merciful."[31] Emotion had taken hold of his being.

At this point, Abu Bakr arrived at the Prophet's home, sat at his bedside, and lifted the blanket that had been laid over the Prophet's body and face. Tears were streaming down his face as he realized that the Prophet had left them. He went out and tried to silence Umar, who, still in a state of emotional shock, refused to calm himself. Abu Bakr then stood aside and addressed the crowd, and this was when he uttered those words, so full of wisdom, that we mentioned in the introduction, that synthesized the very essence of Islam's creed: "Let those who worshiped Muhammad know that Muhammad is now dead! As for those who worshiped God, let them know that God is alive and does not die."[32] Then he recited this verse: "Muhammad is no more than a messenger; many were the messengers who passed away before him. If he died or was killed, will you then turn back? If any did turn back, not the least harm will he do to God. But God will reward the thankful."[33] When Umar heard that verse, he collapsed, and he was later to confess that it was as if he had heard the verse for the first time, even though it had been revealed a long time before. He realized, along with all the Muslims, that the Prophet was gone for good, that he had left them, and that the emptiness that had suddenly set in must henceforth be filled by their faith in the One, Who "is alive and does not die"; they must ask Him to help them find in themselves the strength, patience, and perseverance they needed to go on living without the Messenger, but always in the light of his example.

Umar, despite his strong character and impressive personality, had lost control of himself for a short while, his emotions seizing him so strongly that it brought out a heretofore unsuspected fragility, causing him to react like a child refusing the ruling of God, of reality, of life. By contrast, Abu Bakr, who was normally so sensitive, who wept so abundantly and so intensely when he read the Quran, had received the news of the Prophet's death with deep sorrow but also with extraordinary calm and unsuspected inner strength. At that particular moment, the two men's roles were inverted, thus showing that through his departure the Prophet offered us a final teaching: in the bright depths of spirituality, sensitivity can produce a degree of strength of being that nothing can disturb. Conversely, the strongest personality, if it forgets itself for a moment, can become vulnerable and fragile. The path to wisdom and to strength in God inevitably leads through awareness and recognition of our weaknesses. They never leave us, and the Most Near recommends that we accept them—with confidence, as Abu Bakr did, and with intensity, as Umar did, but always with humility.

In History, for Eternity

Revelation had apprised the Companions, just as it tells Muslims today and for all eternity, throughout history and across manifold societies and cultures: "You have indeed in the Messenger of God an excellent example for him who hopes in [aspires to get close to] God and the Final Day and who remembers God intensely."[1] The Messenger is the master whose teachings one studies, the guide one follows on the Way, the model one aspires to resemble, and, above all, the elect whose sayings, silences, and actions one is invited to ponder.

A Model, a Guide

Throughout the twenty-three years of his mission, Muhammad sought the way to spiritual freedom and liberation. He received Revelation, step by step, in the midst of the circumstances of life, as if the Most High was conversing with him in history, for eternity. The Prophet listened to Him, spoke to Him, and contemplated His signs day and night, in the warm company of his Companions or in the solitude of the Arabian desert. He prayed while the world of humans was asleep, he invoked God while his brothers and sisters despaired, and he remained patient and steadfast in the face of adversity and insult while so many beings turned away. His deep spirituality had freed him from the prison of the self, and he kept seeing and recalling the signs of the Most Near, whether in a flying bird, a standing tree, falling darkness, or a shining star.

Muhammad was able to express love and spread it around him. His wives were gratified by his presence, tenderness, and affection, and his Companions loved him with an intense, profound, and extraordinarily generous love. He gave and offered his presence, his smiles, his being, and if a slave happened to address him or wanted to take him to the other end of the city, he went, he listened, he loved. Belonging to God, he was nobody's possession; he simply offered his love to all. When he gave someone his hand, he was never the first to draw it back, and he knew what light and peace can surge in the heart of a being who is offered a tender word, an affectionate name, comfort. Freed from his own self, he neglected nobody's self. His presence was a refuge; he was the Messenger.

He loved, he forgave. Every day he begged God to forgive his own failings and oversights, and when a woman or a man came to him burdened with a mistake, however serious, he received that soul and showed her or him the way to forgiveness, solace, dialogue with God, and the Most Gentle's protection. He covered other people's mistakes from the sight of others, while teaching everyone the need for personal rigor and discipline. When laziness moved anyone to ask him for minimal practice, he always answered positively and invited them to use their intelligence and their qualities to understand, improve, and free themselves from their own contradictions while accepting their own fragility. He taught responsibility without guilt and adherence to ethics as the conditions for freedom.

Justice is a condition for peace, and the Prophet kept insisting that one cannot experience the taste of equity if one is unable to respect the dignity of individuals. He set slaves free and recommended that Muslims pledge to do so constantly: the faith community of believers had to be a community of free beings. Revelation showed him the way, and, as we have often seen, he never ceased to give particular attention to slaves, the poor, and the lowly in society. He invited them to assert their dignity, to demand their rights, and to get rid of any feeling of inferiority; the message was a call for religious, social, and political liberation. At the close of his mission, in the plain lying at the foot of the Mount of Mercy (*Jabal ar-Rahmah*), men and women of all races, cultures, and colors, rich and poor, were present and listened to this message, which stressed that the best among people are so through their hearts, which are determined neither by class nor by color or culture. "The best among you is the best toward people," he had once said.[2] In the name of human brotherhood—

addressing not just Muslims but all people (*an-nas*), as he did during the farewell sermon—he taught each conscience to transcend the appearances that might hinder its progress toward the Just (*al-adl*). In the presence of God, nothing could justify discrimination, social injustice, or racism. In the Muslim community, a black man called the believers to prayer, and a slave's son commanded the army; faith had freed the believers from judgments based on deceptive appearances (linked to origin and social status) that stimulate unwise passions and dehumanize them.

He had listened to women in his society, who often experienced denial of their rights, exclusion, and ill-treatment. Revelation recalls this listening and this accessibility: "God has indeed heard the statement of the woman who pleads with you concerning her husband and carries her complaint to God. And God hears the argument between both of you. For God hears and sees [all things]."[3] Similarly, he listened to a woman who wanted to divorce her husband because she did not like him anymore; he heard her, looked into the matter, and separated them.[4] He also received another woman who complained that her father had married her off without asking for her opinion; he was ready to separate her and her husband, but she informed him that she was actually satisfied with her father's choice but wanted to make it known "to fathers" that "this was not their decision" and that they could not act in such a way without seeking their daughters' consent.[5] The Messenger conveyed to women the twofold requirement of spiritual training and of asserting a femininity that is not imprisoned in the mirror of men's gaze or alienated within unhealthy relationships of power or seduction. Their presence in society, in public space and in social, political, economic, and even military action, was an objective fact that the Prophet not only never denied or rejected but clearly encouraged. In the light of spiritual teachings, he guided them to assert themselves, be present, express themselves, and claim the real freedom of heart and conscience. They had to choose it by themselves and trace it out for themselves, trusting in the Most Gracious.

The Messenger loved children, with their innocence, gentleness, and ability to be present in the moment. Close to God, close to his own heart, he remained attentive to those who primarily understood the heart's language. He kissed them, carried them on his shoulders, and played with them, reaching toward their innocence, which is in its essence the expression of a permanent prayer to God. Children, like angels, wholly belong to God. They are signs. The Prophet's attitude was a constant reminder of this: thus, if his ritual prayer to God was disturbed by a baby crying—the infant, in effect, praying to God by invoking his or her mother—the Messenger would then shorten his adult's prayer as if to respond to the child's prayer.[6] The Messenger, moreover, drew from children his sense of play and innocence; from them he learned to look at people and the world around him with wonder. From watching children experience beauty he also more fully developed his sense of aesthetics: in front of beauty, he wept, he was moved, he sometimes sobbed, and he was often filled with well-being by the poetic musicality of a phrase or by the spiritual call of a verse offered by the Most Generous, the Infinitely Beautiful.

Freedom and Love

The Prophet came to humankind with a message of faith, ethics, and hope, in which the One reminds all people of His presence, His requirements, and the final Day of Return and Encounter. Though Muhammad came with this message, throughout his life he kept listening to women, children, men, slaves, rich, and poor, as well as outcasts. He listened to, welcomed, and comforted them. An elect among the inhabitants of this earth, he concealed neither his fragility nor his doubts; in fact, God had, very early on, made him doubt himself so that he should never henceforth doubt his own need for Him, and shown him the reality of his failings so that he should seek His perfect Grace and remain indulgent toward his fellow human beings. He was a model not only through his qualities but also through his doubts, his wounds, and occasionally, as we have seen, his errors of judgment, which either Revelation or his Companions would point out.

However, absolutely everything in his life was an instrument of renewal and transformation, from the slightest detail to the greatest events. The Muslim faithful, believers of any faith, and all who study Muhammad's life regardless of personal religious belief can derive teachings from this, thus reaching toward the essence of the message and the light of faith. The Prophet prayed, meditated, transformed himself, and transformed the world. Guided by his Educator, he resisted the worst in himself and offered the best in his being because such was the meaning of *jihad*, such was the meaning of the injunction commanding believers to "promote good and prevent evil."[7] His life was the embodiment of that teaching.

Muhammad's life journey offered at every stage an existence devoted to the worship of God. The heart cannot but commune with such a being as he follows the path to freedom: freedom not only to think or act, for which Muhammad fought with dignity, but also the freedom of a being who had liberated himself from his attachments to superficial emotions, destructive passions, or alienating dependence. Everybody loved, cherished, and respected him because his demanding spirituality enabled him to transcend his ego, to give himself, and, in turn, to love without bondage. Divine love was free from human dependence. He submitted, and he was free: he submitted in the peace of the divine, and he was free from the illusions of the human. He had once told one of his Companions the secret of real love: "Keep away from [do not envy] what men love, and men will love you."[8] God had inspired him to follow the path to the Love that continues this love: "My servant keeps getting closer to Me through freely chosen devotions until I love him; and when I love him, I am the hearing through which he hears, the sight through which he sees, the hand through which he holds, and the foot through which he walks."[9] God's love offers the gift of proximity to the divine and transcendence of the self. God's Love is a Love without dependence, a Love that liberates and elevates. In the experience of this closeness one perceives the presence of the Being, of the divine.

Muhammad had followed a path that entailed a number of different stages: the call of faith, exile, return, and finally departure to the first resting place, the last refuge. All along the way, beginning with his initiation, God had accompanied the Messenger with His love, and He caused human beings to accompany him with their love as well. The Prophet carried a universal message, both in the experience of love present throughout his life and in his reminders to people of the need to adhere to a universal ethics that transcends divisions, affiliations, and rigid identities. This was a true freedom—the freedom of a being who loves with justice and does not allow himself to be entrapped by passions springing from his race, nation, or identity. His love illuminating his ethical sense made him good; his ethical sense guiding his love made him free. Profoundly good among men and extraordinarily free from them—such were the two qualities that all Companions recognized in the last Prophet.

He was beloved by God and an example among humans. He prayed, he contemplated. He loved, he gave. He served, he transformed. The Prophet was the light that leads to Light, and in learning from his life, believers return to the Source of Life and find His light, His warmth, and His love. The Messenger may have left the human world, but he has taught us never to forget Him, the Supreme Refuge, the Witness, the Most Near. Bearing witness that there is no god but God is, in effect, stepping toward deep and authentic freedom; recognizing Muhammad as the Messenger is essentially learning to love him in his absence and to love Him in His presence. Loving, and learning to love: God, the Prophet, the creation, and humankind.

Notes

Introduction

1. It is recommended to Muslims that they offer a prayer for the Prophet whenever his name is mentioned. Therefore, the formula *"Salla Allahu alayhi wa sallam"* (May God's peace and blessings be upon him) usually follows the Prophet's name whenever it appears in classical biographies. Since the present book is addressed to a wide audience, both Muslim and non-Muslim, we shall abstain from mentioning it in the text, and let the Muslim reader personally and inwardly formulate this prayer as he or she reads.
2. Quran, 18:110.
3. Quran, 33:21.
4. Hadith reported by al-Bukhari.
5. Quran, 3:31.
6. Ibn Hisham, *As-Sirah an-Nabawiyyah* (Beirut: Dar al-Jil, n.d.), 6:75–76.
7. Quran, 3:144.

Chapter 1: Encounter with the Sacred

1. Quran, 2:156.
2. Quran, 22:78.
3. Genesis, 15:5 (Revised Standard Version).
4. Genesis, 17:20.
5. Genesis, 21:17–19.
6. Quran, 14:37–39.

7. Quran, 2:124–26.

8. The Islamic tradition is that God asks Abraham to sacrifice Ishmael; in the Bible, the tradition is that Abraham is asked to sacrifice his second son, Isaac.

9. Quran, 37:101–9.

10. Genesis, 22:1–2 and 6–8.

11. In particular, his analysis of Abraham's experience in his *Fear and Trembling* (1843).

12. See our analysis of this point in *Islam, the West and the Challenges of Modernity* (Leicester: Islamic Foundation, 2000), Part Three: "Values and Finalities."

13. Quran, 2:186.

Chapter 2: Birth and Education

1. Muslim tradition draws a distinction between prophets (*nabi*, pl. *anbiya*) and messengers (*rasul*, pl. *rusul*). Prophets bear a message or teachings that they are not meant to transmit to humankind; rather, they remind the people of God's presence and behave accordingly. Messengers, by contrast, receive, live, and transmit the divine message (sometimes to their tribe or people, sometimes to humankind at large). Thus, a messenger (*rasul*) is always a prophet (*nabi*), but not all prophets are messengers.

2. Meaning "pure," "following a faithful or orthodox line."

3. Quran, 4:125.

4. Ibn Hisham (d. 828 CE/AH 213) is the author of the first account of the life of the Prophet Muhammad, which has come down to us as *As-Sirah an-Nabawiyyah (The Prophet's Life)*. This is considered the authoritative work on the subject. Ibn Hisham selected, reproduced, elaborated on, and commented on the facts reported by Ibn Ishaq (d. 767 CE/AH 150) in an earlier work that is now lost. The quotation is from *As-Sirah an-Nabawiyyah* (Beirut: Dar al-Jil, n.d.), 1:294.

5. Tribes were the largest social units in Arabia. They were divided into clans, and then into subclans or families. The term *banu* means "clan."

6. Ibn Hisham, *As-Sirah an-Nabawiyyah*, 1:293. The meaning of the name Muhammad is "he who is often praised" or "he who is worthy of praise."

7. Ibid.

8. The word *Rabb* is often translated as "Lord," but the root of the word includes the notion of education or educator, which is directly present in the word *tarbiyah*, derived from the same root, which means education aimed at building a moral personality.

9. Quran, 93:6–11.

10. Prophetic tradition (hadith) reported by al-Bukhari.

11. Quran, 41:39.

12. Quran, 3:190.

13. Quran, 2:164.

14. Ibn Hisham, *As-Sirah an-Nabawiyyah*, 1:301.

15. Ibid.

16. Ibid., 302.

17. Hadith reported by Muslim. In Islamic tradition, jinns are spirits who can be
     incarnated or not and who can be virtuous or evil. Like human beings, they
     are free to believe or not.

18. The Lotus of the Utmost Boundary is mentioned in the Quran and refers to
     the limit beyond which it is impossible to go while being in the presence of
     God.

19. Al-Mustafa is one of the Prophet Muhammad's names.

20. Quran, 94:1–4.

21. Quran, 94:5–6.

22. Hadith reported by al-Bukhari. See also Ibn Hisham, *As-Sirah an-Nabawiyyah*,
     1:303.

Chapter 3: Personality and Spiritual Quest

1. See Ibn Hisham, *As-Sirah an-Nabawiyyah* (Beirut: Dar al-Jil, n.d.), 1:319.

2. Ibid., 321.

3. The Quraysh were a powerful Meccan tribe, descendants of Qusayy, who
    were prosperous merchants largely controlling trade in the region.

4. Hadith reported by Ibn Ishaq and Ibn Hisham and confirmed as authentic
    by various sources, including al-Hamidi, and partly by Imam Ahmad.

5. Hadith reported by al-Bukhari and Muslim.

6. Ibn Hisham reports an episode with a monk who, having seen Muhammad
    sitting under a tree, told Maysarah that this young man "could only be a
    Prophet." See Ibn Hisham, *As-Sirah an-Nabawiyyah*, 2:6.

7. See Ibn Hisham, *As-Sirah an-Nabawiyyah*, 2:6–8. See also Ibn Sayyid an-Nas,
    Uyun al-Athar (Medina: Dar at-Turath, 1996), 80–81.

8. Muhammad was subsequently often called Abu al-Qasim (father of Qasim),
    and some prophetic traditions refer to the Prophet by this name.

9. He was to bear that name until Revelation commanded that all adoptive chil-
    dren keep their family names when known (Quran, 33:4–5) in order to draw
    a clear distinction between blood kinship and the status of the adopted child.

10. Ibn Hisham, *As-Sirah an-Nabawiyyah*, 2:66–67.

Chapter 4: Revelation, Knowledge

1. Quran, 96:1–5.
2. Hadith reported by Aishah and authenticated by al-Bukhari and Muslim.
3. Ibid.
4. In the above-quoted hadith, Aishah reports that they went together, whereas Ibn Hisham (*As-Sirah an-Nabawiyyah* [Beirut: Dar al-Jil, n.d.], 2:73) states that she first went alone, and that Waraqah ibn Nawfal met the Prophet later.
5. Ibn Hisham, *As-Sirah an-Nabawiyyah*, 2:73–74.
6. Ibid., 2:74.
7. Hadith reported by Aishah and authenticated by al-Bukhari and Muslim.
8. Quran, 2:31.
9. "Your Lord said to the angels: 'I will certainly establish a vicegerent [*khalifah*] on earth'" (Quran, 2:30).
10. Quran, 68:1–6. This surah is often classified as the second in the chronological order of Revelation.
11. Hadith reported by Aishah and authenticated by al-Bukhari and Muslim.
12. Quran, 74:1–5.
13. Al-Bukhari, 91:1.
14. Quran, 93:1–5.
15. They all died when Muhammad was still alive, except for Fatimah, who died six months after him.
16. And the mother of all his children, except for Ibrahim, whom Muhammad had with the Copt Mariyah and who also died in infancy.
17. In a hadith reported by al-Bukhari (1:1), Ibn Abbas relates the painful character of the moment of Revelation: "The Messenger of God tried to appease the suffering occasioned by Revelation" by moving his lips, hence the verses "Do not move your tongue concerning the [Quran] to make haste with it. It is for Us to collect it and to recite it. But when We have recited it, follow its recital" (Quran, 75:16–18).

Chapter 5: The Message and Adversity

1. Quran, 26:214.
2. Ibn Hisham, *As-Sirah an-Nabawiyyah* (Beirut: Dar al-Jil, n.d.), 2:98–99.
3. Because of this status, the Quran answered him in a later Revelation, using the same formula with the additional aesthetic power of assonance and consonance in the Arabic words: *"Tabat yada Abi Lahabin watab"* (let the hands of Abu Lahab perish, let him perish). Quran, 111:1.
4. Quran, 15:94.

5. Quran, 17:110.

6. This surah was revealed later (during the Medina period), but it synthesizes the substance of the believer's relationship to the One Who is merciful and infinitely kind. The Prophet particularly enjoyed this surah, which he once called "*arusat al-Quran*" (the Quran's bride) in allusion to its beauty.

7. Quran, 55:1–13.

8. The elements of the Islamic creed, according to the Quran, include belief in God, angels, prophets, scriptures, and the Day of Judgment.

9. Quran, 16:103.

10. Quran, 73:5.

11. Quran, 59:21.

12. Ibn Hisham, *As-Sirah an-Nabawiyyah*, 2:83.

13. Quran, 73:1–8.

14. Quran, 2:186.

15. Quran, 3:31.

16. Quran, 33:21.

17. Quran, 93:4.

18. Quran, 95:6.

19. Quran, 3:104. In Islamic terminology, *al-maruf* means "what is right" but not in a restrictive way. A central concept, it refers to what is universally known as good, proper, ethical, and moral and is confirmed as such by Revelation. Revelation may specify some teachings, but it primarily relies on the collective and common sense of "what is good."

20. Quran, 3:104.

21. Ibn Hisham, *As-Sirah an-Nabawiyyah*, 2:101.

22. Ibid., 2:132–33.

23. Ibid., 2:159.

24. Ibid., 2:128.

25. Ibid., 2:162.

26. Quran, 80:1–12.

27. The Prophet also said in this sense: "Wealth is not the possession of goods; wealth is the wealth of the soul" (authentic hadith reported by al-Bukhari and Muslim).

28. Hadith reported by Muslim.

Chapter 6: Resistance, Humility, and Exile

1. *Yawm* in Arabic means "day" but also "a period of time" or "a cycle" of sometimes indeterminate duration.

2. Quran, 41:1–10. *Hâ* and *mîm* are Arabic letters; as noted previously, their presence in Revelation is not explained. The appropriate translation is "purifying social tax" which covers the three dimensions of the concept of *zakat*: It is a duty before God and man; it is levied for the benefit of the poor in society; the believer's conscience is appeased in the knowledge that his/her property is purified by fulfilling the right of God and man.

3. Quran, 25:52.

4. Quran, 29:64.

5. Quran, 53:29–31.

6. Hadith reported by al-Bukhari.

7. Quran, 16:106.

8. Quran, 10:78.

9. Quran, 112.

10. Quran, 109. This surah was revealed when some Quraysh leaders suggested a kind of syncretism between their forefathers' polytheistic religion and the monotheism brought by the Prophet. Revelation's answer is clear and final; it determines the inescapable character of the distinction while implicitly opening the way to the injunction of mutual respect.

11. Ibn Hisham, *As-Sirah an-Nabawiyyah* (Beirut: Dar al-Jil, n.d.), 2:140.

12. Quran, 18:23–24.

13. Quran, 17:85.

14. Quran, 18:60–82.

15. Ibn Hisham, *As-Sirah an-Nabawiyyah*, 2:164.

16. Present-day Ethiopia.

17. Quran, 19:16–21.

18. Ibn Hisham, *As-Sirah an-Nabawiyyah*, 2:180.

19. Ibid., 2:181.

Chapter 7: Trials, Elevation, and Hopes

1. Ibn Hisham, *As-Sirah an-Nabawiyyah* (Beirut: Dar al-Jil, n.d.), 2:189.

2. Quran, 20:1–8.

3. Quran, 20:14.

4. Abu al-Hakam was, as mentioned before, the name of the man whom the Muslims had nicknamed Abu Jahl because of his limitless cruelty toward Muslims.

5. From that day on, Umar was nicknamed Al-Faruq (the one who draws a distinction) in reference to his determination to distinguish the Muslim community (having accepted the message as true) from the Quraysh (stubborn in ignorance, *al-jahiliyyah*).

6. Quran, 2:187.

7. Quran, 28:56.

8. Ibn Hisham, *As-Sirah an-Nabawiyyah*, 2:268.

9. Ibid., 2:269.

10. Differences exist in classical sources telling of the Prophet's life as to the chronology of events: the account of the Night Journey sometimes precedes that of the Year of Sorrow.

11. There were initially to be fifty prayers, but the number was reduced to five after successive requests from the Prophet acting on Moses's advice.

12. Quran, 2:285. The return to God refers to the idea of the hereafter and the Last Judgment. A prophetic tradition (hadith) reported by Umar ibn al-Khattab and authenticated by al-Bukhari and Muslim mentions the sixth of the pillars of faith (*arkan al-iman*) that constitute the Muslim creed (*al-aqidah*): belief in fate (*al-qadr wal qada*) whether good or evil.

13. Quran, 17:1.

14. Quran, 53:4–18.

15. Ibn Hisham, *As-Sirah an-Nabawiyyah*, 2:256.

16. Ibadat includes the religious duties of worship required of all Muslims who are of age and of sound body and mind. They include the profession of faith (*shahadah*), prayer (*salat*), purifying social tax (*zakat*), fasting (*sawm*), and pilgrimage to Mecca (*hajj*).

17. Ibid., 2:281.

18. Ibid., 2:281–82.

19. Quran, 60:8–9.

20. Quran, 39:53–54.

21. Um Habibah was later to marry the Prophet.

Chapter 8: Hijrah

1. Quran, 13:11.

2. Quran, 9:40.

3. Hadith reported by al-Bukhari.

4. Muslims still turned toward Jerusalem for ritual prayer.

5. Hadith reported by al-Bukhari and Muslim.

6. Quran, 39:10.

7. Quran, 16:41–42.

8. Hadith reported by Ibn Majah. Ansar (helpers) was the name given to Medina Muslims while Mecca-born Muslims were henceforth called Muhajirun (exiles).

9. Quran, 73:10. The Quran makes use of forms of the word *ha-ja-ra*: *uhjurhum* (exile yourself from them) or *fahjur* (therefore, exile yourself).

10. Quran, 74:5.

11. Quran, 29:25–26.

12. Hadith reported by Ahmad.

13. Ibn Hisham, *As-Sirah an-Nabawiyyah* (Beirut: Dar al-Jil, n.d.), 3:20.

14. The Christian tribes lived on the outskirts of Medina, and this agreement did not directly apply to them.

15. In modern terms, we would say that they enjoyed full citizenship.

16. Ibn Hisham, *As-Sirah an-Nabawiyyah*, 3:31. Polytheists in Mecca kept expressing their hostility and their desire to fight, since Muhammad's settlement in Yathrib amounted to humiliation and defeat for them.

17. In particular, of course, in the different branches of Islam's first applied science (*al-fiqh*, Islamic law and jurisprudence).

18. Quran, 17:34.

19. Hadith reported by al-Bukhari.

20. Quran, 3:2–4.

21. Verses 108 to 116 in surah 4, "An-Nisa" (Women).

22. Quran, 4:112.

23. Quran, 5:8.

24. Surah "Al-Baqarah" (The Cow), which is also the longest surah in the Quran.

25. Ibn Kathir, *Tafsir al-Quran* (*Mukhtasar*) (Cairo: Dar as-Sabuni), 1:27–37.

26. Quran, 2:8–9.

27. Quran, 2:14.

28. Hadith reported by Ahmad and Muslim. A *hadith qudsi* is a Prophetic tradition in which God speaks through the Prophet's words. Unlike the Quran, this is an inspiration verbalized by the Prophet.

29. This is one of God's names.

Chapter 9: Medina, Life, and War

1. Commentators have often made a difference between two types of expeditions: *as-sariyyah* (pl. *saraya*), in which the Prophet did not take part, and *al-ghazwah* (pl. *ghazawa*), in which he was present.

2. Quran, 22:39–40.

3. Quran, 22:40.

4. Quran, 2:251.

5. Quran, 2:30.

6. Quran, 2:144.

7. Uthman ibn Affan would later, after Muhammad's death, become the third caliph.

8. Ibn Hisham, *As-Sirah an-Nabawiyyah* (Beirut: Dar al-Jil, n.d.), 3:161.

9. Ibid., 3:162.

10. Hadith reported by al-Bukhari and Muslim.

11. Hadith reported by Muslim in Muhammad Nasr ad-Din al-Albani, *Al-Jami as-Saghir wa Ziyadah*, 2nd ed. (Beirut: al-Maktab al-Islami, 1988), 2:948.

12. Hadith reported by al-Bukhari.

13. Ibn Hisham, *As-Sirah an-Nabawiyyah*, 3:167.

14. Ibid., 3:175.

15. Authentic hadith reported by al-Mundhiri. See al-Albani, *Al-Jami as-Saghir wa Ziyadah*, 2:955.

16. Hadith reported by al-Bukhari and Muslim.

17. Quran, 3:123.

18. According to some accounts, it was Mughirah ibn al-Harith, an ordinary soldier in the Quraysh army, and not Abu Sufyan.

19. Quran, 111. Abu Lahab is the only person who is condemned by name in the Quran.

20. Quran, 8:67–68.

21. Quran, 8:1.

22. Quran, 8:58.

23. Quran, 8:61.

24. Quran, 8:67.

25. Quran, 8:57.

Chapter 10: Teachings and Defeat

1. Hadith reported by al-Bukhari and Muslim.

2. Hadith reported by al-Bukhari.

3. Hadith reported by Muslim.

4. Hadith reported by al-Bukhari.

5. Hadith reported by al-Bukhari and Muslim.

6. Hadith reported by al-Bukhari and Muslim.

7. Hadith reported by al-Bukhari.

8. According to one version, he brought some dates. Another narrator, called Abd ar-Rahman, said that he did not know what kind of food it was.

9. Hadith reported by al-Bukhari and Muslim.

10. Hadith reported by al-Bukhari and Muslim.

11. Hadith reported by al-Bukhari.

12. Hadith reported by Muslim.

13. Hadith reported by al-Bayhaqi.

14. A bench had been set up for them near the mosque. Some commentators, looking for the origin of the word *Sufi*, have linked it to those *ahl as-suffah*, some of whom had deliberately chosen to be poor and withdraw from the world, its desires, and its possessions.

15. Hadith *hassan* (reliable) reported by Abu Dawud and at-Tirmidhi.

16. Hadith reported by Abu Dawud and an-Nasai.

17. Ibn Hisham, *As-Sirah an-Nabawiyyah* (Beirut: Dar al-Jil, n.d.), 2:112.

18. As Ibn Hisham points out, the first eighty verses of the surah "Ala Imran" (The Family of Imran) deal with this encounter and more generally discuss respective positions about God, messages, and commands.

19. Quran, 3:1–4.

20. Quran, 3:64.

21. Ibn Hisham, *As-Sirah an-Nabawiyyah*, 2:114.

22. Quran, 2:256.

23. Quran, 49:13.

24. The Arabic form *taarafu*, used in the verse, expresses mutual knowledge based on a horizontal, equal relationship.

25. Quran, 5:82.

26. Hadith reported by al-Bukhari and Muslim.

27. Hadith reported by al-Bukhari.

28. Hadith reported by al-Bukhari and Muslim.

29. Hadith reported by al-Bukhari and Muslim (according to another version, he concealed her with his cloak so that she could watch their games).

30. Quran, 24:31 and 33:59.

31. Around the eighteenth year of the revelation (four to five years before its end and the death of the Prophet), the wives of the Prophet were commanded to cover their face in public (with the *niqâb*) and not to address men, as we mentioned, except behind a veil. For the great majority of the scholars, this was understood as a specific command directed to the Prophet's wives because of their specific status in the community and never did apply to all the Muslim women. Later, a tiny minority of Muslim scholars have been – and some still are – of the opinion that this applies to all the women. It is a marginal opinion today.

32. Hadith reported by Muslim.

33. Hadith reported by Muslim.

34. Quran, 24:11–26.
35. Hadith reported by al-Bukhari and Muslim.
36. Hadith reported by Muslim. This referred to Aishah, whose skin was very white. Another version says: "Take half your religion from this red-colored young woman."
37. Ibn Hisham, *As-Sirah an-Nabawiyyah*, 4:30.
38. Another version relates that Wahshi brought her Hamzah's liver, and that she then went to look for his body on the battlefield and disfigured it.
39. Quran, 16:126.
40. As we shall see in the last chapter, he was to give similar orders about animals.
41. Quran, 3:159.
42. Quran, 42:38.

Chapter 11: Tricks and Treason

1. Ibn Hisham, *As-Sirah an-Nabawiyyah* (Beirut: Dar al-Jil, n.d.), 4:138.
2. Quran, 59:5.
3. Ibn Hisham, *As-Sirah an-Nabawiyyah*, 4:145.
4. Quran, 16:90.
5. Hadith reported by Muslim.
6. Quran, 57:1.
7. Quran, 17:44.
8. Quran, 67:19.
9. Quran, 55:5, 6.
10. Quran, 17:74.
11. Hadith reported by al-Bukhari.
12. Hadith reported by at-Tirmidhi.
13. Hadith reported by al-Bukhari and Muslim.
14. Hadith reported by Muslim.
15. Quran, 8:63.
16. Quran, 33:32. The practice of polygamy was widespread and unrestricted as to the possible number of wives. The Quran prescribed a limit of four wives, with strict conditions to be respected when marrying a second, third, or fourth wife.
17. Quran, 33:40.
18. Ibn Hisham, *As-Sirah an-Nabawiyyah*, 4:170.
19. Hadith reported by at-Tirmidhi and Ibn Majah.
20. Quran, 33:10–11.

21. Quran, 33:12.
22. Quran, 33:13.
23. Quran, 33:21.
24. Quran, 33:22.
25. Quran, 4:103.
26. Hadith reported by Muslim.
27. Quran, 20:14.
28. Ibn Hisham, *As-Sirah an-Nabawiyyah*, 4:188.
29. Ibid., 4:193.
30. They did not pray *al-asr* until the last evening prayer (*al-isha*).
31. Ibn Hisham, *As-Sirah an-Nabawiyyah*, 4:198.
32. Jewish law, implemented in war and victory situations, stated: "And when the Lord your God gives it into your hand you shall put all its males to the sword; but the women and the little ones, the cattle, and everything else in the city, all its spoil, you shall take as booty for yourselves" (Deuteronomy 20:13–14).
33. Ibn Hisham, *As-Sirah an-Nabawiyyah*, 4:205.

Chapter 12: A Dream, Peace

1. The month of fast was prescribed in its final form during the second year after the Emigration. It is presented in the Quran as a teaching following in the footsteps "of those who preceded you" (2:183) referring here to the Jews and the Christians.
2. Eight to twenty cycles of prayer, according to the various schools of Islamic law and jurisprudence, performed after the last evening prayer (*al-isha*) and during which all of the Quran so far revealed was recited.
3. The *umrah*, the lesser pilgrimage, can be done at any time during the year, whereas the *hajj* can be done only during one specific period each year.
4. Ibn Hisham, *As-Sirah an-Nabawiyyah* (Beirut: Dar al-Jil, n.d.), 4: 283.
5. Quran, 48:18.
6. Ibn Hisham, *As-Sirah an-Nabawiyyah*, 4:284.
7. Ibid., 4:285.
8. Ibid., 4:287.
9. Quran, 48:1.
10. Quran, 48:18.
11. Quran, 48:27.
12. Ibn Hisham, *As-Sirah an-Nabawiyyah*, 4:291.

13. Abu Jandal, whom we mentioned above, was one of them.

14. Mariyah was to give the Prophet a son, Ibrahim, who died in infancy, to Muhammad's great sorrow (see the next chapter).

Chapter 13: Coming Home

1. He was the son of former slave Zayd ibn Harithah, whom the Prophet had long considered as his adoptive son.

2. Quran, 4:94.

3. Quran, 9:84.

4. As far as Abdullah ibn Ubayy is concerned, some traditions note that he had changed and that the above-quoted verse did not apply to him. Al-Bukhari reports a hadith (23, 78) stating that the Prophet had a particular attitude toward him because of his attitude toward his uncle Abbas. This implies he had changed, and his conversion seemed sincere in the last moments of his life. Whatever the facts may be in reality, what remains is the depth of the teaching we have tried to point out.

5. Hadith reported by Muslim.

6. Mariyah became the Prophet's concubine, a practice that Islamic teachings accepted, while they were proceeding by stages, but very clearly, toward the cessation of slavery.

7. Quran, 66:1; see also the whole of surah 66.

8. Quran, 33:28–29.

9. Quran, 66:10–11.

10. The major pilgrimage, *al-hajj*, is the fifth pillar of Islam. Every Muslim must go to Mecca at least once in her or his life, during specific days of the month of Dhu al-Hijjah.

11. According to some traditionists, twelve men were killed.

12. Ibn Hisham, *As-Sirah an-Nabawiyyah* (Beirut: Dar al-Jil, n.d.), 5:31.

13. Ibid., 5:59.

14. Ibid., 5:66.

15. Quran, 48:1–4.

16. Quran, 17:81.

17. Quran, 42:11.

18. Ibn Hisham, *As-Sirah an-Nabawiyyah*, 5:73.

19. Quran, 49:13.

20. Ibn Hisham, *As-Sirah an-Nabawiyyah*, 5:74.

21. Ibid.

22. Quran, 12:92.

23. Ibn Hisham, *As-Sirah an-Nabawiyyah*, 5:74.

24. Quran, 17:15.

25. Ibn Hisham, *As-Sirah an-Nabawiyyah*, 5:96.

Chapter 14: At Home, Over There

1. Quran, 22:40.

2. Quran, 22:41.

3. Most of those Meccans had recently embraced Islam, but others, such as Suhayl or Safwan, fought along with the Muslims at Hunayn without having become Muslims.

4. Ibn Hisham, *As-Sirah an-Nabawiyyah* (Beirut: Dar al-Jil, n.d.), 5:111 n. 1, 5:128.

5. Ibid., 5:113.

6. Ibid., 5:114.

7. Quran, 9:25–26.

8. Quran, 9:60.

9. Hadith reported by al-Bukhari and Muslim.

10. Ibn Hisham, *As-Sirah an-Nabawiyyah*, 5:166.

11. Ibid., 5:176.

12. Ibid., 5:177.

13. Quran, 109:6.

14. Between three and nine years, since the Arabic word *bid* means any number from three to nine.

15. Quran, 30:2–5.

16. Ibn Hisham, *As-Sirah an-Nabawiyyah*, 5:214.

17. This was exactly how Umar ibn al-Khattab, then the caliph, was to understand it several years later when he gave back to Christian and Jewish tribes the whole *jizyah* they had paid while telling their chiefs, before an upcoming conflict, that he was unable to ensure their protection.

18. Quran, 9:118.

19. Ibn Hisham, *As-Sirah an-Nabawiyyah*, 5:219.

20. Ibid., 5:248. In fact, most probably it was the ninth and the beginning of the tenth year of *hijrah* (end of 630–beginning of 631 CE).

21. Ibn Hisham, *As-Sirah an-Nabawiyyah*, 5:229.

22. *"BismiLLah ar-Rahman ar-Rahim"* ([I begin] in the name of God, the Most Gracious, the Most Merciful). The reasons for this absence have been given

various interpretations by Muslim scholars: some consider that it is due to the very contents of the surah, which deals with idolaters and war, while others think that it is merely the continuation of surah 8.

23. Some traditionists place the Najran Christian delegation's visit during that year of the delegations, i.e., long after Badr. Others, such as Ibn Hisham, consider that a second encounter took place at that time and that the Najran Christians afterward converted to Islam.

24. Quran, 9:18.

25. Some scholars, however, particularly those of the Maliki school, consider that the prohibition applies to all mosques.

26. Hadith reported by al-Bukhari and Muslim.

27. Hadith reported by al-Bukhari and Muslim.

28. Zaynab had also died some time before, and the Prophet had personally given instructions as to how her body should be washed.

29. Hadith reported by al-Bukhari and Muslim.

30. Ibn Hisham, *As-Sirah an-Nabawiyyah*, 5:211.

31. Quran, 9:107–8.

32. Hadith reported by al-Bayhaqi.

33. Quran, 3:8.

34. Hadith reported by Ahmad and at-Tirmidhi.

35. Quran, 110:1–3.

36. Hadith reported by al-Bukhari.

37. Hadith reported by Muslim.

38. The number of pilgrims was between 124,000 and 144,000, according to different accounts.

39. In March or April 632 CE.

40. Ibn Hisham, *As-Sirah an-Nabawiyyah*, 6:9.

41. Ibid.

42. Ibid.

43. Ibid., 6:10.

44. Ibid.

45. Quran, 5:3.

Chapter 15: Debtless

1. During the ninth year of Hijrah, according to the majority of traditionists and scholars in Islamic law and jurisprudence (*fuqaha*).

2. Hadith reported by at-Tirmidhi and Abu Dawud.

3. Some traditionists mention, among the Prophet's Companions who were to

take part in that expedition, the names of Abu Bakr, Ali, and Uthman; however, they are not unanimous about who actually went.

4. Ibn Hisham, *As-Sirah an-Nabawiyyah* (Beirut: Dar al-Jil, n.d.), 6:12 n. 3.

5. Literally, "Let the blood of women, children and old people never soil your hands."

6. Ibn Jarir at-Tabari, *Tarikh ar-Rusul wal-Muluk* (Cairo: al-Matbaah al-Husaniyyah, 1905), 3:213–14.

7. Ibn Hisham, *As-Sirah an-Nabawiyyah*, 5:127.

8. Hadith reported by Ibn Hanbal.

9. Quran, 8:61.

10. Hadith reported by Ahmad and Ibn Majah.

11. The Prophet said in this respect: "When a believer performs ablutions and washes his face, all the sins he has committed with his eyes are washed away; when he washes his hands, all the sins he has committed with his hands are washed away; when he washes his feet, all the sins toward which he has stepped are washed away" (hadith reported by Abu Dawud).

12. The preoccupations of the two ecologies are eventually bound to meet even though their sources differ.

13. Hadith reported by Ahmad.

14. Hadith reported by al-Bukhari and Muslim.

15. Hadith reported by al-Bukhari and Muslim.

16. Hadith reported by al-Bukhari.

17. "When you do something, do it with mastery [in the best possible manner]" (hadith reported by al-Bukhari and Muslim).

18. Hadith reported by an-Nasai.

19. An elevated chair from which the imam addresses the faithful in a mosque.

20. Hadith reported by al-Bukhari.

21. All the facts narrated here are reported by all of the reference traditionists, but there are sometimes differences in their chronology or the time when they actually took place: the speech in the mosque, the transfer to Aishah's, the prayers in the mosque, etc.

22. Hadith reported by Malik.

23. This injunction never to lapse into the worship of human beings explains why prophets cannot be represented in classical Islamic tradition. Pictures, like carved statues, are by essence liable to fix human imagination on an object or a being that can come to be idealized or worshiped because of, and through, their representation. One should follow the prophets' teaching and not their persons: they are paths that guide people and bring them closer to God. A believer reaches toward God's presence and love, but the Being and His Presence transcend all that humans can represent or imagine.

Faith is thus a disposition of the heart, not of the imagination and its images.

24. Ibn Hisham, *As-Sirah an-Nabawiyyah*, 6:64.
25. Ibid. (hadith also reported by al-Bukhari).
26. Hadith reported by al-Bukhari.
27. Hadith reported by at-Tirmidhi.
28. Quran, 4:69.
29. Ibn Hisham, *As-Sirah an-Nabawiyyah*, 6:73 n. 1.
30. Quran, 33:56.
31. Quran, 9:128.
32. Ibn Hisham, *As-Sirah an-Nabawiyyah*, 6:75–76.
33. Quran, 3:144.

In History, for Eternity

1. Quran, 33:21.
2. Hadith reported by al-Bayhaqi.
3. Quran, 58:1.
4. Several women came to him asking for divorce (*khul*), for instance Jamilah bint Ubayy ibn Salul, Habibah bint Sahl al-Ansariyyah, Barirah, and Thabit ibn Qays's wife. In this last case, Ibn Abbas recounts that Thabit's wife came to the Prophet and told him that she had nothing to reproach her husband with as far as religion was concerned, but that she did not want to be guilty of infidelity regarding Islam (by failing to respect his rights as a husband or betraying him through her thoughts or behavior). The Prophet asked her whether she was willing to return the garden that he had given her as dowry, and she accepted. The Prophet then asked Thabit to accept the separation (hadith reported by al-Bukhari).
5. This is found in a hadith reported by Ahmad. In another hadith reported by al-Bukhari, an-Nasai, and Ibn Majah, the Prophet is said to have simply canceled a marriage contract established without the woman's consent.
6. "Sometimes," the Prophet had said, "I prepare for prayer, intending to make it last, but when [during prayer] I hear a child cry, I shorten it for fear of distressing his mother" (hadith reported by Abu Dawud).
7. "*Al-amr bil-maruf wa an-nahy an al-munkar*" (see, e.g., Quran, 22:41).
8. Hadith reported by Ibn Majah.
9. Hadith reported by al-Bukhari.

Index